Butterworths Compliance Series
Market Abuse and Insider Dealing

D1323225

Butterworths Compliance Series

General Editor: Professor Barry A K Rider, LLB (Lond), MA (Cantab), PhD (Lond), PhD (Cantab), LLD (Hon) (Penn State), LLD (Hon) (UFS), Barrister

Series Editor: Graham Ritchie MA (Cantab), Solicitor

Other titles available in this series include:

Risk-Based Compliance Stuart Bazley, Dr Andrew Haynes, Tony Blunden

Money Laundering Toby Graham, Evan Bell, Nick Elliott QC, Sue Thornhill

Investigations and Enforcement Dr Peter Johnstone, Richard Jones QC

Conflicts of Interest and Chinese Walls Dr Chizu Nakajima, Elizabeth Sheffield

Managed Funds Daniel Tunkel

Butterworths Compliance Series
Market Abuse and Insider Dealing

Barry A K Rider
Professor of Law and Director of the Institute of Advanced Legal Studies,
University of London

Kern Alexander
Senior Research Fellow, Institute of Advanced Legal Studies,
University of London

Lisa Linklater
Barrister, Chancery House Chambers, Leeds

Butterworths
London
2002

United Kingdom	Butterworths Tolley, a Division of Reed Elsevier (UK) Ltd, Halsbury House, 35 Chancery Lane, LONDON, WC2A 1EL, and 4 Hill Street, EDINBURGH EH2 3JZ
Argentina	Abeledo Perrot, Jurisprudencia Argentina and Depalma, BUENOS AIRES
Australia	Butterworths, a Division of Reed International Books Australia Pty Ltd, CHATSWOOD, New South Wales
Austria	ARD Betriebsdienst and Verlag Orac, VIENNA
Canada	Butterworths Canada Ltd, MARKHAM, Ontario
Chile	Publitecsa and Conosur Ltda, SANTIAGO DE CHILE
Czech Republic	Orac sro, PRAGUE
France	Editions du Juris-Classeur SA, PARIS
Hong Kong	Butterworths Asia (Hong Kong), HONG KONG
Hungary	Hvg Orac, BUDAPEST
India	Butterworths India, NEW DELHI
Ireland	Butterworths (Ireland) Ltd, DUBLIN
Italy	Giuffré, MILAN
Malaysia	Malayan Law Journal Sdn Bhd, KUALA LUMPUR
New Zealand	Butterworths of New Zealand, WELLINGTON
Poland	Wydawnictwa Prawnicze PWN, WARSAW
Singapore	Butterworths Asia, SINGAPORE
South Africa	Butterworths Publishers (Pty) Ltd, DURBAN
Switzerland	Stämpfli Verlag AG, BERNE
USA	LexisNexis, DAYTON, Ohio

© Reed Elsevier (UK) Ltd 2002

A CIP Catalogue record for this book is available from the British Library.

ISBN 0 406 93249 2

Typeset by Columns Design Ltd, Reading, England
Printed and bound in Great Britain by Hobbs The Printers Ltd, Totton, Hampshire

Visit Butterworths LexisNexis *direct* at www.butterworths.com

Preface

Concern about the harm to confidence in the integrity of the markets, caused by those who take advantage of privileged information in their own dealings, is nothing new. Indeed, in the United Kingdom, insider dealing has been a specific and serious criminal offence since 1980 and other controls have been on the statute book since 1967. The Financial Services and Markets Act 2000, however, introduces a much wider 'offence' of market abuse, which can be committed by using information in investment activity, which is not publicly, or for that matter widely, available. Furthermore, the new legislation provides the Financial Services Authority with new and very far reaching investigative and enforcement powers. Under the Criminal Justice Act 1993, insider dealing and related activity is sanctioned only by the criminal law, but under the new law, the Financial Services Authority is able to impose civil penalties and seek restitution in cases where privileged information is abused.

It is also important, for those operating in the markets and advising investors, to appreciate that the criminal law and new provisions do not exist in a vacuum. The civil law in certain circumstances may render a person who abuses their position or uses confidential information improperly liable in damages or obliged to make restitution. The relevant civil law has been developed to a significant extent in recent years and is a very real issue for those operating in the financial services industry. Furthermore, financial intermediaries remain subject to a number of other obligations imposed by virtue of their contracts of employment, professional and other codes and the provisions of the Companies Act 1985. While it is perhaps not necessarily helpful to regard the abuse of inside information as a type of fraud, there are a large number of criminal offences which relate directly and indirectly to the promotion and maintenance of integrity in the financial markets.

The new law on market abuse, the old law on insider dealing and the host of other legal, regulatory and compliance obligations impose a complex web of responsibilities and, indeed, risks on those who engage in financial transactions or advise and assist others. In this work, the authors, who have considerable practical experience of the relevant law, seek to set out in a comprehensive, accurate and constructive manner not only the relevant and current law, but also how best to avoid being on the 'sharp end' of a criminal prosecution, civil enforcement action or civil suit.

While the views expressed in this book are those of the authors, they would like to acknowledge advice and assistance they have received from a number of individuals, including many who are very much involved in 'policing' the new law.

Barry A K Rider
Kern Alexander
Lisa Linklater

Contents

Table of statutes

References in this table are to paragraph numbers

Table of cases

References in this table are to paragraph numbers

PARA

CHAPTER I

The nature of insider dealing and market abuse

Insider dealing in perspective

1.1 The commonly held view is that insider dealing is a problem of the twentieth century and, more specifically, the last quarter of the century. It is certainly the case that, over the last 30 years, there has been considerable interest in the topic in many countries. The media and, in particular, the press regularly carry stories of those in positions of trust taking advantage of price-sensitive information to further their own interests. Most jurisdictions have in recent years enacted legislation specifically to deal with the problem of directors and officers of companies taking advantage of information that they receive by virtue of their privileged positions by dealing in their company's securities. Insider dealing is not, of course, confined to those holding office in a company and many regulatory systems impose prohibitions on anyone who acquires such information with knowledge that it is from a privileged source. On the other hand, despite the amount of law that has been created, there is considerable scepticism as to whether it does provide sufficient protection for investors and the markets.

1.2 In fact, the problem of insiders abusing information that they obtain by virtue of the special relationship that they have with their company is not a new one. It is possible to find references to insiders taking advantage of their privileged position to dump over-valued securities on the market in official reports as early as the seventeenth century[1]. Furthermore, the taking advantage of privileged information or, at least, information that the other party could not obtain, is as old as human nature. While history may not record examples of the abuse of such information on securities markets, there are countless examples from many countries of people profiting in one way or another from such information. Indeed, in many cultures, no opprobrium necessarily attached to such conduct and in some it would have been regarded inopportune, if not ungracious, not to have utilised the advantage in question. It is still the case that very few jurisdictions seek to impose constraints, let alone legal prohibitions, on the use of privileged knowledge in dealings other than in securities.

1   See, for example, B Rider, C Abrams and M Ashe, *Guide to Financial Services Regulation* (3rd edn, 1997, CCH) at Chapter 1 and, in particular, House of Commons Journals, 20 November 1697 and G Gilligan, *Regulating the Financial Services Sector* (1999, Kluwer) Chapter 4.

1.3   While most systems of law do, to some degree, protect the confidentiality of information, they do not necessarily interfere in transactions with third parties who have been disadvantaged by the use of information obtained in breach of a duty of confidentiality. Few legal systems go anywhere near imposing an obligation on someone in possession of superior information to disclose this to another contracting party. Even when that other party could not have obtained the same information even with the greatest diligence, in most jurisdictions there will be no duty to disclose or warn him. To require equality of information in such circumstances would undermine any incentive that a person would otherwise have to conduct research or acquire material information. Regarding decisions relating to the disposal of property and the conduct of commerce, it is necessary to have the best information that is available and therefore the acquisition of superior information should not be discouraged, let alone penalised.

1.4   Why should we, therefore, be concerned when such transactions occur in regard to intangible property and, in particular, in securities of public companies? Of course, the development of corporate enterprise has necessitated that we look at our ordinary laws and their application to new areas. While it is convenient for us to attribute a legal personality to the corporation for a variety of sensible and important reasons, this legal fiction inevitably gives rise to implications for those who deal with, or are involved in, the enterprise. For example, the corporation is interposed between the shareholders and the enterprise's property. In the vast majority of legal systems, shareholders do not own the company's property. It is only the company as a separate legal person that owns its assets. The shareholders' property is confined to their 'share' in the enterprise. The value of this 'share' will depend on many things, albeit most significantly, the value of the enterprise's assets and the productivity of their use. The important thing to note, however, is that we are not dealing with absolutes and value in this context will be determined by what another is willing to pay or exchange for the share in question. Of course, when we consider the value of other securities such as bonds and derivatives, the relationship with quantifiable and assessable property becomes even more remote. It is clear, therefore, that, in determining the value of securities, knowledge of events that are likely to affect the decision of others as to whether to acquire or dispose of ownership and upon what terms plays a much greater role than in regard to many other forms of wealth. It is also clear that there will be persons who, by virtue of their position in or in relation to the enterprise, will be in a very privileged position in obtaining and assessing price-relevant information. Thus, quite early on in the development of the common law, obligations were cast upon those responsible for issuing new securities and, in particular, shares, to ensure fair and adequate disclosure of all material information relating to the enterprise and not to take advantage of their privileged position. In most jurisdictions today, such obligations have been placed on a statutory footing[1].

1 See, for example, the Financial Services and Markets Act 2000, Pt VI.

1.5 Where such insiders deal in the market in the securities of the issuer with which they enjoy this privileged access to its information, it is not difficult to see why many consider they should be held to similar responsibilities. While the situation is not quite the same as when the issuer itself offers securities of unknown value to the market, in the perception of those in the market, the dissimilarity is not fundamental. Those in a position of stewardship over the company's enterprise are taking advantage of their position to derive profit that is taken at the expense of those in the market. Given the conceptual and practical difficulties in fitting this sort of conduct within the scope of traditional civil or criminal causes of action, it is hardly surprising that most countries have enacted legislation specifically prohibiting those in possession of inside information from taking advantage of it. Indeed, in most systems, the prohibitions extend somewhat further than to those who would ordinarily be considered to occupy positions of trust within a company. While the unfairness of such misconduct more than justifies the intervention of the law to discourage abuse, it does not necessarily justify the development of remedies for those who happen to transact with an insider. Obviously, in practical if not legal terms, there are considerable differences between the matching of parties to a particular transaction, on or off the market.

1.6 In the result, the regulation of insider dealing has and will no doubt continue to throw up a host of issues that would not ordinarily be encountered in the control of other anti-social conduct. The sophistication of the financial environment within which the law and regulatory mechanisms operate, compounds the practical and legal difficulties confronting those seeking to administer and apply the law. While the control of insider abuse has much in common with the prevention and interdiction of money laundering and even corruption, the crafting of legislation and the development of supporting regulatory mechanisms involve issues of peculiar complexity and sensitivity. Despite these problems, the efficacy of anti-insider dealing regulation has, in many countries, become almost a litmus test for the efficiency and competence of the wider regulatory structure overseeing the markets and the conduct of business in the financial sector.

1.7 Consequently, in practical and political terms, the control of insider abuse is a significant issue. While the various philosophical justifications for regulation may be argued about, it is the case that in many countries it is now recognised that the presence of such laws is required if investor confidence in the integrity of the markets is to be preserved and promoted. From perhaps a somewhat cynical perspective, it matters little if such empirical evidence as there is, is equivocal as to the extent of the problem of insider dealing and the harm it occasions. If enough people think it occurs and for whatever reason, including jealousy, consider this is unfair, confidence in the reputation and therefore the efficiency of the market will be eroded. Consequently, those who are responsible for the protection of the markets have a responsibility to act. Whether this be through the medium of the criminal law or some other mechanism, it is in the 'public good' that it be seen that insider dealing is not condoned.

What is insider dealing?

The classic case

1.8   The classic example that is often given of insider dealing is where a director of a company learns in a board meeting that his company's profit forecasts are about to be revised to a significant extent and then goes onto the stock market and trades on the basis of this information before it is made publicly available. In such circumstances, he has clearly taken advantage of his position and the information that came to him by virtue of his seat on the board. He has manifestly misused the confidential information that was entrusted to him in the proper performance of his duties as a director or, in the words of US federal law, misappropriated it. It would also be generally regarded as falling within the notion of insider dealing if he persuaded another person to deal in the securities of his company or disclosed the information to a third person knowing that he would be likely so to deal or otherwise misuse the information.

1.9   It is accepted that this notion of insider dealing would extend to the misuse of confidential information to avoid a loss as well as to make a profit. It matters not whether the director takes advantage of the information to buy more securities in his company in the expectation that their price will rise on publication of the information or whether he sells securities in the fear that the market price will decline. It should, however, be noted that the law might not always offer a remedy or sanction in the latter case. It requires a degree of sophistication that is not always found in the law, to regard a loss avoided as a profit, which should be rendered accountable to the company.

Other primary insiders

1.10   It is not, of course, only company directors that will in the ordinary course of their duties acquire price-sensitive information. Indeed, it is probably more likely that in most companies there are many other insiders who will come into possession of such information rather more regularly than the directors. Having regard to the obvious relationship that a director has to his company, it remains to be seen whether such persons would be rash enough to risk exposure to public criticism by engaging in insider dealing. Furthermore, it cannot be taken for granted that most company directors would be willing to risk their position and the financial and other benefits that arise as a result of their office by engaging in abusive deals.

1.11 The notion of insider dealing is broad enough to encompass all those who, by virtue of their position in the company or who, by their business or professional relationship with the company, are likely to have access to privileged information. For the sake of convenience, it is perhaps useful to describe such persons as primary insiders. They are all subject to the common denominator of enjoying a special relationship with the company that gives them access to the price-sensitive information in question. Indeed, in US jurisprudence, they have often been referred to as 'access insiders'. Debate has taken place as to whether those who obtain such information in breach of their duties attaching to the relationship in question should be regarded as primary insiders. For example, is it appropriate to regard an office cleaner, who, while having access to a company's premises by virtue of her employment directly or indirectly with the company, obtains price-sensitive information by rummaging in the rubbish bins, as a primary insider? Although it is arguable that all those who abuse price-sensitive information should be sanctioned, for the sake of convenience in drafting rules and laws, most jurisdictions distinguish between those who obtain such information in the proper and lawful exercise of the duties attaching to the relationship that they have with the relevant company and those who do so essentially outside the scope of those responsibilities.

1.12 In practice, it is usual to throw the net rather wider and regard primary insiders as insiders, not only of the company with whom they are in this relationship, but also issuers that are closely related to it and to other issuers, such as a potential offeree company. Thus, it will be considered to be insider dealing when a director of a company, having learnt that his company intends to make an attractive takeover offer for the shares of another company, acquires shares in that other company before the offer is announced.

Secondary insiders

1.13 It is also considered to be insider dealing when a person, while not in an access relationship to the issuer, acquires the relevant information in circumstances where he knows that it is unpublished price-sensitive information and comes from an insider source and then deals or encourages another to deal. Thus, although the office cleaner in the example referred to above might not be considered to be a primary insider, her abuse of the information obtained from what she appreciates is an 'inside source', would generally be considered to amount to insider trading. In some cases, it will even be considered objectionable for this tippee or secondary insider to pass the information on to yet another person in circumstances where they know or should appreciate that the information is likely to be misused.

Inside source

1.14   The law and, indeed, morality in most societies therefore necessitates proof of a relationship between the source of the information and the person who is to be accused of insider dealing. The price-sensitive information must be obtained by virtue of this relationship. It is the relationship that taints it and renders improper its use for personal benefit. Of course, the notion of relationship is stretched far beyond what the law would normally consider to be relationships of a fiduciary quality or, for that matter, necessarily giving rise to a duty of confidentiality. The extent to which it is necessary to establish that the relevant information is obtained by virtue of the privileged access that the relationship gives to the person concerned is a matter for debate. Logically, if the information can be shown to have been obtained from some other and outside source, then its use by a person who is clearly in a special relationship with the company should not be considered to be insider dealing. However, in most systems of law, there will be a 'presumption' that if a primary insider is in possession of price-sensitive information in regard to the securities of the issuer with which he has an access relationship, then the 'inside information' was obtained pursuant to this relationship.

Inside information

1.15   Information is a very vague and ill-defined concept in most legal systems. However, in the context of insider dealing, it is generally not necessary to refine a definition that does more than indicate that it possesses a quality sufficient to influence the decision of the person who has access to it to deal in particular securities. In other words, the information that the person accused of insider dealing has in his possession must be such as would influence his decision to buy or sell. In the UK, as in most legal systems, it is enough if the information would influence the mind of a person who would be likely to deal in the relevant securities. Thus, materiality is objective and is determined by reference to the particular class or group of investors that would ordinarily be likely to deal in the securities in question. This gives the test of materiality sufficient flexibility to accommodate narrow and highly specialised markets. The more specific and precise the information is, the more likely it is that it will influence the mind of a reasonable person.

1.16   Some systems of regulation seek to define materiality not so much in terms of the impact on the investor, but on the market. Obviously, the more significant the impact that the information once disclosed is likely to have on the price of the securities, the more influential it will be on the mind of an investor. On the other hand, tests that focus on whether the information is likely to affect the decision of an investor encompass not only the relevance of price, but also other market factors. Generally speaking, it is enough to establish materiality of information that it would be a factor in taking a decision; it need not be the determinant or an especially significant factor.

1.17 The information must be inside information. In other words, it must have a quality which ties it to the issuer in whose securities the dealing takes place. We have already discussed this issue in terms of the relationship that the person accused of insider dealing must have, directly or indirectly, with the source of the information. Obviously, relevance will be bound up with materiality in most conceivable cases. The information need not be generated within, by or for the benefit of the issuer in whose securities the dealing takes place. For example, it would be objectionable for a director of a company which intends to make an attractive takeover offer for the securities of another company to deal in the securities of that other company on the basis of this knowledge. The information in such a case may be regarded as being inside information obtained through his insider nexus with his company, but its relevance is to the market in that other issuer's securities.

1.18 While the information involved in most cases of insider abuse will be confidential or at least obtained in a relationship that might be expected to give rise to obligations of confidentiality, it is not always that the information will be such that could be protected as 'confidential' information. Indeed, there will be cases where the information is too tentative to be protected as proprietary information, but which would still meet the test of materiality. It is also the case that there will be situations when the information is not confidential to a particular person or entity. In the result, it is clear that inside information is not always confidential information. Of course, in the United States, the courts have fashioned the so-called 'misappropriation theory' to justify liability for insider dealing. This approach sanctions the 'misappropriation' of information that belongs to another person. Dealing on the basis of such information will constitute a misappropriation, as will improperly disclosing it to another in circumstances where that other utilises it. The notion that information belongs to another person who will often obtain the same by the inside source is a difficult one for many legal systems. For example, while many legal systems are prepared to protect confidential information as if it were a form of property, not all by any means consider information capable of being a species of property[1].

1   See, for example, *Oxford v Moss* (1978) 68 Cr App R 183, in which it was held information was not property for the purpose of the law of theft.

1.19 Inside information has sometimes been described as 'privileged' information. In the legal sense, privileged information is a concept even narrower than that of confidential information. Consequently, it is preferable to contemplate the notion of privilege, as referring to the circumstances in which it is acquired, rather than the information itself. Where a person in a special relationship or an access relationship acquires information by virtue of his position, then his access may be described as having been made possible in privileged circumstances. To describe, however, inside information as being privileged information in the traditionally accepted legal sense of the word is misleading.

1.20 The information to be inside information must not be in the public domain. Obviously, the value of the information to the person who deals upon it is that it is not publicly available. While it is not necessary for the information to be secret in the sense of being confidential, as we have seen, it must not be accessible to those who could ordinarily be expected to deal in the relevant securities. Many regulatory systems provide that the information should, at the time of its misuse, be unpublished. Much will therefore depend upon what publication means in this context. At one end of the spectrum, if information has been released into the public domain through a press announcement or a regulatory disclosure, then it ceases to be inside information. On the other hand, what if the company is prepared to make the information available only to analysts or other market professionals, possibly on a selective basis? The nature of the market and the sophistication of the financial environment within which the disclosure takes place will inevitably bear upon the question whether the information has been sufficiently published or not.

1.21 It is the case, however, that in most jurisdictions including the UK, provided that the information is freely available to those who would be likely to deal in the relevant securities, there is adequate public disclosure. It has been argued that the fact that the information is publicly available does not entitle those who had pre-publication knowledge to deal before there is an opportunity for the information to be adequately disseminated and even 'digested'.

The transaction

1.22 Insider dealing requires that the person in possession of the information does something partly, at least, in reliance on the information in question. It is not necessary that he does something that he would not have done had he not possessed the information. This would require a much too high standard of materiality and introduce difficult issues of causation. On the other hand, it is generally accepted that for insider dealing to occur the person concerned must enter into a transaction himself, procure or encourage another to enter into a transaction or disclose the information to another in circumstances where that other is likely to abuse the information. Merely desisting from trading would not, in most people's perception, amount to insider dealing. Of course, if a transaction has already been initiated, failing to complete it might well be sufficient.

1.23 The buying or selling need not necessarily relate to securities of the company with which the person concerned is in an access relationship. We have already referred to the fact that many systems of regulation would sanction the use of information pertaining to a transaction or arrangement between the insider's own company and another corporate issuer. It is also the case that dealing in the securities of related companies on the basis of relevant unpublished information would also be considered insider dealing. Dealings in securities other than equity securities that are price-affected by the information would be considered to be insider dealing in the UK and most other jurisdictions. Thus, acquiring options to acquire or dispose of underlying securities would be objectionable, as would dealing in other types of derivative securities. The question is simply whether the decision to deal in the relevant securities is influenced by the information that the person concerned has acquired and is using improperly.

1.24 The term 'insider dealing' is wide enough to encompass deals on or off an organised securities market. While a number of legal systems have effectively confined the operation of their legal rules to transactions that occur on an organised securities exchange or on or through an organised over-the-counter market, the elements of the abuse are the same whether the transaction is on a market or in a private direct transaction. One of the reasons why jurisdictions have confined the operation of their laws to public markets is the idea that the wrong indicated by insider dealing is one against the market as a whole. It saps confidence in the integrity and fairness of the market. Consequently, some have made available only their criminal justice system to sanction this essentially public wrong or, rather, crime. Off-market transactions are left to the ordinary law which governs the commercial dealings of private persons. The fallacy is to attribute the description of insider dealing to one type of transaction and not to the other. While there may be justifications for distinguishing market and off-market insider transactions in regard to the remedies that are made available and in relation to enforcement, the nature of the abuse and its elements are the same. Therefore, it is appropriate to regard insider dealing as taking place on organised markets as well as in private and even face-to-face transactions.

Unauthorised disclosures

1.25 It has already been pointed out that most systems of insider dealing regulation would regard disclosing inside information to another person, without the appropriate authority, in circumstances where that other person is likely to abuse the information, as a form of insider dealing. Of course, merely disclosing information even if there is an expectation that the recipient will himself deal, is not 'dealing' in any real sense of the word. While it is possible and common place to attribute the transactions of an agent to the principal and therefore the deals of the agent to the deals of the 'insider', it is less easy to describe procuring or encouraging the dealing of another as insider dealing. Nonetheless, the term insider dealing is often employed in such an expansive manner, as it is in the UK.

1.26 Where a person, without authority, discloses unpublished and material information in the knowledge that the recipient might well utilise the information for dealing, then it is at least arguable that the person should be held responsible for what is indirectly the exploitation of the information in question. In the UK, as in most systems of law that regard such unauthorised disclosures as tantamount to insider dealing, it matters not whether the recipient actually engages in transactions which would themselves be considered insider dealing. For example, while the informant might be culpable, the recipient who deals on the basis of the information may not be aware that the information emanates from an inside source. Of course, a failure to appreciate the status of the information might well in any case bring into issue its materiality.

1.27 Such conduct will, however, only be considered objectionable when the primary insider discloses the relevant information without proper authority. It is not always easy to decide if a particular disclosure is legitimate or not. As a general rule, if the disclosure is made with the actual or implied authority of the person concerned to make or authorise disclosure, then it will not be objectionable. There may be cases where, while the relevant officer of the company has authority to disclose information, he does so not for a proper purpose, but perhaps to facilitate improper transactions on the part of another. In most systems of law, agents have authority only to engage in actions that are properly motivated. Therefore, a disclosure that is motivated by improper considerations, such as a desire to promote a false market, would not be legitimate and justifiable even when a primary insider has no authority to disclose information. It may well be on the facts appropriate and legitimate for him to do so, for example, 'blowing the whistle' on misconduct. Provided that such is done for a purpose that would be considered proper and is not dishonest, it is hard to see that such conduct could be described as fostering insider abuse. The line between what is acceptable and what is not is not always clear. Difficulties have arisen in the case of selective disclosures to analysts and private briefings, as we shall see.

The inside nexus

1.28 While over the last two decades most jurisdictions have enacted laws specifically prohibiting insider dealing and penalising infractions of the law, outside the US and one or two other jurisdictions, such as the UK and France, prosecutions have been rare and have only occasionally resulted in convictions. The reasons why such few cases of insider abuse end in convictions are many and varied. However, it is not uncommon to find that the specific offences that have been created to address the problem of insider abuse require the prosecution to prove, to the high standard of the criminal law, a set of facts which in practice renders many cases incapable of prosecution. For example, the former offence of insider dealing in the UK required the prosecution to establish no fewer than 12 separate facts. Proof of the requisite state of mind, or mens rea, was particularly onerous. The record of successful prosecutions for fraud and economic crime involving complex factual situations and sophisticated business activities is not impressive in almost any country. On the other hand, there is the perception that insider dealing does occur at a sufficiently significant level in many markets to be a matter of concern to those who are charged with promoting and maintaining their integrity and, therefore, attempts have been made to simplify the essential elements for establishing the 'offence' of insider dealing.

1.29 Consequently, attempts have been made, most noticeably through the European Commission's company law harmonisation programme and then later as part of its initiative to ensure equivalence of protection and the creation of a level 'playing field', for the financial services industry to recast the law so as to render it more useable and effective in addressing insider abuse. In doing so, there has been, apart from in the United States, a tendency to move away from the need for an essentially fiduciary nexus and to base the prohibition on what might be described as 'fraud on the market' concepts. In doing so, the emphasis has been placed, at least as far as the law is concerned, on the misuse of privileged information from the standpoint of those in the market and not from the position of the company. Although the European directive[1] which seeks to co-ordinate anti-insider dealing laws within the EU is very much orientated to the market and ensuring the integrity of dealings in a market context, it still adheres in part to the more traditional notion that insider dealing signifies the involvement of persons who would be considered by virtue of their positions to be corporate insiders, ie directors, officers and substantial shareholders, albeit these primary insiders need not have this relationship with the issuer of the securities to which the abuse relates. Thus, we are still in the realm of company law and traditional issues of governance, although conceptually somewhat on the periphery.

1   Council Directive 89/592/EEC (13 November 1989).

1.30 Although there is a tendency, in at least some jurisdictions, to fasten upon the unfair use of all information that is not adequately disseminated, at this point in time, the notion of insider dealing involves three basic elements. First, the existence of information which is not publicly available, or at least is not available to those who would be likely to deal in the securities to which it relates, but, if it were, it would be likely to influence their decision to deal and upon what terms. In other words, there must be material, non-public information. Secondly, those in possession of the information must be aware that it emanates, directly or indirectly, from an inside source. Thirdly, they must then deal in the securities that would be affected by the information. It is also usually thought to be insider dealing when the possessor of the information encourages another to deal or improperly discloses the information to another in circumstances where it is likely that that other person will deal or encourage another to deal.

Who are insiders?

1.31 We have looked at what might be described as the constituent elements of what is ordinarily conjured up by the term 'insider dealing'. Before proceeding with our discussion, it would be useful to explore the various arguments as to who should be regarded as an insider. Of course, we have already looked at the traditional categories and raised the distinction between primary or access insiders and those who obtain the relevant information through such a person and are thus more appropriately described as secondary insiders. However, even in relation to this simplistic distinction, there are issues which would be useful to discuss in the wider context of who may properly and appropriately be considered to be an insider and thereby subjected to additional obligations. It is also important to remember that, under the laws of most jurisdictions, the determination of who and who is not to be considered an insider has serious implications for those dealing with them and, in particular, receiving and utilising information from them. A person who deals with an insider is dealing with an inside source and, consequently, any communication from that insider will be from an inside source subjecting that person to the obligations of being an insider himself.

Access insiders

1.32 The classic notion of insider dealing, as we have already indicated, involves a person closely associated with an issuer, taking advantage of material unpublished information that has come into his possession by virtue of his relationship to the company. While there are no doubt instances of persons in an access relationship to an issuer engaging in such conduct, as we have already indicated, it must surely be unlikely that corporate insiders would be prepared to risk their position and employment by engaging in such egregious conduct. Consequently, most of the cases that have come to light involving primary insiders acting in such an unsophisticated and blatant manner have involved individuals whose conduct may fairly be described as an aberration, possibly motivated by exceptional pressures or financial needs. In fact, in a high proportion of cases, the amounts of money involved have also been relatively small. Most corporate insiders would not in the ordinary course of events be able to raise very significant amounts of money to risk on insider trading within the requisite time frame. Those insiders who are prepared to violate the trust reposed in them and engage in a more systematic abuse of their position would tend to utilise nominees, sell or even barter the information in question. Obviously, the more sophisticated the attempts are to evade detection, the less likely it is that the insider will be identified or rendered amenable to sanctions. In those jurisdictions that have developed regimes for the control of insider abuse, in the case of primary insiders, it is on the whole only the relatively 'innocent' and foolish that get caught.

Those in the market

1.33 Professor Henry Manne suggested in 1966, in his book *Insider Dealing and the Stock Market*[1], that primary insiders would, because of the risks that they face, be far more likely to exchange items of inside information rather than trade on it themselves. While this was thought somewhat fanciful, there are examples of insiders indulging in this activity or selling information. Obviously, the more disassociated the eventual dealing is from the relationship through which the information was obtained, the more difficult it is for action to be taken against the insider who has betrayed his fiduciary obligations. In countries where anti-insider dealing regulation is developed, a significant proportion of cases involve dealing on unpublished price-sensitive information by financial intermediaries. Such persons are often in a much better position to evaluate the impact of information and exploit it, as compared with the ordinary corporate executive. They are also able to organise exploitation to maximum effect through the use of derivatives and other trading devices. The relevant information in many of these cases is either obtained from a primary insider or relates to the financial activity of the issuer in question.

1   Free Press (US).

1.34 There has been debate as to the extent to which 'market information', as opposed to information that is generated from within the company, can properly be regarded as inside information. For example, the decision of a substantial shareholder to liquidate his holding, while not inside information in the conventional sense of the word, could well be highly price-sensitive. While it would generally be thought inappropriate to stigmatise the actual transaction by the substantial shareholder as objectionable, as he is possessed of nothing more than the knowledge of his own intentions, those who are privy to this might be thought to be in a rather different situation. It should be noted, however, that many systems impose disclosure obligations, primarily to the market, when a transaction would have implications for the control of a company[1]. In addition to the disclosure of shareholdings above a certain level, most developed regulatory systems impose obligations on individuals and companies, once certain thresholds have been crossed, to announce their intentions and or make a public offer[2]. There are also provisions for the mandatory aggregation and disclosure of shareholdings in cases where persons act in concert to 'warehouse' securities if the aggregated holding exceeds the requisite 'disclosure threshold'[3].

1   See the Companies Act 1985, Pt VI.
2   See General Principle 10 and Rule 2.2 of the Takeover Code.
3   See the Companies Act 1985, ss 203–208 and the Takeover Code.

1.35 There are a number of important considerations, however, that need to be addressed if the regulatory net is thrown over market information, that does not have some additional quality to it, other than being merely material and non-public. Mention has already been made of the important role that analysts and other intermediaries play in the financial services industry. It is important that what are widely considered to be quite proper and even beneficial operations in the market are not undermined. The position of market makers is particularly sensitive. In many markets, certain professionals will be charged with a responsibility to provide a market, either way, in a selection of securities. This facilitates liquidity and stability and assists in the maintenance of an orderly market. It is the case, however, that such dealers will, because of their specialised relationship with the issuers in whose securities they make a market, come into possession, or themselves generate, information of a price-sensitive nature. Having said this, however, it is also important to note that market makers, given their obligation to remain in the market, albeit within certain limits and be willing to trade, are particularly exposed to insider dealing and manipulative practices on the part of others. Consequently, market makers in many countries have often been at the forefront of those calling for stricter control of insider dealing. Generally speaking, the beneficial role performed by such market professionals is recognised in law by effectively exempting what they do in the ordinary and proper course of business as a market maker.

The corporate issuer

1.36 Discussion has also taken place in several jurisdictions as to whether the issuer can be regarded as an insider of itself. There is no objection, under the laws of most countries, to a company being considered an insider and to legal liability attaching to the corporation in the ordinary way. What has been said in regard to the intention of a person to act in a certain manner applies as much to a company as it would to an individual. However, where the issuer intends to act in a manner which would affect the price of its own securities or for that matter a related company's, the view in some of the more developed jurisdictions is that it is properly cast in the role of an insider. Of course, the circumstances in which a company can deal in its own capital are strictly limited and in many countries it is illegal for a company to acquire its own securities or give any third person financial assistance to do so[1]. However, in certain circumstances, companies may be able to repurchase and cancel stock or redeem preference shares. Where this is permitted, the issuer would be bound to ensure that the holders of these securities are in no way prejudiced by the existence of unpublished information which might affect the value of the securities to be acquired or redeemed. Consequently, the company would have to make a full and fair disclosure. Of course, in such circumstances, the directors of the company would also have a duty to ensure that whatever is done by the company is done in its best interests.

1   See the Companies Act 1985, Pt V, Chapters VI and VII.

'Scalpers' and 'gun jumpers'

1.37 From a conceptual standpoint, a somewhat related issue is that of 'scalping'. In its simplest form, 'scalping' involves what a journalist or analyst trading in securities has written up or, for that matter, expressed reservations about, in an article or report prior to its publication. Depending upon the circumstances, there is little doubt that comments of a favourable or negative character can have a profound and predictable impact on the price of the securities. The problem is that the information upon which the journalist trades has no insider nexus with the relevant issuer. It may well amount to nothing more or less than the fruits of his own work and reflections based upon widely available and verifiable facts. On the other hand, using advance knowledge that the article is likely to have an impact on the market to make a profit or, for that matter, avoid a loss, is objectionable. It has the character of betting on a certainty which is compounded by an abuse of position. Where the dealing is by an individual other than the person who wrote it, then it is often relatively easy to construct an argument that would bring that person within the reach of the ordinary theories of insider liability. It is where the journalist or analyst himself trades that the real difficulty arises.

1.38 While most systems of regulation would consider this unethical, few actually attempt to impose specific legal sanctions. In the United States, the 'misappropriation theory' has been used with effect to impose liability on anyone who uses, without proper authority, 'inside' information that belongs to another. Consequently, if the article has been prepared by the journalist in the course of his employment or under commission, then it is arguable that the information can only be used for his employer's purposes. If he seeks to take personal advantage of it by trading prior to publication, then he would be guilty of insider dealing. Of course, in many jurisdictions and in particular common law legal systems, it is probable that the ordinary law would impose liability on an employee who sought to profit in such a manner.

1.39 In the present context, the term 'gun jumping' is often applied to the same sort of conduct as 'scalping'. However, it is wider in the sense that it involves those, other than the person or persons responsible for the creation of the information or opportunity, seeking to take advantage of it before it is published. It is also applied to those who deal immediately on publication of the information before others have had an opportunity to assess it properly. Those who are privy to unpublished price-sensitive information and then, without authority, seek to exploit it, may well fall within the purview of anti-insider dealing laws. Under the European directive on insider trading, provided that the person seeking to exploit the information is aware that the source of the information is classified as a primary insider, even though they may have no relationship with the issuer of the securities in question, an offence would be committed. As we have already pointed out, the directive creates a class of primary insiders, members of which may or may not happen to be in an access relationship to the company in question. Where, however, the information is not obtained from a person who happens to be a director, officer or substantial shareholder of any company, the issue of liability is rather more problematical. Where the dealing takes place after the information has been disclosed, then, very few jurisdictions require those with advance knowledge to hold back for a period to allow dissemination, let alone digestion.

1.40   While 'jumping the gun' may be considered to be unfair, it must also be remembered that analysts do play an important role in refining information and thereby improving the quality of investment decisions. The costs of providing this service to the market needs to be met and it is important not to place those who develop such information at a competitive disadvantage in reaping the benefits of their own work. Perhaps the appropriate dividing line between what is acceptable use by the originators of such information and what is not, is the distinction between utilising the work product itself, as opposed to seeking to benefit from its market impact, once it becomes known.

Shareholders

1.41   Primary insiders are those who have a clear and defined relationship with the company to which the inside information 'belongs' or, in the case of those jurisdictions that have followed the European directive, any company. Although, as we have seen, it can be misleading to describe this relationship as always resembling a fiduciary or confidential relationship, in the majority of cases, those in an access relationship to the relevant information will be subject to legal obligations similar to those of a fiduciary or an agent. Many jurisdictions, however, include in the class of primary insiders substantial shareholders and, in some cases, all shareholders. In the vast majority of legal systems, the relationship between a shareholder and his company is purely contractual and does not involve obligations of a fiduciary or confidential character.

1.42   In the laws of many states, shareholders have no special or privileged access to corporate information. Indeed, in many cases they have no right even to inspect the books of the company. Creditors, other than pursuant to special contractual arrangements that may be made, have even less access to the company. It is appreciated, however, that some shareholders, by virtue of the size or relevance of their holdings, may well have an influence on the management of the issuer and thereby, in some respects, be in the same position as an 'access insider'. In such cases, it may be appropriate simply to consider them to be potentially secondary insiders. Having said this, however, there is a tendency, which is not particularly logical, to expand the category of 'presumed insider' to encompass those shareholders with a substantial interest in a class of equity or to, at least in Europe, all shareholders.

CHAPTER 2

Insider reporting and disclosure obligations

Introduction

2.1   As discussed in Chapter 1, insider dealing involves the exploitation of information which has not yet been effectively discounted by the market, or in direct personal transactions, by the person with whom the insider is dealing. Minimising and regulating the release of price-sensitive information to the market will result in less opportunity for those seeking to exploit it[1]. It has already been observed that insiders are likely to manipulate events so as to avoid prompt disclosure of information which they can exploit for their own ends[2]. This is a particular problem in situations where those in a position to influence the management of a company are also substantially interested in its securities. Thus, in many developing countries, the manipulation of information about a company is far more common than efforts by insiders seeking merely to beat the market. The overall objective of encouraging as much dissemination of relevant information into the market as possible to facilitate sensible investment decisions means that issuers should be required to disclose, through appropriate procedures, all information which might be reasonably considered to have an impact on the price of their securities.

1   See B A K Rider and M Ashe, *Insider Crime* (1993, Jordans) p 10.
2   See *Insider Crime*, p 4.

2.2   A highly evolved system of disclosure by company insiders of 'relevant information' (in the sense used in the Financial Services and Markets Act 2000 ('FSMA 2000') market abuse regime) provides an effective method of enhancing market transparency. Where the obligations of disclosure are observed, the scope for market abuse is correspondingly reduced. The significance of disclosure obligations is recognised by the FSA in its Code of Market Conduct. The FSA's emphasis upon disclosure is in harmony with the approach of the Securities and Exchange Commission in the USA, which has adopted a new regulation (Regulation FD) directed at the practice of selective disclosure by companies to analysts in order to maintain favour with the latter and the draft European directive on market abuse[1] at art 6(2).

1   2001/118 (COD).

2.3 As will be seen in Chapter 6, the FSA has expanded upon the FSMA 2000, s 118 definition of misuse of information in its Code of Market Conduct. The FSA considers that in order for information to amount to market abuse 'the information must relate to matters which the regular user would reasonably expect to be disclosed to users of the particular prescribed market … this includes both matters which give rise to such an expectation of disclosure or are likely to do so either at the time in question, or in the future'[1]. This includes information that has to be disclosed in accordance with any legal or regulatory requirement. Moreover, the FSA has expanded upon the s 118 definition of market manipulation by defining certain behaviour as market abuse if it involves the knowing dissemination of false or misleading information that is relevant to the market[2]. Consequently, an understanding of disclosure obligations assists in clarifying the offence of misuse of information.

1   MAR 1.4.4(4).
2   MAR 1.5.15E(1)–(3) and MAR 1.6.7.

2.4 This chapter considers certain statutory and common law obligations of disclosure, before turning to certain regulatory provisions requiring disclosure and how the FSA may interpret these guidelines.

Statutory disclosure and reporting obligations

2.5 A company will encounter statutory disclosure obligations at various stages, such as, for example, when it seeks to raise capital it will have disclosure obligations relating to offer and sale of securities. Continuous disclosure requirements are also designed to provide those dealing with the company to have adequate information concerning the term and conditions of their agreements and overall relationship. The requirement of continuous disclosure relies significantly on the medium of financial statements which, even if accurate and comprehensive, are essentially retrospective in their focus on past events. Accordingly, timely disclosure is of great importance to the efficient functioning of financial markets. This involves the immediate release of information to the market in a readily understood form, which may lead to more effective price dissemination in the market resulting in less volatility in prices because of unexpected and significant events[1].

1   See B A K Rider and H L French, *The Regulation of Insider Trader* (1979, Macmillan) Chapter 4 (discussing development of timely disclosure policies).

Directors' statutory duties of disclosure

2.6 The significance of disclosure obligations in reducing the opportunity for insider dealing has long been recognised. There have been statutory obligations upon directors to disclose share transactions and holdings for longer than there has been a prohibition against insider dealing in this jurisdiction. These obligations of disclosure are recognised as important in ensuring that the markets are informed of primary insiders' transactions.

2.7 The Companies Act 1985, ss 324–329 contain the main statutory requirements of directors' duties of disclosure in relation to their share transactions. The Companies Act 1985, Sch 13 supplements and amplifies these sections[1]. These sections lie within the Companies Act 1985, Pt X which is concerned with the enforcement of fair dealing by directors. The Law Commission in its paper entitled 'Company Directors: Regulating Conflicts of Interests and Formulating a Statement of Duties'[2] noted these provisions 'play an important role in terms of monitoring whether directors are properly subordinating their personal interests to those of the company'[3].

1 Companies Act 1985, ss 324(3) and 325(5).
2 Law Commission No 261.
3 Paragraph 11.19.

2.8 The Companies Act 1985, s 324(1) requires a director to notify the company in writing of the subsistence of certain interests in the company and sets out the details that must be given in such notification. When giving notification under either s 324(1) or (2), the notice must be expressed to be given in fulfilment of the obligation[1]. This disclosure obligation arises where the director 'is interested in' shares in or debentures of the company or any other body corporate, being the company's subsidiary or holding company or a subsidiary of the company's holding company. The phrase 'is interested in' is expanded upon at some length in the Companies Act 1985, Sch 13, Pt I. Regard must also be had to the Companies (Disclosure of Directors' Interests) (Exceptions) Regulations 1985, SI 1985/802. The Companies Act 1985, Sch 13, Pt II sets out the periods within which obligations must be fulfilled. This obligation must be fulfilled before the expiration of the period of five days beginning with the day following the day on which he becomes a director if he knows of such interest at such time[2]. Otherwise, the obligation must be fulfilled within five days beginning with the day on which the existence of the interest comes to his knowledge[3]. 'Days' for these purposes excludes Saturdays, Sundays and bank holidays in any part of Great Britain[4].

1 Companies Act 1985, s 324(5).
2 Companies Act 1985, Sch 13, para 14.
3 Companies Act 1985, Sch 13, para 14.
4 Companies Act 1985, Sch 13, para 16.

2.9 The director is also under a continuing obligation to notify the company of the occurrence while he is a director of certain events set out in the Companies Act 1985, s 324(2). These relate essentially to changes relating to his shareholding or prospective shareholding in the company and are broadly worded. For instance, an assignment by the director of a right granted to him by the company to subscribe for shares in or debentures of the company are included[1]. The director must not only notify the company of the fact of such occurrence, but also, pursuant to the Companies Act

1985, Sch 13, Pt III, of further detail, including, for instance, the consideration received for such an assignment. The time limits applicable to s 324(2) are similar to those applying to s 324(1)[2]. A director is not obliged to notify an event whose occurrence comes to his attention after he has ceased to be a director[3].

1 Companies Act 1985, s 324(2)(c).
2 Companies Act 1985, Sch 13, para 15.
3 Companies Act 1985, s 324(4).

2.10   The Companies Act 1985, s 324 applies to shadow directors as it does to directors[1]. A person who either fails to make notification within the prescribed period or in purported discharge of an obligation to which he is subject makes a statement to the company which he knows to be false or recklessly makes a statement which is false is guilty of an offence and liable to imprisonment or a fine or both[2]. Proceedings may only be instituted by or with the consent of the Secretary of State or the Director of Public Prosecutions[3]. The validity of transactions, however, is unaffected by non-compliance with this section[4].

1 Companies Act 1985, s 324(6).
2 Companies Act 1985, s 324(7).
3 Companies Act 1985, ss 324(8) and 732.
4 *Chitty on Contracts* (28th edn) para 17–150.

2.11   The Companies Act 1985, s 328 extends the Companies Act 1985, s 324. This section deems the position of a wife or husband of a director or infant son or infant daughter (which include stepsons and daughters) of a director in shares and debentures of the company to the director. The section also extends the duty of notification to the company in relation to events particular to the members of the director's family. The obligations and sanctions relating to the notification obligation created by this section are the same as those under s 324.

2.12   Following notification by the directors, all companies are required to record the information received and the date of the entry in the register that it is obliged to keep under the Companies Act 1985, s 325. Whenever the company grants a director or shadow director a right to subscribe for shares in or debentures of the company, it is required to record prescribed details relating to such option in the company's register pursuant to s 325(3) and (6). Similarly, whenever the director or shadow director exercises such right, the company is required to register certain details pursuant to s 325(4). The Companies Act 1985, Sch 13, Pt IV sets out how the register is to be compiled, where it is to be kept, who may require a copy of such register and the fact that it is to be produced at the commencement of the AGM. The provisions relating to the copying of the register should be read together with the Companies (Inspection and Copying of Registers, Indices and Documents) Regulations 1991, SI 1991/1998. The manner in which the register is to be kept should be read in conjunction with the Companies Act

1985, ss 722(1) and 723(1) and the Companies (Registers and Records) Regulations 1985, SI 1985/724.

2.13 The Companies Act 1985, s 326 creates a number of offences for which the company and every officer of it who is in default of various provisions of the Companies Act 1985, s 325 and Sch 13, Pt IV may be liable to a fine and, for continued contravention, a daily fine. In addition, the court is empowered by s 326(6) to compel an immediate inspection of such register where inspection as permitted by the Companies Act 1985, Sch 13, para 25 is refused or to direct that a copy is sent to a person requiring it where there is default under Sch 13, para 26.

2.14 A company whose shares are listed on a recognised investment exchange ('RIE') as defined by the Companies Act 1985, s 329 is also required by that section to notify such exchange of any matter notified to it by a director pursuant to the Companies Act 1985, ss 324 and 328 that relates to shares or debentures listed on such exchange. The RIE may then publish in such manner as it determines any information received by it pursuant to such section. The company's obligation must be fulfilled before the end of the next day following that on which it arises pursuant to s 329(2). However, Saturdays, Sundays and bank holidays in any part of Great Britain are disregarded for these purposes[1]. The company and every officer of it who is in default are guilty of an offence and liable to a fine and to a daily default fine for continued contravention pursuant to s 329(3).

1   Companies Act 1985, s 329(2).

2.15 These disclosure requirements have been criticised for their length and complexity and the Company Law Review hopes that it will be possible to simplify the drafting[1]. Overall, the Company Law Review has adopted the recommendations of the Law Commission on this topic. The most significant issue in the present context is the recommendation that a company's obligation to notify an RIE pursuant to the Companies Act 1985, s 329 should be extended so that a company is bound to transmit information that is registered pursuant to the Companies Act 1985, s 325(3) and (4) (relating to a director's share and debenture options) whether or not the director has yet notified the company[2].

1   'Modern Company Law Review for a Competitive Economy: Developing the Framework' at Annex C, p 419 and 'Modern Company Law for a Competitive Economy: Final Report' at para 6.16, n 87.
2   Law Commission, para 11.44 and 'Developing the Framework' at Annex C, para 27.

Prohibition on directors dealing in share options

2.16 The Companies Act 1985, s 323 prohibits directors (including shadow directors) from buying put or call options in the listed securities of a company of which he is a director or of another within the same group. The Companies

Act 1985, s 327 extends this section to the wife or husband of a director or the infant son or daughter of a director, which includes stepsons and stepdaughters. In 'Modern Company Law for a Competitive Economy: Final Report' at para 6.15, the Company Law Review Steering Group notes that the DTI inspectors' report on Mirror Group Newspapers plc[1] recommended that there be additional regulation of directors dealing in options, by reason of concerns about market manipulation. The Company Law Review has concluded that s 323 is a matter for the FSA and HM Treasury rather than the Review. The Law Commission has concluded that there is nothing intrinsically objectionable to directors dealing in such options if there is full disclosure and has recommended the repeal of this section, notwithstanding that the Crown Prosecution Service recommended its retention by reason of its scope being wider than the criminal prohibition against insider dealing[2]. The Law Commission's view is that the gap in the law covered by s 323 (namely off market dealings) is better addressed either through an extension of the Criminal Justice Act 1993 or self-regulation such as the Model Code or by companies themselves by contract. However, if s 323 is repealed, the Law Commission recommends that the activities in question should be subject to disclosure obligations by directors under the Companies Act 1985, s 324.

1   'Mirror Group Newspapers plc: Investigation under ss 432(2) and 442 of the Companies Act 1985: Report by the Honourable Sir George John Laugharne Thomas and Raymond Thomas Turner FCA, Inspectors Appointed by the Secretary of State for Trade and Industry' (March 2001, HMSO).
2   Law Commission, para 11.7.

Reporting directors' shareholdings

2.17   By the Companies Act 1985, s 234(3) and Sch 7, Pt I, the company is required to give information in the directors' report or by way of notes to the company's annual accounts. The information to be given is similar to that required to be notified by directors pursuant to the Companies Act 1985, ss 324 and 328 and kept in the register the company is obliged to keep by the Companies Act 1985, s 325.

General obligations of disclosure of shareholdings

2.18   The Companies Act 1985, Pt VI creates a number of general obligations of disclosure in relation to public companies that apply to company insiders and outsiders. These provisions are of two types: those that require automatic disclosure in certain prescribed circumstances (Companies Act 1985, ss 198–210) and those that enable the company to investigate interests in its shares (Companies Act 1985, ss 212–216). Although these sections were traditionally regarded as important to a public company in ascertaining the true ownership of its shares and thus identifying a potential takeover threat, more recently they have been recognised as important to market transparency.

Offers of securities

2.19   The duties of disclosure when a company is created are also important. The FSMA 2000, Pt VI retains the statutory duties of disclosure that were set out in the Financial Services Act 1986, Pt IV. The FSMA 2000, s 80 creates the general statutory duty of disclosure in listing particulars, with the FSMA 2000, s 90 providing a mechanism for compensation in the event of non-compliance. The Public Offers of Securities Regulations 1995, SI 1995/1537 make similar provision in relation to offers of unlisted securities.

European directives

2.20   The European Directive on the admission of securities to official listing on a stock exchange[1] provides that a listed company must inform the public as soon as possible of any major new development in its sphere of activity which is not public knowledge and which may, by virtue of its effect on its assets and liabilities or financial position or on the general course of its business, lead to a substantial movement in the price of its shares. It also allows the relevant national authorities responsible for regulating the market to exempt an issuer from this obligation, if the disclosure of a specific item of information would prejudice the legitimate interests of the company. The FSA 1986, s 153(1) implemented these provisions by authorising the Stock Exchange to adopt such an obligation in its Listing Rules. Article 7 of the Insider Dealing Directive, however, requires that the obligation to make prompt disclosure of material events in the Admissions Directive should be applied for securities to which, although not officially listed, are admitted to trading on a regulated market. In 1993, the UK Treasury adopted regulations pursuant to the UK European Communities Act that implements the obligation of the 1991 Insider Dealing Directive that issuers must make prompt disclosure in regard to securities which are officially listed by the Stock Exchange *or* are traded on the Unlisted Securities Market[2].

1   Directive 79/279, Sch C5(9).
2   But this did not extend to issuers whose securities are traded on SEAQ.

2.21   Issuers that are publicly listed on a recognised investment exchange are required to make proper and timely disclosure. The FSMA 2000 imposes a public law duty on issuers – whether authorised persons or not – to make timely disclosure. Furthermore, it is required that the rules of all recognised investment exchanges must, at least, provide that, in the event of a failure by an issuer to comply with its rules, to publish and make known that the issuer has breached its obligations and proceed to publish the information itself. Indeed, the imposition of such an obligation on issuers, and the threat of sanctions under the FSMA 2000, conform with the requirements of art 13 of the Insider Dealing Directive 'to promote compliance'.

Disclosure obligations at common law

2.22 At common law, a general principle of contract law was that in the absence of a specific duty to make disclosure of material facts, there was no general duty to disclose material information[1]. Essentially, silence did not constitute a misrepresentation. Moreover, the traditional rule was that a company director had no duty of good faith and fair disclosure to an individual shareholder of the company[2]. Logically, then, the director would not have such a duty to an individual who is not a shareholder. When directors do disclose, of course, they must not mislead shareholders[3].

1   *Chase Manhattan Equities Ltd v Goodman* [1991] BCLC 897.
2   *Percival v Wright* [1902] 2 Ch 421 at 427–428.
3   This duty derives from the law of deceit, see *Gore-Brown on Companies*, s 12.17 and *Prudential Assurance Co Ltd v Newman Industries Ltd (No 2)* [1981] Ch 257.

2.23 The common law is therefore of far greater significance in the context of private companies, where arguments have focussed upon fiduciary duties. The starting point of an analysis of this branch of the law is the classic case of *Percival v Wright*[1]. The court held that directors of a company are not trustees for individual shareholders and may purchase their shares without disclosing pending negotiations for the sale of the company's undertaking – a director's duties are owed to the company and not to individual shareholders. This case has been actively criticised in New Zealand and Australia. The New South Wales Court of Appeal in *Brunninghausen v Glavanics*[2] recently refused to follow the decision, thus following the lead taken by the New Zealand Court of Appeal in *Coleman v Myers*[3].

1   [1902] 2 Ch 421.
2   (1999) 32 ACSR 294.
3   [1977] 2 NZLR 225.

2.24 *Percival v Wright* has not been without its detractors in this jurisdiction either. In fact, the rule was severely criticised by the Cohen Committee[1] and rejected by the Jenkins Committee[2]. The law has now evolved to a position where the courts recognise that a fiduciary duty may be owed by directors to individual shareholders where there are special circumstances[3]. The claimants failed to establish special circumstances sufficient to resist an application to strike out in *Peskin v Anderson*. However, in the course of judgments both at first instance and in the Court of Appeal, indications were given that particularly in 'the specially strong context of the familial relationships of the directors and shareholders and their relative personal positions of influence in the company concerned', special circumstances might be established.

1   Cmnd 6659.
2   Cmnd 1749.
3   See, eg, *Peskin v Anderson* [2000] 2 BCLC 1 at 14 per Neuberger J and [2001] 1 BCLC 372 at 379, CA per Mummery LJ.

Directors

2.25   There have been a number of attempts to argue that a director owes a duty of disclosure to the party with whom he contracts in the course of buying or selling shares in a company of which he is a director. The attacks have variously relied upon misrepresentation (eg *Chase Manhattan Equities Ltd v Goodman*[1]) and breach of fiduciary duty (see most recently *Peskin v Anderson*[2]). In the context of listed companies (as distinct from private companies), the starting point of an argument based on non-disclosure will probably be based either on statute or regulatory provision. This view is supported by the decision of Knox J in *Chase Manhattan*. In that case, a market maker sought to repudiate a sale of shares of a company in circumstances where a director of the company in question had failed to comply with the Model Code. The market maker in question alleged that the director owed it a duty to disclose all facts material to the making of the sale agreement between them. This argument failed to persuade Knox J. He was of the view that:

> 'there is too long and tenuous a chain of legal obligation between the duty of a director under the Model Code to report a proposed dealing in a security to the board at one end and a market maker in that security at the other end to justify the finding of a duty owed to the latter by the former to speak'[3].

The learned judge was more concerned as to the position of 'ordinary investors'. In the context of such ordinary investors, the new powers created by the FSMA 2000 in relation to market abuse are particularly relevant. If it were possible to identify any 'victims' in such circumstances, the FSA could impose a restitution order administratively or apply to the court for such an order.

1   [1991] BCLC 897.
2   [2001] 1 BCLC 372.
3   At 929c.

Promoters

2.26   Special mention should also be given to another type of insider, the company promoter. Prior to any statutory intervention, the courts had sought to reduce potential abuse by such persons and held that company promoters owed a fiduciary duty to the company with all the duties of disclosure that accompany such duty[1].

1   See, eg, *Erlanger v New Sombrero Phosphate Co* (1878) 3 App Cas 1218.

Financial Services Authority interpretation and Model Codes

2.27   The FSMA 2000 contains a new market abuse framework that extends the current insider dealing regulatory regime in two important respects: (a) its coverage extends to unauthorised as well as authorised persons, so that all market participants will be subject to the same requirements and (b) greater transparency and disclosure is required for the regulated community. To accomplish this, the FSA has issued a Code of Market Conduct that provides guidelines for the regulated community in determining what information is relevant and thereby should be disclosed to the market. The Code of Market Conduct provides an insight into the FSA's overall approach of identifying market practices that fall short of the standards expected by a reasonable regular user of the market and which undermine a key FSMA 2000 objective of promoting market confidence. The section of the Code dealing with situations when information will not be generally available relies primarily on the sections in CP 10 dealing with 'disclosable information' and 'privileged possession'.

2.28   Market abuse includes behaviour which is likely to give a false or misleading impression of the price or value of qualifying investments. Regarding the dissemination of information, the Code provides that behaviour will constitute market abuse when a person:

- disseminates information which is, or if true would be, relevant information;
- knows, or could reasonably be expected to know, that the information disseminated is false or misleading; and
- disseminates the information in order to create a false or misleading impression, which need not be the sole purpose for disseminating the information, but must be an *actuating purpose*[1].

In determining whether the person in question had an actuating purpose, the FSA will apply several factors, including whether that person had an interest in a qualifying investment or relevant product to which the information was relevant[2]. The presence of this factor will tend to suggest that the person had disseminated the information in order to create a false or misleading impression. In contrast, the FSA has emphasised that the absence of this factor does not conclusively demonstrate that the behaviour in question does not amount to market abuse. Chapter 7 will discuss examples that apply this principle in the Code of Market Conduct.

1   MAR 1.5.15E(1)–(3).
2   MAR 1.5.16E.

2.29   The disclosability of information with respect to future developments is another important concern that is addressed by the FSA. Generally, the issue of whether information is disclosable or announceable must relate to matters which a regular user would reasonably expect to be disclosed to other users on an equal basis, irrespective of whether those matters occur in the present or will occur in the future. In other words, there are circumstances in which it is apparent that information will have to be disclosed, but the use of information may be restricted before it is formally required to be disclosed (eg confidentiality requirement in a disclosure rule). The point in time when information becomes disclosable will depend on the wording of the particular disclosure rule in question. If there is no rule prohibiting disclosure, the possessor of information would not have to disclose relevant information before a regular user in the market would expect that information to be made available. The FSA takes the view in CP 70 that once it becomes reasonably certain that a disclosure requirement will be triggered or that publication will take place, such information should be treated as if it were already disclosable or announceable.

2.30 The FSA has acknowledged that practitioners have concerns about the difficulty of determining when information is 'potentially' disclosable and the impact that such uncertainty could have on the flow of information to the market. In respect of this issue, the FSA has adopted a test of the relevance of such potentially disclosable information that requires that the information in question provides, with reasonable certainty, a basis to conclude that the possible future developments will in fact occur[1]. It appears that the test may be formulated so that the misuse of information which will clearly become disclosable or announceable is restricted in the same way as information which is disclosable or announceable.

1   See CP 70, para 6.35.

2.31 An example where uncertainty arises involves merger negotiations where no agreement in principle has been reached regarding price and structure. The issue of whether merger negotiations result in disclosable information, as defined in the Code, will depend on the facts of each case. It will be relevant whether there is interest in the transaction at the highest corporate levels. For example, board resolutions, senior management involvement and communications with potential investors will be important factors. Also of significance will be communications with legal advisers and auditors and their participation in preparation for the merger and actual negotiations between principals and the involvement of intermediaries in preparing documents related to the proposed merger. No single factor will be conclusive in determining whether the facts serving as the basis for merger negotiations constitute disclosable information[1].

1   Similar factors will apply in the case of takeover bids, which will be discussed in Chapter 10.

Information obtained by research or analysis

2.32 The FSMA 2000, s 118(7) provides that information obtained by research or analysis that is conducted by, or on behalf of, users of a market is to be regarded as being generally available, thereby allowing free use of such information with no obligation of disclosing it before it is acted upon in the market. Accordingly, a firm which trades before the publication of its own research report will not have engaged in market abuse[1]. It should be noted, however, that certain 'conduct of business' rules will govern certain disclosures to clients in circumstances where a firm has dealt on its own account before the publication of its own research[2].

1 CP 70, para 6.38.
2 See Conduct of Business Sourcebook, Rule 7.3.

The FSA Listing Rules and disclosure

2.33 The FSA has decided that certain behaviour will not attract liability under the FSMA 2000 market abuse regime where such behaviour conforms to an FSA rule that includes a provision to the effect that behaviour conforming to that rule does not amount to market abuse[1]. Behaviour will be regarded as conforming to an FSA rule when it is required or expressly permitted by that rule. To qualify for this safe harbour, there must be a specific rule that either requires or expressly permits a person to engage in the behaviour in question. The FSA policy rationale for these safe harbours is that issuers would find it very difficult to conduct their affairs without a relaxation of the disclosure requirements contained in Chapter 9 of the Listing Rules.

1 FSMA 2000, s 118(8). These exceptions to liability are known as 'safe harbours' and will be discussed in more detail in subsequent chapters.

2.34 Chapter 9 of the Listing Rules contains provisions that allow or require issuers and their directors to make selective disclosures of relevant information which is not generally available in certain specified circumstances. The parts of the Listing Rules that have been given safe harbour status and relate to the timing, dissemination or availability, content and standard of care applicable to a disclosure, announcement, communication or release of information are provided in MAR 1, Annex 1G. Listing Rule 9.3A provides that disclosures will not be a breach of the market abuse regime if such disclosures are expressly required or expressly permitted by the Listing Rules. The FSA policy is that if an issuer makes disclosures, which are expressly required or permitted by the Listing Rules, such disclosures should not be considered as misleading in the context of the market abuse regime. For example, Listing Rule 9.1 requires issuers to notify the Company Announcement Office ('CAO') without delay of any major developments in its activities which are not public knowledge. An issuer's dissemination of information in this situation would attract safe harbour status and probably not result in liability as market abuse. On the other hand, if an issuer fails to comply with a Listing Rule in making a disclosure and the disclosure is misleading, the FSA would have to apply its statutory principles and rules to determine whether the behaviour amounted to market abuse.

2.35 Listing Rule 9.10(j) provides safe harbour status for disclosures regarding the timing of announcements, documentation and dealings[1]. It permits issuers to delay announcing the results of new issues where the securities are subject to an underwriting agreement. The delay creates an opportunity for issuers to sell to the secondary market the portion of the issuance that has not been distributed before the announcement of the results of the issue.

1   MAR 1, Annex 1G.

2.36 Listing Rules 9.4 and 9.5 permit issuers to pass information concerning impending developments or matters in negotiation to a number of specified persons, including professional advisers or counterparties to proposed commercial, financial or investment transactions. Listing Rule 9.15 deals with an issuer's disclosure obligations when the CAO is not open. During these times, issuers are required to provide adequate coverage of relevant information by distributing such information to at least two newswire services and two UK newspapers operating in the UK and to notify the CAO as soon as it reopens. These disclosure obligations are intended to provide alternative modes of dissemination instead of the RNS. However, the FSA has noted that these procedures create the risk that such information may be misused, especially given the fact that the newswires and newspapers are under no legal or regulatory obligation to pass on the information to the market. Industry has expressed the concern that issuers required to follow the requirements of Rule 9.15 could be subject to liability for 'requiring or encouraging' if the recipients of the information at, for instance, a newspaper deal on the information before it has been made generally available. The FSA has expressed doubt as to whether the issuer's behaviour would amount to market abuse in the case on the basis that the issuer would have distributed the information for the purpose of fulfilling its obligations under the Listing Rules and not for the purpose of encouraging another to deal on the basis of relevant information that is not generally available.

The Model Code

2.37   The Model Code on conduct for securities transactions by directors of listed companies[1] contains important provisions regarding disclosure requirements for connected persons of UK companies. Paragraphs 11 and 12 of the Model Code require directors to disclose to all persons connected with them in the company of the names of all companies and business entities of which they are directors. They must also disclose the periods during which they are not to deal in the listed securities of those companies. During consultation, the FSA noted the concern that such notification could alert those connected persons to the fact that a particular company was in a prohibited period (as defined under the Listing Rules) and therefore raise the concern that the notification itself could amount to 'requiring or encouraging' market abuse. The FSA has addressed this issue by stating that para 12 of the Model Code would be amended to ensure that connected persons receive a statement that the information passed to them was in confidence, but the FSA had made clear that directors will only be protected to the limited extent that such information that was passed was information that was specifically required to be provided in any FSA guidance and paras 11 and 12 of the Model Code.

1   The Model Code is in the Appendix to Chapter 16 of the UK Listing Rules. In May 2000, the Financial Services Authority assumed the role of UK listing authority with responsibility for administering the Listing Rules of the London Stock Exchange.

2.38   The US Securities and Exchange Commission adopted Regulation FD (Fair Disclosure) in October 2000 which addresses important issues regarding the selective disclosure by issuers of material, non-public information[1]. Regulation FD addresses selective disclosure for new issuers by providing that when an issuer, or person acting on its behalf, discloses material, non-public information to certain enumerated persons (generally, securities market professionals and holders of the issuer's securities who may well trade on the basis of the information), it must make public disclosure of that information. The timing of the required public disclosure depends on whether the selective disclosure was intentional or non-intentional. Where there is intentional selective disclosure, the issuer must promptly make public disclosure[2]. Regulation FD seeks to address the problem of issuers disclosing important non-public information, such as advance warnings of earnings results, to securities analysts or selected institutional investors or both before making full disclosure of the same information to the public[3]. In issuing Regulation FD, the SEC draws close parallels between issuer selective disclosure and ordinary 'tipping' and insider trading.

1   17 CFR, ss 243.100–243.103 (2000). The new rules and amendments consisting of Regulation FD were proposed in Exchange Act Release No 42259 (20 December 1999) and cited in 64 Fed Register 72590.
2   The Regulation requires that public disclosure be made by filing a Form 8-K or by other approved methods that are reasonably designed to effect broad, non-exclusionary distribution of the information to the public.
3   The SEC has become increasingly alarmed because those who were privy to the information beforehand were able to make a profit or avoid a loss at the expense of those who were not informed.

2.39   Regulation FD also aims to address the problem of corporate management treating material information as a commodity to be used to gain or maintain favour with particular analysts or investors. The SEC noted in its release that the absence of a prohibition on selective disclosure would result in analysts being pressured to report favourably about a company or otherwise in order to maintain continued access to selectively disclosed information. Regulation FD addresses these concerns by establishing new requirements for full and fair disclosure by public companies. Regulation FD is similar to the new UK Listing Rules, which the Financial Services Authority inherited from the London Stock Exchange in May 2000, that require that any information which might be price sensitive must be announced to the market as a whole without delay and 'must not be given to anyone else before it has been so notified'.

CHAPTER 3

Dealing on the basis of inside information

Introduction – the general criminal law

3.1   In the United Kingdom, insider dealing can be defined as trading in organised securities markets by persons in possession of material non-public information and has been recognised as a widespread problem that is extremely difficult to eradicate. Some of the insider dealing is based on corporate information, ie information about a company's finances or operations. In recent years, however, most of the important dealing cases have concerned mergers and acquisitions due largely to the explosive growth in takeover activity during the past decade. The community of bankers, lawyers, public relations advisors and others who receive advance knowledge of proposed takeovers, which invariably occur at a substantial premium over the existing market price of the acquired company's shares, face a strong temptation to make a quick profit from inside information.

3.2   The general criminal law has always sought to protect the integrity of public markets[1]. In recent years, the offences outlawing interference with proper operation of the markets were covered by the Financial Services Act 1986, s 47, which deals with false statements, manipulative practices and the crime of conspiracy to defraud. In practice, however, these more general offences relating to interference with the market would not be applicable in cases of simple insider dealing unless there had been manipulation and fraudulent conduct.

1   See B A K Rider and M Ashe, *Insider Crime* (1993, Jordans) p 20.

3.3   Until 1980, the restrictions on insider dealing in the United Kingdom were extremely limited. There was no statutory prohibition of the practice, nor did the common law make insider dealing actionable[1]. In the leading case of *Percival v Wright*[2], the Court of Chancery held that a corporate director only owed a fiduciary duty to the company and not to its individual shareholders and that therefore the director was ordinarily not obliged to disclose information about the company to the shareholders before trading with them. Nevertheless, if a director expressly or impliedly becomes an agent for one or more shareholders in a particular transaction, the fiduciary duties arising out of the agency relationship may prevent him from realising a profit on the acquisition of securities to his own advantage. Although the City Panel on Takeovers and Mergers[3] and the London Stock Exchange[4] had adopted rules and guidelines that restricted insider dealing and the 'tipping' of inside information, these self-regulatory bodies never strictly enforced these measures[5].

1 By contrast, the United States enacted anti-market manipulation legislation in 1934 in the form of the Securities and Exchange Act 1934, s 10(b).
2 [1902] 2 Ch 421.
3 City Code on Takeovers and Mergers, Rule 4.1.
4 LSE, 'Model Code for Securities Transactions by Directors of Listed Companies' (1987, 'Yellow Book') 5.43–5.48.
5 See Hull and Bridges, 'End of the Line for Insider Traders?' (1981) 14 Brackton L Rev 13, 17.

3.4 After two unsuccessful legislative attempts to outlaw insider dealing in the 1970s[1], in 1980 Parliament amended the Companies Act to make insider dealing a criminal offence[2]. These provisions outlawing insider dealing were consolidated in 1985 when the Companies Act was revised. The insider dealing provisions of the Companies Act 1985 became known as the Companies Securities (Insider Dealing) Act 1985[3]. These provisions were supplemented the following year by new provisions in the Financial Services Act 1986 that were intended primarily to strengthen the government's enforcement powers[4].

1 In 1973, the Conservative government published a Companies Bill that would have out-lawed insider trading, but it failed when the government was defeated in the February 1974 general election. The Companies Bill that was proposed by the Labour government in 1978 suffered a similar fate after that government went down to defeat in the May 1979 general election.
2 Companies Act 1980, ss 68–73.
3 Company Securities (Insider Dealing) Act 1985 (hereinafter the 'Insider Dealing Act').
4 Financial Services Act 1986, ss 173–178.

3.5 The Insider Dealing Act 1985 prohibited persons who had access to material non-public information by virtue of their position with a company (including directors, officers, employees and various kinds of agents of the company) from trading in the securities of the company while in possession of such information. These insiders were also prohibited from making selective disclosure of such information to others ('tipping') and it prohibited their tippees from trading on the basis of such inside information. The Act also prohibited persons in possession of non-public information about a proposed takeover of a company from trading in that company's stock.

3.6 The Insider Dealing Act 1985 established only criminal liability and its prohibitions applied only to individuals who acted while knowingly in possession of inside information. Although the Insider Dealing Act was an important step in outlawing the offence of insider dealing, the scope and impact of the British legislation was rather narrow. In fact, despite the fact that insider dealing had been an offence since 1980, there were no convictions under the Act's provisions (as amended by the Financial Services Act 1986) until the late 1980s.

3.7   The following sections will discuss the existing criminal legislation that makes insider dealing a criminal offence, which is contained in the Criminal Justice Act 1993, Pt V and applies only to the trading of securities. The following section will generally discuss the market abuse regime under the Financial Services and Markets Act 2000 ('FSMA 2000'), which imposes criminal and civil liability for market abuse. The FSMA 2000 defines the specific offence of market abuse to occur in a situation where a user of the market has been unreasonably disadvantaged (whether directly or indirectly) by others in the market who: (a) have used to their own advantage information which is not generally available, (b) created a false or misleading impression or (c) undertook activities that distort the market.

The offence of insider dealing

3.8   The Criminal Justice Act 1993 ('CJA 1993') replaced the Company Securities Act (Insider Dealing) Act 1985 and represented an extension of the basis of liability for the insider dealing offence. The CJA 1993 contains a wider definition of 'securities' and 'insider' than the 1985 Act and the nature of the inside information necessary to impose liability has been altered.

The Criminal Justice Act 1993, Pt V

3.9   The CJA 1993, Pt V came into force on 1 March 1994 together with two ancillary statutory instruments (both reproduced in the 'Rules and Regulations'): the Insider Dealing (Securities and Regulated Markets) Order 1994 and the Traded Securities (Disclosure) Regulation 1994. The relevant provisions are in the 'ancillary Acts'.

3.10   The CJA 1993, Pt V provides for the offence of insider dealing that seeks to prevent individuals from engaging in three classes of conduct in particular circumstances. First, the Act prohibits dealing in price-affected securities on the basis of inside information[1]. Secondly, it prohibits the encouragement of another person to deal in price-affected securities on the basis of insider information and, thirdly, it prohibits knowing disclosure of insider information to another[2]. To prove an offence under s 52, it was necessary to demonstrate two elements: (a) the status of the person charged as an insider and (b) the type of information in its possession to be inside information. Section 52 provides in the relevant part:

'(1)   An individual who has information as an insider is guilty of insider
         dealing if, in the circumstances mentioned in subsection (3), he

deals in securities that are price- affected securities in relation to the information.

(2)   An individual who has information as an insider is also guilty of insider dealing if –

   (a)   he encourages another person to deal in securities that are (whether or not that other knows it) price-affected securities in relation to the information, knowing or having reasonable cause to believe that the dealing would take place in the circumstances mentioned in subsection (3); or

   (b)   he discloses information, otherwise than in proper performance of the functions of his employment, office or profession, to another person.

(3)   The circumstances referred to above are that the acquisition or disposal in question occurs on a regulated market, or that the person dealing relies on a professional intermediary or is himself acting as a professional intermediary'.

1   CJA 1993, Pt V, s 52(1).
2   CJA 1993, Pt V, s 52(1) and (2).

3.11   Criminal liability for each offence may only attach to an individual because the term 'individual' is defined to exclude corporations and other entities (eg public authorities). The definition of individual did cover, however, unincorporated partnerships or firms comprising a collection of individuals. Moreover, it should be noted that a company could be liable for insider dealing by committing the secondary offence of encouraging another person to deal[1].

1   See an analysis of the encouragement offence in Chapter 4.

Insider

3.12   To commit the offence of insider dealing, an individual must have information 'as an insider', which is defined in the CJA 1993, s 57 as follows:

'(1)   … a person has information as an insider if and only if –

   (a)   it is, and he knows that it is, inside information, and

   (b)   he has it, and knows that he has it, from an inside source.

(2)   For the purposes of subsection (1), a person has information from an inside source if and only if –

   (a)   he has it through

      (i)   being a director, employee or shareholder of an issuer of securities; or

      (ii)   having access to the information by virtue of his employment, office or profession; or

   (b)   the direct or indirect source of his information is a person within paragraph (a)'.

3.13   The CJA 1993, s 57 created a distinction between a primary insider (a person who has direct knowledge of inside information) and a secondary insider (a person who learns inside information from an inside source). The primary insider usually obtains inside information through being a director, employee or shareholder of an issuer of securities or any person who has information because of his employment or office. A secondary insider obtains inside information either directly or indirectly from a primary insider. Section 57 would impose liability on brokers or analysts as secondary insiders if they act on 'market intelligence' that comes from a primary insider[1].

1   See the discussion of 'tippee' liability in Chapter 6.

3.14   The insider dealing offence, only in so far as dealing and encouragement are concerned, could only be committed if the acquisition or disposal of securities occurs on a regulated market or if the person dealing relied on a professional intermediary or is himself a professional intermediary[1]. The CJA 1993 defines 'professional intermediary' as a person who carries on a business of acquiring or disposing of securities (whether as principal or agent) or a business of acting as an intermediary between persons taking part in any dealing in securities[2]. An individual employed by such a person to carry out these activities are also defined as 'professional intermediaries'. The definition of professional intermediary does not include a person whose activities are merely incidental to other activities or if those activities are only conducted occasionally[3].

1   CJA 1993, s 52(3).
2   CJA 1993, s 59(1)(a).
3   CJA 1993, s 59(3)(a)–(b).

3.15   The CJA 1993, s 59 defines professional intermediary as follows:

'(1)   … a professional intermediary is a person –
  (a)   who carries on a business consisting of an activity mentioned in subsection (2) and who holds himself out to the public or any section of the public (including a section of the public constituted by persons such as himself) as willing to engage in any such business; or
  (b)   who is employed by a person falling within paragraph (a) to carry out any such activity.
(2)   The activities referred to in subsection (1) are –
  (a)   acquiring or disposing of securities (whether as principal or agent); or
  (b)   acting as an intermediary between persons taking part in any dealing in securities'.

3.16   Under this definition, a person will rely on a professional intermediary only if the professional intermediary either acquires or disposes of securities (whether as principal or agent) in relation to the dealing or acts as intermediary between persons taking part in the dealing[1]. If deals in securities do occur on a regulated market (ie investment exchange), the insider dealing offence will be relevant unless the transaction is truly a private deal off the market without the intervention of a market professional.

1 CJA 1993, s 59(4).

3.17 The offence of insider dealing cannot apply to anything done by an individual acting on behalf of a public sector body in pursuit of the government's economic policies (eg managing monetary policy through the adjustment of exchange rates, interest rates or the public debt or foreign exchange reserves)[1]. The purpose of these exclusions is to permit government policymakers to have sufficient discretion to manage the economy in the public interest. These exclusions, however, would not apply to the government's sale of shares in a privatisation.

1 CJA 1993, s 63(1).

The elements of the dealing offence

3.18 The two essential requirements for the dealing offence are that: (a) an individual must have information as an insider and (b) the insider must deal in securities that are price-affected securities in relation to the information[1]. With respect to inside information, the prices of price-affected securities will likely be significantly affected if information related to such securities is made public[2]. Accordingly, if an insider has inside information, he must not deal in the securities to which that information relates. The CJA 1993 adopts a broad definition of 'dealing in securities' to cover any acquisition or disposal of a security, including an agreement to acquire or dispose of a security and the entering into a contract which creates the security or the bringing to an end of such contract[3]. Moreover, such acquisitions or disposals are within the definition irrespective of whether they are made by an individual as principal or as agent.

1 CJA 1993, s 52(1).
2 CJA 1993, s 56(2).
3 CJA 1993, s 55(3)(b).

3.19 The securities to which the Act applies are price-affected securities which are defined in the CJA 1993, Sch 2. They include shares and debentures in companies, as well as their derivatives. They also include gilts and local authority stock (even of foreign public bodies) and their derivatives. Contractual rights of differences (eg derivatives) are also included[1]. The list conforms to the EC Directive on Insider Dealing[2], so that not only corporate securities and instruments based on such securities are included, but also that other contractual rights in other futures and derivatives markets are covered.

1 The list contained generally most of the investments that had been designated under the Financial Services Act 1986, Sch 1, Pt I.
2 Council Directive 89/552/EEC, art 1(2).

3.20   The relevant time at which to consider whether or not an offence has been committed would appear to be at the time of agreement to acquire or dispose of the security. At that time, if the individual had inside information about these securities he will have committed an offence. However, if he received inside information only after making the agreement, he will probably not have violated the provision if he completes the deal and actually acquires or disposes of the securities[1]. On the other hand, if the individual had the inside information at the time when he agreed to acquire or dispose of the security, it would seem that he will still have committed an offence, even if he does not complete the bargain.

1   See a discussion of the defences under the CJA 1993, s 53(1)(c) in Chapter 9 for an alternative approach.

3.21   The acquisition or disposal may be made by an individual acting either as principal or agent. Accordingly, if an agent has inside information, he will be within the scope of the offence if he deals in the relevant securities even though, in a direct sense, he will not gain from the transaction. This has special relevance to a trader who is engaged in a transaction as agent to benefit his principal. The fact that the individual deals as agent and not principal is irrelevant. However, where the agent deals on an execution basis only, such an approach hardly seems justified and is unfair to the principal who gave the instruction if the agent then feels inhibited from processing the order. Fortunately, it appears that a defence in this situation would allow the agent to act on instructions notwithstanding that, incidentally, he has inside information[1].

1   CJA 1993, s 53(1)(c).

3.22   A person is also regarded as dealing in securities if he procures, directly or indirectly, an acquisition or disposal of the securities by another person[1]. Such procurement may occur in a number of ways, including where the person who actually acquires or disposes of the security is acting as an agent, nominee or at the direction of another in relation to the acquisition or disposal of a security[2]. This aspect of the definition of 'dealing in securities' is designed to cover transactions through an agent or nominee where the principal has relied on inside information without purchasing or selling the securities himself. Transactions are also covered that are undertaken at the direction of a sole shareholder who uses its influence over a company to deal in its shares[3].

1   CJA 1993, s 55(1)(b).
2   CJA 1993, s 55(4).
3   See Parliamentary Debates, House of Commons, Standing Committee B, 10 June 1993, column 171 (per the Economic Secretary).

3.23   The broad scope of the procurement prohibition was recognised in debates in the House of Commons Standing Committee during passage of the Criminal Justice Bill in which the phrase 'a person who is acting at his direction' may likely result in liability for a principal who has inside information, but whose investment portfolio is handled by someone else on a discretionary basis. For example, this might occur in the case of a fund manager who had the authority to deal in a discretionary manner in securities to which his principal's insider information relates, thus resulting in liability for the principal, despite the principal's lack of knowledge of the specific transaction.

3.24 The government's Economic Secretary responded by stating that whilst it was possible for a person who had transferred its holdings of a portfolio to an investment manager to be exposed to liability as a procurer, 'it may well be that'[1] a person who gives a general direction to another to manage its affairs would not be considered to have directed and, therefore, to have procured dealings in securities which were undertaken by the person with responsibility for managing the fund. Moreover, the minister stated that in cases where there were circumstances to suggest that a person had procured a transaction, the holder of the shares would have a statutory defence if the holder had not genuinely influenced the dealing[2].

1 See Parliamentary Debates, House of Commons, Standing Committee B, 10 June 1993, columns 171 and 172 (per Peter Ainsworth).
2 See the CJA 1993, s 53(1)(c).

The characteristics of insider information

3.25 Each of the three offences provided for in the CJA 1993 and the FSMA 2000 require that insider information be an essential element of the offence. Commentators have acknowledged, however, that, notwithstanding the statutory definition, inside information is a difficult concept to define in practice. For example, at any one time, a substantial amount of information will be generated within a company and be available to its directors, employees and advisors. Much of this information will be confidential and may have some impact on share prices. Generally, insider dealing law should not be concerned with this type of information, but rather it should focus on information that is essentially extraordinary in nature and which is reasonably certain to have a substantial impact on the market price of securities[1]. Indeed, during debate over the original UK insider dealing law, ministers acknowledged that the kind of knowledge they were concerned with was that of dramatic events and major occurrences that would transform a company's prospects[2].

1 See Rider et al, *Insider Dealing*, p 29 (citing US Supreme Court case *SEC v Texas Gulf Sulfur Co* 401 F 2d 833, 848 (2nd Cir, 1968)).
2 Parliamentary Debates, House of Commons, Standing Committee A (debates on the Company Bill), 6 December 1979, column 394.

3.26 The CJA 1993 and the FSMA 2000 both assess the quality of information to determine whether it is inside information by use of criteria that seek to ascertain whether or not information has a 'significant effect' on the market price of the security. The CJA 1993 defines inside information by reference to four characteristics as provided in the CJA 1993, s 56:

'(1) ... inside information means information which –

    (a) relates to particular securities or to a particular issuer of securities or to particular issuers of securities and not to securities generally or to issuers of securities generally;

    (b) is specific or precise;

    (c) has not been made public; and

    (d) if it were made public would be likely to have a significant effect on the price of any securities.

(2) ... securities are "price-affected securities" in relation to inside information, and inside information is "price-sensitive information" in relation to securities, if and only if the information would, if made public, be likely to have a significant effect on the price of the securities'[1].

The FSMA 2000 has also adopted this meaning of the term 'inside information'.

1   CJA 1993, s 56. Under the Company Securities (Insider Dealing) Act 1985, inside information was referred to as 'unpublished price-sensitive information' that contained the following elements:
- the information was not generally to be known to those persons accustomed or likely to deal in the company's securities;
- the information should be likely to affect the price of the securities; and
- the information was such that it would be reasonable to expect a primary insider not to disclose it, except in the proper performance of its functions.

3.27   The characteristics and elements of inside information are such that they should cover information which relates to a specific sector as well as to a specific security, while excluding general information. General information has been defined, for example, under the FSMA 2000 as information which can be obtained by research or analysis conducted by or on behalf of users of a market[1].

1   FSMA 2000, s 118(7).

3.28   The approach of the CJA 1993 and the FSMA 2000 conforms with that of the EC Directive on Insider Dealing[1] and even seems to accomplish the objective of promoting an efficient market through the timely disclosure of information more effectively than the Directive, which has been criticised on the grounds of obscurity.

1   Council Directive 89/592/EC, art 1(1).

Particular securities and particular issuers of securities

3.29   The first of these four characteristics as set out in the CJA 1993 makes clear that information which relates to a specific sector is included, as well as that which relates to a specific security. Accordingly, information may still be inside information, although it has nothing specifically to do with a particular company or its shares, but rather relates to the industry in which that company operates[1]. Similarly, inside information relating to an issuer will include information which comes directly from the issuer. Thus, for example, information about a substantial increase or reduction in profits of a company, which clearly has its source within the organisation, will certainly be information which relates to an issuer. The information, however, referred to in the CJA 1993 also includes information that arises from a source outside of the issuer. This may occur in a takeover bid where the proposal to acquire the company's shares emanates from the bidder. Similarly, information relating to securities may be internal, such as dividends, but may be external, such as a decision by the company to be listed on the Stock Exchange.

1   See B A K Rider and M Ashe, *Insider Crime* (1993, Jordans) p 30.

3.30   There are situations, however, when the question will not be so straightforward regarding when information relates to a particular security or particular issuer or issuers. Although it is clear that the definition does not include information which relates to securities generally or to issuers generally, there is much information which, although not of that general quality, is not related to a particular security, but may, nonetheless, have a significant effect on its price if disclosed to the public.

3.31   If, for example, an employee of Microsoft has, in the course of her employment, gained knowledge that Microsoft is about to submit a bid for the shares of another publicly-held company, this information is likely to be advantageous if she were to purchase shares in the other company. Undoubtedly, the information has its most direct relationship with Microsoft and, because the employee has the information as an insider (and assuming it to be price sensitive, negatively, in relation to Microsoft's shares) she should not deal in Microsoft's shares by selling them before the news becomes generally available with the likely result that their price will drop. Similarly, the information may also have been considered to relate to the target company. It would be curious, if not illogical, if the employee, having obtained the information as an insider, had committed an offence by selling the shares in Microsoft, but not have committed an offence by purchasing shares in the target company. In both cases, the employee was acting on the same information obtained as an insider and in both cases that information would have a significant effect on the prices of each share. Yet, it is arguable that the information did not relate to the target company, rather it only related to Microsoft. It would seem, however, that such a result would offend common sense.

3.32   The CJA 1993, s 60(4) provides clarification on this issue by stating:

'For the purposes of this Part, information shall be treated as relating to an issuer of securities which is a company not only where it is about the company but also where it may affect the company's business prospects'.

This provision appears to apply to the above example by ensuring that the information relates not only to Microsoft, but also to the target company because it will affect the target company's prospects, ie Microsoft's proposed purchase of the shares will likely enhance the value of the target company's shares.

3.33 The statutory provision was criticised as being too broad because of its inclusion of the term 'business prospects' in the definition of insider dealing. The statute's inclusion of the term 'business prospects' was defended by the Earl of Caithness on behalf of the government in debate in the House of Lords when he said:

'It is included because the government believes that it is essential our insider dealing legislation catches as inside information, information which, while not relating directly to a company, would nonetheless be likely to have a significant effect on the price of its shares. An example of information in this category might be important regulatory decisions and information about a company's major customer or supplier'[1].

1 Parliamentary Debates, House of Lords, 3 December 1992, column 1501 (per the Earl of Caithness).

3.34 It is generally accepted that the CJA 1993 adopts a broad-based approach to the definition of inside information, together with an expanded approach to who is an insider[1], but the exclusion from the definition of information which relates to securities generally, or to issuers of securities generally, appears to mean that, for example, confidential information of a particular government economic policy which will impact on the market generally is outside the definition of inside information. In this regard, the CJA 1993 appears to be less strict than the EC Directive on Insider Dealing, art 1(1), which places no such restriction and specifically includes such general news. The Directive, therefore, has a broad scope, as compared to the narrower approach of the CJA 1993. As discussed in Chapter 6, the FSMA 2000 seeks to address this discrepancy by adopting an approach that includes information that affects the market generally, but which may have a specific effect on the issuers of specific securities.

1 CJA 1993, s 57(2)(a)(ii).

'Specific' or 'precise'

3.35 Inside information may also be characterised by the terms 'specific' or 'precise'. The CJA 1993 includes the word 'specific' because the word 'precise', by itself, may not have covered, for example, information that there will be a huge dividend increase because the lack of details concerning the quantum increase would not amount to inside information. Information is precise when it is exact. The word 'specific' is intended to ensure that information that, for example, involves a large drop in a company's earnings would be considered inside information, while mere rumour and untargeted information cannot[1].

1 Parliamentary Debates, House of Lords, 3 December 1992, column 1501 (per the Earl of Caithness).

3.36 Moreover, the use of the word 'specific' may eliminate more than mere rumour and untargeted information. An Australian case held that the phrase 'specific information' meant not merely that the information was precisely definable, but that its entire content can be precisely and 'unequivocally expressed and discerned'[1]. The court concluded that specific information had to be specific in itself and not based on the process of deduction[2]. On this approach, a company that was prepared to purchase a large tranche of shares from several persons would not be considered specific in relation to a similar purchase from one person. Although this view may be attractive, it is often inferences drawn from facts which affect market price and, theoretically, if the facts are not made public, the insider who has them needs also to be restrained from trading on inferences made from those facts.

1 *Ryan v Triguboff* [1976] 1 NSWLR 588 at 596 (per Lee J).
2 *Ryan v Triguboff* at 597.

3.37 Whatever the correct approach for inferences, information may still be specific even though, as information, it has a vague quality. Thus, information concerning a company's financial problems has been held to be specific[1]. Moreover, information as to the possibility of a takeover may be regarded as specific information[2] and will likely rank as precise, given that it is more than a mere rumour. The House of Commons Standing Committee that was considering the Criminal Justice Bill provided some examples of what the words 'specific' and 'precise' would cover.

1 *Public Prosecutor v Choudhury* [1980] 1 MLJ 76 at 78 (Singapore).
2 See *Green v Charterhouse Group of Canada Ltd* (1976) 12 OR (2d) 280. The Ontario Court of Appeal held such information to be specific even though it may not have been worthy of credence or not have been of sufficient weight to justify any positive action by the board (at 306).

Example 1

3.38 As the chairman of a company and an analyst walked into a car park, they saw the chairman's battered BMW. The analyst said to the chairman, 'Isn't it time you got a new car?' The chairman replied that he would not buy a new car that year.

3.39 The Economic Secretary considered that these circumstances would lead neither to specific nor precise information in relation to the company, given that there could be many reasons for the statement, including the fact that the chairman may have been experiencing personal financial troubles[1].

1   Parliamentary Debates, House of Commons, Standing Committee B, 10 June 1993, column 174.

Example 2

3.40   In contrast, if the chairman had remarked that 'Our results will be much better than the market expects or knows' it would not be precise information because there was no disclosure of the company's results, but it would likely be specific information because the chairman would have disclosed information about the company's result, whilst making it clear that the information was not public[1].

1   See the comments of the Economic Secretary, Parliamentary Debates, House of Commons, Standing Committee B, 10 June 1993, column 175.

3.41   Some commentators have also noted that the CJA 1993, s 56's requirement that information be specific or precise was drafted more broadly than EC Directive 89/592, which required in art 1 that the information be of 'a precise nature' only[1].

1   See the discussion in J Fisher and J Bewsey, *The Law of Investor Protection* (1997, Sweet & Maxwell) p 291.

'Made public'

3.42   For the purposes of defining inside information under the CJA 1993, s 56, another characteristic of it is that it has not been made public[1]. Under the CJA 1993, s 58(2) and (3), inside information is made public or is to be treated as made public in the following circumstances:

- if the information is published in accordance with the rules of a regulated market for the purpose of informing investors and their professional advisors;
- if the information is contained in records which, by virtue of any enactment, are given to inspection by the public;
- if the information can be readily acquired by those likely to deal in any securities to which the information relates or of an issuer to which the information relates; or
- if the information is derived from information which has been made public.

1   The original drafts of the Criminal Justice Bill that were introduced in the House of Lords provided no guidance for defining what was meant by the phrase 'made public'. See B A K Rider and M Ashe, *Insider Crime* (1993, Jordans) p 34.

3.43   In addition, the CJA 1993 provides five circumstances when information may be treated as having been made public, even though it has not[1]. These are where information:

- can only be acquired by persons exercising diligence or expertise;
- is communicated to a section of the public and not to the public at large;
- can only be acquired by observation;
- is only communicated on payment of a fee; or
- is only published outside the UK[2].

1   CJA 1993, s 58(2).
2   CJA 1993, s 58(3).

3.44   The above definitions state that information may be treated as public, even though further efforts have to be made to obtain the information. This accords with the broad scope of the definition of 'made public' in EC Directive 89/592, which provides that information derived from publicly available data cannot be regarded as inside information and any transaction executed on the basis of such information would not constitute insider dealing under the broad definition of the Directive.

Information published according to the rules of a regulated market

3.45   Publication of insider information will not necessarily deprive insiders of their advantages because markets often take time to absorb information. It is generally accepted in financial markets that prices of securities do not always adjust immediately upon the release of material information. Accordingly, US securities law recognises this market reality by imposing liability on insiders for transactions undertaken before the market has assimilated the information[1]. Similarly, before the CJA 1993, the UK Companies Securities (Insider Dealing) Act 1985 would probably have prohibited insiders from immediately dealing on insider information after announcement until prices had adjusted to the information. The insiders were thus required to wait for the market to assimilate the information. The EC Directive on Insider Dealing has also been given this interpretation[2].

1   *SEC v Texas Gulf Sulfur Co* 401 F 2d 833 (2nd Cir, 1968); *SEC v MacDonald* 699 F 2d 47 (1st Cir, 1982).
2   See Klaus J Hopt, 'The European Insider Dealing Directive' (1990) 27 CMLR 51. The recital to the Directive states that investors should be 'placed on equal footing'.

3.46   The CJA 1993 clarifies the procedure for insiders to know when they can trade on information just released to the market. It adopts a procedure for notifying information to the Stock Exchange[1] that contains the following requirements: (a) the information which issuers wish to release to the public must be delivered in the form of an announcement to the Company Announcements Office, (b) the Stock Exchange then arranges for the prompt publication of announcements through its Regulatory News Service and (c) at this point, for example, there could be an announcement on TOPIC that the information will be 'made public' for the purposes of the CJA 1993.

1   The Listing Rules, Chapter 9.

3.47   The FSA Listing Rules provide that no information may be released to a third party before such information is released to the Company Announcements Office. If announcements are made outside the operational hours of the Regulatory News Service[1], however, the information must be given to two or more UK national newspapers and to two news services to ensure adequate coverage. This information must also be lodged with the Company Announcements Office no later than it is given to the other parties. In these circumstances, the information would appear to have been made public on publication of the newspapers.

The CJA 1993 definition of 'made public' provides the advantage of clarity because it avoids the uncertainty of waiting for the market to absorb the news by providing a clearer set of standards as to the time when insiders may deal.

1   In recent years, the Regulatory News Service operates between 7.30 am and 6.00 pm and announcements notified up until 5.30 pm are released on the day of receipt.

Information contained in public records

3.48   Information will be regarded as being made public if it is contained on records which, by virtue of any enactment, are open to inspection by the public. This covers registers set up under the statute, such as companies' or patents' registers or in publications such as the Official Gazette[1].

1   Parliamentary Debates, House of Commons, Standing Committee B, 10 June 1993, column 184 (per the Economic Secretary).

Information readily acquired by people 'likely to deal' in securities

3.49   Information is considered 'public' when it can readily be acquired by those likely to deal in any securities to which or to whose issuer the information relates[1]. The phrase 'likely to deal' in securities is a term of art having its origin in the Company Securities (Insider Dealing) Act 1985, which defined it as 'unpublished price-sensitive information'[2]. Although it could be argued that the phrase only embraces the market professionals who deal in securities, such as market makers who are clearly 'likely to deal', it is also possible that it refers to the market in the shares itself. If information can readily be acquired by the market, that information is already likely to have made its price impact and is, therefore, not properly to be regarded as inside information. Thus, it is treated as having been 'made public'.

1   CJA 1993, s 58(2)(d).
2   Company Securities (Insider Dealing) Act 1985, s 10(b).

Information derived from information made public

3.50   Information is considered 'public' if it originates from information which has been 'made public'[1]. Although this may seem obvious, expert analysis of information may still have regard to many other factors, including the exposure of facts that had not been in the public domain. The CJA 1993 addresses the problem posed by an analyst who has knowledge of the company and industry and who can put together seemingly inconsequential data with public information into a mosaic which reveals material non-public information. Whenever managers, advisors and analysts meet in non-public places, there will be a risk that the analysts will take away knowledge of material information which is not publicly available. This should not be a violation of UK law so long as the mosaic, which contains inside information, is derived from information which has been made public.

1 CJA 1993, s 58(2)(d).

Price sensitivity

3.51 The final aspect of the definition of 'insider information' is the price sensitivity of the information. The test is that if the information were made public, it would be likely to have a significant effect on the securities. This is the most essential feature of the statutory definition of inside information. This criterion, rather than the issue of how qualitative the information actually is, is what really matters and which, ultimately, will be the determining factor when a jury considers whether information is inside information. Price sensitivity can only be determined at the moment of the deal when, by definition, the information is not known to the public and can have no impact on the price. In cases where the insider has dealt close to the time when the information was 'made public', the courts may rely on evidence that measures price sensitivity by the effect of the information on the market[1]. Because the CJA 1993 provides no further guidance, the UK courts may apply a 'reasonable investor' test relative to the securities in question and leave the matter to the jury. A Singapore court held that information will become price sensitive if it is information which would influence the ordinary reasonable investor to buy or sell the security in question. The UK courts will probably apply a careful analysis of the evidence supporting what is alleged to be a significant effect on any price.

1 *Chase Manhattan Equities Ltd v Goodman* [1991] BCLC 897 at 931 (per Knox J).

Territorial scope of the offence

3.52 The statute is narrowly aimed at insider dealing that takes place in the United Kingdom and will not apply if an essential element of the offence takes place outside UK territory[1]. The jurisdictional provisions of the Act are contained in the CJA 1993, s 62, which requires that some element of the offence under the CJA 1993, s 52(1) or (2) must take place in the United Kingdom or the dealing was on a UK regulated market or the broker or investment firm was carrying on business in the UK.

1 CJA 1993, s 62(1)–(2).

3.53   The prohibitions contained in these provisions are subject to territorial restrictions, though the restriction 'regulated markets' included all of the major stock markets of the European Community and any other designated by order[1]. It is important to note, however, that purely private deals, even involving securities covered by the CJA 1993, fell outside the scope of the offence. By contrast, the FSMA 2000 market abuse regime covers both transactions by regulated persons and dealing by private persons off regulated exchanges.

1   The territorial scope of the offence is provided in the CJA 1993, s 62. A full list of proposed regulated markets appears in Appendix 2, Sch, Regulated Markets, Pt I.

3.54   Generally, an offence will be committed under the following circumstances: if the insider is in the United Kingdom when he deals, or when the dealing takes place on a UK regulated market, which operates in the United Kingdom, or if the person dealing in the price-affected securities relies on a professional intermediary on a regulated UK market or is himself a professional intermediary.

Market abuse and the FSMA 2000

3.55   The new FSMA 2000[1] represents an important extension of the powers currently available to regulators to combat market abuse and insider dealing. As discussed in Chapter 1, the UK's position as a leading international financial centre depends not only on the openness and competitiveness of its markets, but also on its reputation as a clean and fair place to do business. Market confidence will be undermined where participants and users believe markets are susceptible to abuse. This reduction in market confidence will impair market efficiency, thus disadvantaging market participants. The FSMA 2000 defines three broad categories of behaviour which may amount to market abuse: (a) misuse of information that is not generally available to users of the market, (b) the dissemination[2] of false or misleading information and (c) market distortion[2]. The FSMA 2000, s 119 requires the FSA to issue a code that provides guidance for determining whether behaviour amounts to market abuse.

1   FSMA 2000, s 8.
2   FSMA 2000, s 8.

3.56   Insider dealing is a form of market abuse, which may occur when market participants have improperly used relevant information which is not generally available, created a false or misleading impression or distorted the market. This will have the effect of reducing confidence in the market and impairing its efficiency. Under the statute, market confidence will be undermined if market users feel unreasonably disadvantaged – either directly or indirectly – by others in the market who have used to their own advantage information which is not generally available, created a false or misleading impression or distorted the markets.

3.57   The Act's legal framework complements the existing criminal offences of market manipulation and insider dealing that is set out in the CJA 1993. The Act confers on the FSA broad powers to combat market abuse, in particular to fill the gap that had existed in previous legislation. The FSA is also empowered to prosecute the criminal offences of insider dealing and market manipulation as set out in the FSMA 2000, ss 397 and 402. Although these particular offences cover a relatively narrow range of very serious misconduct where there is an intention to abuse the market and other users, it is also recognised that market confidence, integrity and efficiency can also be damaged by a broader range of misconduct and by the effects of that misconduct on the markets. It is this broader range of conduct that was not covered by previous legislation. Such misconduct was only addressed by the regulatory framework (including the rules of the RIEs), in particular the FSA's Principles for Business which required authorised firms and registered individuals to observe high standards of market conduct.

3.58   The new framework, however, covers both unauthorised and authorised persons and, through the Code of Market Conduct, introduces greater transparency and clarity than existed under the previous legislation and regulations in determining what behaviour is acceptable or not. It is intended that those who use the markets will have a clear benchmark against which to measure their standards of behaviour. The benchmark is based in market standards that were developed through the consultation process and through the 'regular user' test. The 'regular user' test is an essential element in the definition of market abuse and which is discussed more fully in Chapter 6.

What is market abuse?

3.59   The Act's new market abuse and insider dealing framework extends the current regulatory regime in two important respects: (a) extends its scope of coverage to unauthorised persons as well as to authorised persons and (b) introduces greater transparency and clarity in the area of market conduct than was currently available to the regulated community. The insider dealing provisions of the Act are significant because they apply not only to authorised persons, but also to all those who deal in investments traded on certain prescribed markets. These prescribed markets are expected to be those operated by the seven UK recognised investment exchanges (RIEs). With respect to clarity and transparency, the Act requires the FSA to publish a Code of Market Conduct ('the Code') to supplement the statutory provisions defining market abuse and insider dealing in the Act. The Code is intended to give guidance to those who may determine whether or not behaviour amounts to market abuse, as required by the Act. This section will discuss generally the three main elements of the new market abuse and insider dealing regime, ie the misuse of relevant information that is not generally available to other market users, the giving of false or misleading impressions and market distortion.

3.60 The FSMA 2000, Pt VIII contains provisions relating to market abuse. Market abuse is defined[1] in the FSMA 2000, s 118(1) as behaviour (whether by one person alone or by two or more persons jointly or in concert):

- which occurs in relation to qualifying investments traded on a market to which this section applies;
- which satisfies any one or more of the conditions set out in subsection (2); and
- which is likely to be regarded by a regular user of that market which is aware of the behaviour as a failure on the part of the person or persons concerned to observe the standard of behaviour reasonably expected of a person in his or their position in relation to the market.

1 It is important to note that all definitions must be consistent with the Regulated Activities Order, the Prescribed Markets and Qualifying Investments Order, the Interpretation Act and other FSA final rules and regulations.

3.61 The three conditions set out in subsection (2) are:

- the behaviour is based on information which is not generally available to those using the market, but which, if available to a regular user of the market, would or would be likely to be regarded by him as relevant when deciding the terms on which transactions in investments of the kind in question should be effected;
- the behaviour is likely to give a regular user of the market a false or misleading impression as to the supply of, or demand for, or as to the price or value of, investments of the kind in question; and
- a regular user of the market would, or would be likely to, regard the behaviour as behaviour which would, or would be likely to, distort the market in investments of the kind in question.

3.62 Based on the above language, three tests must be satisfied in order to determine whether behaviour is market abuse: (a) that the behaviour must occur in connection with a qualifying investment traded on a prescribed market (ie recognised investment exchange), (b) one or more of the following: 'misuse of information', 'false or misleading impressions' or 'market distortion' and (c) the behaviour must fall below the standard of behaviour that a regular user of the market would reasonably expect of a person in the position of the person in question. Behaviour will amount to market abuse only if it satisfies all three of these tests. The FSA considers these descriptions to cover behaviour which, in its view, constitutes market abuse. Therefore, for such behaviour to be considered market abuse, it must correspond to one of these three elements and be likely to be regarded by a regular user of the market as a failure on the part of the person or persons concerned to observe the standard of conduct reasonably expected of a person in his or their position in relation to the market.

Regular user test

3.63 The definition of the term 'regular user' plays an essential role in defining 'market abuse'. Market abuse is defined in reference to standards of behaviour that a regular user would reasonably expect of a person in the position of a person concerned. A regular user is defined in the FSMA 2000, s 118(10) as 'in relation to a particular market, a reasonable person who regularly deals on that market in investments of the kind in question'. The Code describes how the FSA will apply the 'regular user' test by making clear that the 'regular user' is, in legal terms, a hypothetical user of the market, rather than a particular or actual user. Behaviour will not, therefore, amount to market abuse unless it falls short of the standards of behaviour which the hypothetical regular user of the market in investments of the kind in question would be likely reasonably to expect from a person in the position of the person concerned, ie unless the behaviour in question falls short of acceptable standards of behaviour in the particular context.

3.64 In addition, the Code recognises that, although the actual standards of conduct which prevail in a particular market at a particular time are relevant to the decision as to whether conduct meets or falls short of the standards expected by the regular user, these standards are not defined by the Code. The rationale is that there may be occasions when regular users of the market may not deem the standards which are acceptable by actual users of the market to be objectively acceptable. This may occur in a situation where the actual user of a market would tolerate the misuse of information, whereas the objective reasonable regular user would not find such behaviour acceptable.

3.65 Although the regular user test is based on a hypothetical user, it will not operate in a vacuum unaffected by the standards that do prevail in markets. The regular user will take into account compliance with the rules of an RIE or other rules or codes of conduct and good practice when deciding whether behaviour amounts to market abuse because it falls short of reasonably expected standards. Moreover, the rules of an RIE will include the rules and standards of overseas markets when conduct on those markets is relevant to determining whether or not there has been an abuse of the standards of a prescribed UK market. Similarly, it should also be pointed out that there may be consequences for market participants who operate in different national markets where standards of conduct may vary across different national markets. Specifically, it is possible that conduct which is tolerated in one jurisdiction may be considered as behaviour which amounts to market abuse if that behaviour has an adverse effect on a UK prescribed market. The Code recognises that the local rules, practices and conventions prevailing in a non-UK market will be an important factor in determining the standards that the regular user will expect of a person dealing from that market onto a prescribed market. However, compliance with local rules will not automatically insulate a market user from liability since such conduct may still fall below the standards expected by the regular user. An analogy can be provided by the FSA's Price Stabilising Rules[1], which will only recognise non-UK financial authorities' stabilisation rules if they provide broadly equivalent protection to the FSA's rules. Where such foreign stabilisation rules provide equivalent protection, a person's compliance with those rules entitles it to benefit from a safe harbour, but where such foreign rules do not provide similar protections, then there is no safe harbour protection.

1   See FSA CP 40, s 2.24.

3.66   The FSA has stated, as a general proposition, that 'normal market practices' will not amount to market abuse provided that the behaviour in question meets the standards reasonably expected by the reasonable user. There may be circumstances, however, when it becomes clear that, although a market, or class of users in a market, accepts a particular practice, that practice may still not rise to the standard reasonably expected by the regular user, as defined in the Act. The FSA does not expect such circumstances to arise frequently, but it should be noted that such a case arose in 1991 concerning trading in property futures contracts on the London FOX market. In this case, the Securities and Futures Authority took disciplinary action against five firms which admitted carrying out transactions for the purpose of creating a false appearance of increased activity and liquidity in property futures contracts. Moreover, senior officials of the London FOX (which was, at the time, an RIE) directed and encouraged that such transactions be carried out. This is an example of conduct that was accepted by market participants and senior officials of the exchange, but which fell beneath the standards that were acceptable to the regular user[1].

1   See SFA Board Notice 58 (17 December 1991).

3.67   The focus of the market abuse regime remains centred on the effects of behaviour and not on the intentions behind such behaviour. Accordingly, to impose civil liability, it is not necessary for any intention or purpose to be demonstrated in order for the regular user to conclude that behaviour amounts to market abuse. Notwithstanding, there will be some situations where the purpose of the person responsible for the behaviour will be relevant to the regular user's conclusions as to whether the behaviour falls below that of expected standards. In order to determine acceptable standards of behaviour for a person, the regular user must take into account that person's position in relation to the market. The Code prescribes no universal standard. Rather, the standards expected of the regular user will vary according to, inter alia, a person's skill, level of knowledge and experience. For example, the standards expected of a professional market participant will be more demanding in many instances than those of a retail investor who trades infrequently. Because the Code does not seek to set out the standards of behaviour expected for every conceivable type of market participant, the FSA has determined that it will apply the appropriate differentiation on a case-by-case basis.

3.68 The FSA has stated that it will assess behaviour in the light of the circumstances which applied at the time of the transaction. There will likely be cases where, with the benefit of hindsight, conduct that was previously accepted in a particular market becomes regarded as market abuse. If the behaviour was reasonable at the time, however, taking account of all circumstances, then the regular user will not consider the person as having engaged in market abuse at that time.

The Prescribed Markets and Qualifying Investments Order

3.69 The market abuse regime applies to behaviour in connection with qualifying investments traded on a market to which the FSMA 2000, s 118 will apply. HM Treasury has the power to prescribe the markets to which s 118 will apply and the investments which are qualifying investments in relation to those markets. The Prescribed Markets and Qualifying Investments Order specifies which investments and markets will be subject to the statute. HM Treasury issued a draft of this Order in June 1999[1]. Article 2 of the draft Order prescribes the markets to which s 118 will apply as any market established under the rules of the UK RIEs. These UK RIEs include: the London Stock Exchange Ltd, London International Financial Futures and Options Exchange Administration and Management, the London Metal Exchange Ltd, the International Petroleum Exchange of London Ltd, OM London Exchange Ltd and Tradepoint Stock Exchange. Article 3 of the draft Order prescribes as qualifying investments any investment of a kind which, at the time the Order is made, is admitted to trading under the rules of any of the prescribed markets.

1　See Annex, CP 76.

3.70 In summary, the Act defines market abuse as the misuse of relevant information that is not generally available to other market users, the giving of false or misleading impressions and market distortion. The first element, 'the misuse of information', applies to behaviour based on information not generally available to those using the market, but which, if it were available to a regular user, would be regarded by him as relevant in making investment decisions. The rationale is that market users expect certain classes of information to be made available to all market users on an equal basis. Trading on the basis of such insider information will undermine confidence in the integrity of the market if certain market participants have access to such information before it becomes generally available and can trade on it to their own advantage.

3.71 The second element involves behaviour which is likely to give a regular user a 'false or misleading impression' as to the supply of, or demand for, or price or value of investments. Market users who trade on the markets covered by the Act can reasonably expect to rely on the accuracy of certain types of information and transactions that are reported to the wider market.

The third element of market abuse concerns 'market distortion' in which the behaviour of a person impeding the proper operation of market forces and the interplay of demand and supply would be regarded by the regular user as distorting the market.

Conclusion

3.72 This chapter provides a general analysis of the various legal provisions that seek to protect investors against insider dealing and other types of manipulation of the financial markets. The two major pieces of legislation are the provisions against insider dealing in the CJA 1993 and the market abuse and insider dealing provisions of the FSMA 2000. The CJA 1993 imposes criminal liability for insider dealing, but did not provide a civil remedy for the company or unsuspecting outsider. This chapter discussed how insider information is derived from the company and often results in damages for those outsiders who bought and/or sold shares in ignorance of the information, which, if made public, would have affected the price of company securities. Although the possibility existed for civil remedies for insider dealing on the basis of constructive trusteeship, fiduciary accountability or breach of confidence, it was generally accepted that no comprehensive regime for civil liability was available for those investors who had suffered a diminution in value of their securities as a result of dealing on the basis of inside information. As a response, the FSMA 2000 market abuse regime represents an important extension of the powers currently available to regulators to combat market abuse. The new market abuse regime is a more significant change in approach for unauthorised market participants than for authorised persons. This is because the former were subject to the criminal regime alone, whereas authorised firms must already operate within the regulatory regime. The Code is intended to provide clarity and guidance to the high level of conduct that is considered acceptable behaviour for the regular user of the market. The FSA is concerned to ensure that the Code is effective in helping address market abuse so as to maintain confidence in the standards of UK markets and thereby to promote the UK competitive position in global financial markets[1].

1 The FSA will do so by endeavouring to respond promptly to reasonable requests for further guidance on interpretations of the Code.

CHAPTER 4

Encouraging and requiring insider dealing and market abuse

Introduction

4.1   As discussed in previous chapters, UK law regards the disclosure of information to another person as a type of insider dealing when such disclosure is made without appropriate authority *and* in situations where that other person is likely to abuse the information. Indeed, UK law employs a broad definition of insider dealing to include both the attribution of insider information from agent to principal regarding a particular transaction and also an individual's procuring or encouraging the dealing of another. Most systems of law regard such unauthorised disclosures as a form of insider dealing. In the case where the recipient deals on the basis of inside information, but is not aware of the tainted source of the information, there might well be an issue regarding the materiality of the information. Under UK law, such disclosure will only be considered objectionable when the primary insider discloses the material information without proper authority. This chapter analyses recent developments in the law concerning the encouragement offence and how the new Financial Services and Markets Act 2000 ('FSMA 2000') market abuse regime defines encouragement in the context of imposing civil liability on those who encourage or require others to commit market abuse.

Encouragement under the Criminal Justice Act 1993

4.2   The encouragement offence is found in the Criminal Justice Act 1993, s 52(2)(a) ('CJA 1993') and it prohibits a person from encouraging another person to deal in securities based on knowing or having reasonable cause to believe that the person receiving the encouragement would deal in securities in the circumstances covered by the dealing offence[1]. It is not a requirement of the offence for the individual who has information as an insider to pass information to the other person, nor is it necessary that the other person should know that the securities it is encouraged to buy are price-affected securities. The offence covers the classic situation where a tip is given by an insider to another, for example, 'sell as many shares of Marconi as you can before tomorrow's profit report'. Naturally, this could occur in a number of other situations.

1 CJA 1993, s 52(2)(a).

4.3 If the insider knows or has reasonable cause to believe that the other person will deal on a regulated market or through a professional intermediary, the offence will be committed even if, in fact, the other person does not undertake an insider dealing transaction. In practice, however, a successful criminal prosecution will be likely to require a deal or transaction to ensure a conviction. A deal in securities is relevant not only to the dealing offence, but also to the encouragement offence in so far as the encouragement has to be targeted at a particular transaction. Although not of direct relevance to the form of the disclosure offence, a defence is available where no dealing was expected[1]. This is because the type of dealing with which the CJA 1993 is concerned is limited[2].

1 CJA 1993, s 52(3).
2 Defences under the CJA 1993 and the new FSMA 2000 will be discussed in Chapter 9.

4.4 The encouragement offence can also create intermediary liability. For example, if deals in securities do not occur on a recognised investment exchange, they will only be within the insider dealing legislation if the person dealing relies on a professional intermediary or is himself a professional intermediary. A person will rely on a professional intermediary only if the professional intermediary either acquires or disposes of securities (whether as principal or agent) in relation to the dealing or acts as intermediary between persons taking part in the dealing[1]. Therefore, if the securities dealt in fall within the above categories, the insider dealing offence will be relevant unless the transaction is truly a private deal off the market without the intervention of a market professional.

1 CJA 1993, s 59(1)(a).

Encouraging and requiring market abuse – the FSMA 2000

4.5 The FSMA 2000 also prohibits those persons who encourage or require others to engage in conduct that amounts to market abuse. The FSMA 2000, s 123(1)(b) authorises the FSA to impose a penalty on a person if it is satisfied that that person, by taking or refraining from taking any action, has required or encouraged another person or persons to engage in behaviour which, if engaged in by the encourager, would amount to market abuse. For example, s 123(1)(b) authorises the FSA to impose a penalty on a person, 'A', who by taking or refraining from taking any action, 'has required or encouraged another person or persons to engage in behaviour which, if engaged in by A, would amount to market abuse'. To demonstrate market abuse under s 123(1)(b), the following must be shown:

- that the behaviour would have amounted to market abuse if carried out by the person who requires or encourages; and
- that the person, by action or inaction, required or encouraged another to engage in the behaviour in question[1].

1   Code of Market Conduct, 1.8.2.

4.6   The FSMA 2000, s 123(1)(b) is clearly an effort to prevent persons from circumventing the market abuse prohibition by prohibiting behaviour that encourages or requires other persons to engage in market abuse. It is not necessary to show that the person who encouraged or required has in fact benefited from the action of the person who was required or encouraged to commit the conduct in question[1]. The FSA is authorised to undertake a civil and/or criminal enforcement action against persons who breach the encouragement or requirement standard. The FSA may perhaps adopt a test that assesses whether the conduct undertaken by the person who was encouraged or required amounts to market abuse *and* whether such conduct would also have amounted to market abuse if committed by the person who purportedly did the encouraging or requiring.

1   Code of Market Conduct, 1.8.2.

4.7   Under the FSMA 2000, s 123(1)(b), the FSA may determine if the behaviour of another person amounts to market abuse if such behaviour had been engaged in by the encourager. In deciding this question, the FSA will apply the general principles set out in the Code of Market Conduct[1]. It should be noted that although the regular user test applies to the market abuse offence in the FSMA 2000, s 118, it does not apply to the encouraging and requiring offence. The Code provides guidance to the extent that in determining whether a person's behaviour falls short of expected standards (so that it would have amounted to market abuse if engaged by that person), consideration will be given to the knowledge, skill and experience to be expected of a person in the position of the alleged encourager[2]. This is an objective reasonable person standard to be applied to the person whose conduct has allegedly encouraged or required another to undertake conduct that amounts to market abuse as defined in the statute and the Code.

1   See the Code of Market Conduct, 1.8.1, requiring or encouraging.
2   FSMA 2000, s 119 states that the FSA guidance is not legally a part of the Code and therefore does not have binding effect.

4.8   The Code also provides that whether a person's taking or refraining from taking action might be regarded as requiring or encouraging others will depend on circumstances such as acceptable market practices, the expertise of the person concerned and the control or influence the person has in relation to the person who engages in the behaviour in question[1]. In the case of intermediaries, the primary focus will be on the originator of any abusive behaviour or transaction, including when the originator uses an intermediary to execute the transaction[2]. For example, the mere execution of a customer's order by an intermediary will not result in liability for *requiring* or *encouraging* the customer to engage in behaviour which amounts to market abuse if the contact between the intermediary and the customer is limited to the placing of the order with no indication that the transaction in question is an abusive transaction.

1   Code of Market Conduct, 1.8.4.
2   Code of Market Conduct, 1.8.8.

4.9   There may be circumstances, however, in which an intermediary executes a transaction when it knows, or has reason to know based on an objective standard, that the effect of the transaction on the market will be to abuse the market and allows the transaction to proceed[1]. Under these circumstances, the intermediary's behaviour will amount to market abuse under the FSMA 2000, s 118, but liability will not be based on the intermediary *requiring* or *encouraging* the customer to engage in abusive behaviour. To demonstrate liability in this context, it will be necessary to show that the intermediary failed to observe the standard of behaviour reasonably expected of a person in the intermediary's position. The relevant considerations for determining this will be, inter alia, the extent to which the intermediary had followed the rules of the relevant recognised investment exchange and the extent to which the intermediary had made (or should have made) some assessment of the abusive nature of the customer's behaviour.

1   Code of Market Conduct, 1.8.8.

4.10   The Code discusses several examples in which a person may require or encourage another person to engage in behaviour which, if engaged in by the former, would amount to market abuse. The Code provides some examples where liability might arise under the FSMA 2000, s 123(1)(b):

- a company director who is in possession of information which is both relevant and disclosable (other than trading information) and which is not generally available to market users, instructs a company employee to *deal* in qualifying investments or relevant products in respect of which the information is relevant information; and
- if A recommends or advises B to engage in behaviour which, if engaged in by A, would amount to market abuse or if A seeks to persuade or otherwise entice B to engage in such behaviour[1].

Furthermore, the draft Code addressed the issue of employer liability for employee breach of financial regulation by providing as an example of the requiring or encouraging offence the situation where an employer is aware that one of its employees, or any other person under its authority or control, is engaged in market abuse and then permits that person to continue to engage in the relevant behaviour[2]. The FSA then omitted this example in the issued version of the Code[3], leaving one to surmise that perhaps it did not intend to create employer liability in this situation or that it did not wish to address this difficult issue until further consultation. When considering this issue, however, it should be remembered that the SIB's Core Rule 28 imposed civil liability on a firm 'when it knows of circumstances when one of its associates, or an employee, is prohibited from effecting' a firm 'transaction by the statutory restrictions on insider dealing'[4]. Moreover, Rule 34 required authorised firms to take reasonable steps, including the maintenance of procedures, to ensure that their officers and employees, and officers and employees of their appointed representatives, comply with the obligations that the law imposes regarding insider dealing and market manipulation[5]. In addition, the FSMA 2000, s 200 contains provisions that create a type of vicarious liability for firms whose employees commit breaches of the Act. The FSA is expected to issue more guidance concerning the circumstances in which liability for market abuse can be attributed vicariously to the firm or employer for breaches committed by employees.

1   Code of Market Conduct, 1.8.3.
2   Draft Code of Market Conduct, 1.9.3.
3   Code of Market Conduct, 1.8.3.
4   Securities and Investments Board, Core Rules 28(1) and 36(3). See the discussion in para **[10.8]**.
5   See also the Investment Management Regulatory Organisation, Rule 1.5(2) (providing that each member must take reasonable steps to ensure that none of its officers or employees, or those appointed as representatives, either on its own account or that of any connected person, effects any transaction which is an investment at a time when he knows, or should reasonably know, that this would violate the law on insider dealing).

4.11   In considering whether a person's behaviour falls below certain standards of conduct with respect to market abuse, it will be necessary to inquire as to the knowledge, skill and experience of not only the person who actually committed the offence, but also the person who is alleged to have *required* or *encouraged* the offence. Another important factor in determining whether the person taking or refraining to take action might be regarded as requiring or encouraging others will depend on circumstances (eg acceptable market practices), the expertise of the person concerned and the control or influence the person has in relation to the person who has engaged in the misconduct. Unlawful requiring or encouraging may also occur where a person disclosed information which a *regular user* would expect market users to have on an equal basis, other than in accordance with the rules of a prescribed market, in order to manipulate market prices. For example, unlawful encouragement or requiring would occur where a potential bidder selectively disclosed certain information prior to dissemination of that bidder's intention, except as permitted according to the rules of a prescribed market or recognised investment exchange[1].

1   Code of Market Conduct, 1.8.5.

4.12   The FSA has stated in the Code that it will not regard a person as requiring or encouraging others to deal if he passes information which is relevant information and not generally available to the following:

- his employees (or, where appropriate, his fellow employees) for the purpose of enabling them to perform their functions in circumstances where the possession of the information in question is necessary for the proper performance of those functions; or
- his professional advisors and/or the professional advisors of any persons involved or who may be involved in any transaction or takeover bid with or involving him, for the purpose of obtaining advice; or
- any person with whom he is negotiating, or intends to negotiate, any commercial, financial or investment transaction (including prospective underwriters or placees of securities) for the purposes of facilitating the proposed transaction; or
- representatives of his employees or trade unions acting on their behalf in fulfilment of a legal obligation; or
- any government department, the Bank of England, Competition Commission or any other statutory or regulatory body or authority for the purposes of fulfilling a legal or regulatory obligation or otherwise in connection with the performance of the functions of the body to which the information has been passed[1].

The above list does not cover all the circumstances where liability may arise because of a person passing information which is relevant information and not generally available to the public and the FSA will assess the facts of each case on an individual basis.

1 Code of Market Conduct, 1.8.6.

4.13 Regarding a takeover bid, a person will not be regarded as having required or encouraged another person to engage in behaviour that amounts to market abuse in the following circumstances: (a) where A is an advisor to B and B is an actual or potential offeror in a takeover bid and (b) where A advises B to acquire an equity stake in a target company for the purposes and in the manner specified[1].

1 Code of Market Conduct, 1.8.7(1) and (2).

Conclusion

4.14 The CJA 1993 encouragement offence is a significant component in attacking sophisticated webs of communication between insiders, their associates and agents, whereby insider dealing transactions have been perpetrated. Moreover, the FSMA 2000 market abuse regime attacks market abuse by going after those persons who encourage or require others to undertake conduct (by action or inaction) that amounts to market abuse. As discussed in subsequent chapters, the requiring or encouraging standard is broad as it covers all types of market abuse, as defined under the statute, such as misuse of information, false and misleading disclosures or conduct that involves market distortion. The following chapters will analyse the market abuse provisions and what standards should be applied for determining whether conduct is market abuse and what safe harbours and exceptions to the market abuse regime may be invoked based on standards that have developed in other UK exchanges and codes.

CHAPTER 5

Tippee liability

Introduction

5.1   The third type of insider liability[1] created by the Criminal Justice Act 1993 ('CJA 1993') and expanded upon and applied in the market abuse regime of the Financial Services and Markets Act 2000 ('FSMA 2000') is tippee liability[2]. Tippee liability arises when a person who has information as an insider derives such information, either directly or indirectly, from a person who falls within one of the other two categories of insider, namely, directors, employees or shareholders of issuers or those who have access to inside information by virtue of their employment, office or profession. The essential elements of tippee liability are that the tippee must know that the information is inside information and that such information is derived from an inside source. In many cases, tippees and sub-tippees will not know that information is inside information. Indeed, the classic tip will involve a statement such as, for example, 'sell X Ltd' or 'buy Y Ltd'. Under these circumstances, no inside information will have been conveyed because, although the individual who gave the tip will have committed an offence, the tippee will not have obtained the 'information as an insider' (even though the tippee knows the tip came from an inside source) and would, therefore, appear to be outside the scope of the provision's coverage.

1   CJA 1993, s 57(2)(b).
2   In fact, when the word 'tippee' was included in the Criminal Justice Bill in 1992, it drew strong opposition from their Lordships and the word was eventually withdrawn before the Bill was approved in the House of Lords; see Parliamentary Debates, House of Lords, 19 November 1992, columns 756–767 and 3 December 1992, column 1496. See the discussion in B A K Rider and M Ashe, *Insider Crime* (1993, Jordans) p 46.

5.2   This chapter addresses the issue of tippee liability and the extent of its coverage under both the CJA 1993 and the FSMA 2000 market abuse regime. UK law has regarded tippee liability as a necessary element for protecting investors by making the provision of price-sensitive information available to investors on an equal basis. The FSMA 2000 market abuse regime provisions expand the scope of coverage of tippee liability to include all persons who trade on the basis of inside information in shares listed on recognised investment exchanges.

Primary and secondary insiders

5.3 The CJA 1993 was a significant expansion of the scope of the criminal law to define 'insider' to include primary and secondary insiders, such as tippees who did not have a connection with the company whose securities were traded. As discussed in Chapter 3, primary insiders are those individuals who have inside information through being a director, employee or shareholder of an issuer of securities or by having access to the information by virtue of their employment, office or profession[1]. The latter category of primary insider could be a person who obtained inside information and thereby became a primary insider by virtue of his or her employment, office or profession without necessarily having any direct professional, fiduciary or contractual connection with the company whose securities were traded. The category of persons having access to inside information by virtue of their employment, office or profession could be large indeed and includes professional advisers such as lawyers, merchant bankers, accountants, public relations specialists and the like. Whilst it would not be unreasonable to expect such persons to assume the responsibilities of insider status on a temporary basis, the section's language is wide enough to cover many others performing rather more peripheral services to an issuer. These types of temporary insiders might be office cleaners, temporary secretarial staff, postmen and couriers who have access to inside information by virtue of their employment. Although these groups would certainly have the opportunity to acquire inside information by engaging in the activities of their employment, it is arguable whether the scope of insider liability should be cast so widely.

1   CJA 1993, s 57(2)(a).

Secondary persons and tippee liability under the CJA 1993

5.4 The CJA 1993 defines a person as having information as an insider if, and only if, the person subjectively knows that it is inside information and possesses such information, and subjectively knows that he has it, from an inside source. As discussed in Chapter 3, before a person can be convicted of the offence of insider dealing, the prosecution must prove beyond all reasonable doubt that the individual concerned was fully aware that the information was 'inside information' as defined under the CJA 1993, s 56 and that the individual received the information from an inside source. The CJA 1993, s 57(2) provides the legal basis for tippee liability as a criminal offence. It describes the ways in which tippee liability may arise as follows:

'(2) For the purposes of subsection (1), a person has information from an inside source if and only if –

(a)   he has it through –
   (i)   being a director, employee or shareholder of an issuer of securities; or
   (ii)   having access to the information by virtue of his employment, office or profession; or
(b)   the direct or indirect source of his information is a person within paragraph (a)'.

5.5   The CJA 1993, s 57(2)(b) thus creates tippee liability or secondary person liability for someone who receives inside information directly or indirectly from a director, employee, shareholder or other insider of the issuer. Secondary insiders are essentially persons who know that the 'direct or indirect source' of that information is a primary insider. Some uncertainty exists as to whether the recipient must know the exact identity of the source and the circumstances under which the disclosure occurred or must merely be aware that the disclosure came from a primary source. It is not necessary to show that the secondary insider or tippee actively sought the information or that the primary insider discloses the information in an unlawful manner.

5.6   A person can only be charged with the offence of being a secondary insider or tippee, if it can be proved that the person was aware that the source of the information was one of these primary insiders or someone who had access to non-public, price-sensitive information. Before the CJA 1993, the Company Securities (Insider Dealing) Act 1985, ss 1(3), (4) and 8 made it a criminal offence, subject to exceptions and conditions, where 'an individual has information which he knowingly obtained (directly or indirectly) from' a person connected with a company and then deals on the Stock Exchange with shares in that company knowing that the information is confidential and unpublished price-sensitive information in relation to those shares. The CJA 1993 differs from the Company Securities (Insider Dealing) Act 1985 by eliminating the requirement of a connection between the insider and the issuer. Moreover, the CJA 1993 made it clear that tippee liability could arise even if the recipient of the information received it passively and did not attempt actively to obtain it[1].

1   See *Re A-G's Reference (No 1 of 1988)* [1989] AC 971 at 973–77 and 986, HL (holding that the defendant, who had been given unsought, unpublished, price-sensitive information, had 'obtained' that information within the meaning of the Company Securities (Insider Dealing) Act 1985, s 1(3) on the basis that the term 'obtained' in s 1(3) meant no more than 'received' and thereby had a wider meaning than 'acquired by purpose and effort').

5.7   The wider scope of liability can be attributed to a philosophy that seeks to penalise the exploitation of advantages in information that arise from insider access. According to this view, a journalist or bank analyst who deals before the release of his recommendation will be guilty of insider dealing, even though the price-sensitive information amounts to nothing more than his own recommendation. Some commentators, however, argue that such dealing is not an offence under the CJA 1993 because a precondition for liability requires the relevant information to be from an inside source[1]. For example, a director or employee may obtain inside information from an inside source if the information was received by virtue of the director's or employee's position with the issuer. Based on this analysis, information created by an employee would not be regarded as information to which the employee had access by virtue of employment. Thus, having access to information would appear to require that the information in question exists independently of the person seeking to obtain it or to access it. The recommendations of a journalist or analyst would not therefore be inside information in so far as that individual is concerned because he is not allowed to access his own information.

1   See *Gore-Browne on Companies*, regulation of dealing in securities, s 12.23.

5.8   It should be emphasised that under UK law the establishment of tippee liability does *not necessarily* depend on the liability of the individual who tips. For example, if, in the course of negotiations, inside information is passed bona fide to another person and the recipient then deals on the basis of that information, the tippee who dealt will be likely to have committed an offence, even though the tipper passed the information in a lawful manner. Thus, for example, if a partner of a large law firm that is advising a corporation on a takeover overhears inside information during negotiations, the lawyer will possess that information as an insider if he knows it is inside information and knows that the information is derived from an inside source. Similarly, an individual who knowingly becomes aware of inside information and knows it to be from an inside source, but who is not an insider (by virtue of employment, office or profession), will incur tippee liability as well.

5.9   In the case of sub-tippees, circumstances arise where information has passed through several hands and has consequently lost some of the qualities that made it inside information (ie precision and specificity) with the result that it may be difficult to establish that the tippee has inside information. Aside from proving the tippee's state of knowledge, it may be difficult to prove that the information is in fact inside information because at this stage it may have lost much of its accuracy and novelty. Moreover, even if the information, after passing through several hands, still retains its accuracy and novelty, it may be difficult to show that the sub-tippee knew that the inside information was from an inside source.

US insider trading law

5.10   US law applies a complex test for determining the liabilities of insiders, which essentially narrows the circumstances in which persons are potentially liable for trading, disclosing or procuring insider transactions as compared with those in other jurisdictions. In cases not involving takeovers, primary insiders are prohibited from trading on the basis of material, non-public information in a company's securities if such trading breaches a duty under *either* the fiduciary or misappropriation theories. Under the fiduciary theory, the prosecution must prove that the trading constituted a breach of duty to the firm whose securities were traded and that the firm suffered injury on account of the breach. Under the misappropriation theory, an insider of firm A can be held liable for damages arising from trading in the shares of firm B if such trading breached firm A's policy prohibiting personal use of information produced or derived on behalf of firm A[1]. Insider trading, however, is allowed in fiduciary cases if the party to whom the duty is owed consents[2] and allowed in misappropriation cases if the party to whom the duty is owed has knowledge. Regarding misappropriation theory, the Supreme Court ruled in *US v O'Hagan*[3] that there can be no misappropriation if the fiduciary has fully disclosed to the principal his intention to trade.

1 *US v Carpenter* 791 F 2d 1024 (2nd Cir, 1986) (upholding a journalist's conviction of insider trading under the misappropriation theory based on trading in advance of a newspaper column, finding that he had breached the newspaper's policy prohibiting personal use of information produced or derived on behalf of the newspaper).
2 See Donald Langevoort, *Insider Trading: Regulation, Enforcement and Prevention* (West) s 6.05[3] at 6–33 to 6–35.
3 521 US 642 (1997).

5.11 A secondary insider trading violation only occurs if the tippee knows, or should know, that: (a) the information given to them is insider information, (b) the primary insider passed the information in breach of the primary insider's fiduciary duty[1] and (c) the primary insider derives either a direct or indirect personal benefit from making the disclosure[2]. The courts have adopted a rationale in which secondary insiders should only be liable for trading and primary insiders liable as accessories where the primary and secondary insiders have acted together to form a joint venture to exploit inside information[3].

1 See a similar fact scenario in *SEC v Switzer* 590 F Supp 756 (WED Okla, 1984).
2 *Dirks v SEC* 463 US 646 (1983). The Supreme Court held (at 664) that there were three types of possible personal benefit: pecuniary benefit, reputational benefit and gift.
3 The joint venture has been criticised. See Langevoort, *Insider Trading: Regulation, Enforcement and Prevention*, s 6.07 at 6–39.

5.12 Regarding sub-tippees, it would be unlawful for a person who receives inside information from a secondary insider to trade only where that person is aware that the information is material and non-public and knows, or has reason to know, that the information was obtained by virtue of a breach of fiduciary duty by the primary insider. It should also be noted that because the US legislation only covers transactions in securities, secondary insiders may lawfully refrain or cancel trade orders.

5.13 The complexity of these issues was demonstrated in *US v Musella*[1], where a word processing supervisor of a New York law firm was regularly passing inside information onto a broker, who then passed it to one Dominick Musella, who then tipped his brother, John Musella, a New York City policeman, who then recommended share purchases to two of his police colleagues, O'Neill and Martin. Neither O'Neill nor Martin knew of the original source of the inside information, nor were they aware of the specific basis of the tip. Not even Dominick Musella knew the identity or the position of the person who was the source of the information[2]. The Musella brothers and O'Neill and Martin were found guilty of the crime of insider dealing. The court noted that tippee liability would arise under anti-insider dealing laws for any person who receives suspicious information and that they would not be able to raise as a defence lack of knowledge of the identity or the position of the original source of the information. The court held that by deliberately not wanting to know, the remote tippees (defendants) had the requisite awareness of the original breach of fiduciary duty to incur liability on the basis of inside information. Most US circuits observe the rule that a person who receives suspicious information must *either* abstain from trading or establish that the information is not tainted by the original breach.

1   678 F Supp 1060 (SDNY, 1988); see also *SEC v Musella* 748 F Supp 1028 (SDNY, 1989).
2   In this case, the person, who was the source of the inside information, was known in conversations with the broker, who was the go-between, as 'the goose who laid the golden egg'.

5.14   If one were to apply the UK law on tippee liability for insider dealing to the facts discussed above in the *Musella* case, it would appear that an English court would have found Dominick Musella to have had the insider information, to have known that the information was inside information and also to have known that there was an indirect source of his information, but not to have known either the source's identity or its position. Most commentators observe that it would be unlikely for an English court to hold that knowledge of identity was necessary to prove tippee liability[1]. It would also not be necessary to show that the tippee knew the position of the original source of the information, ie whether the tippee knew it was a director, employee or shareholder of the issuer or a person having access to the information by virtue of his employment, office or profession. The court would probably not require that it be shown that the original source was an inside source and that the tippee knew it was an inside source. What would matter to the court would be whether the tippee received the inside information – either directly or indirectly – from the source that happened to be an inside source, unless it were rebutted to show that the requisite degree of knowledge was lacking. This issue will be explored further in Chapter 9.

1   But see *Re A-G's Reference (No 1 of 1988)* [1989] AC 971 (per Lord Lowry).

5.15   Although the position of John Musella would be likely to result in liability, it is submitted that neither O'Neill nor Martin knew that the information was inside information and, therefore, because the statute requires that it must be proved that they knew that the information was inside information and that a recommendation to buy shares cannot per se be inside information, it is submitted that O'Neill and Martin would be acquitted under the CJA 1993.

The FSMA 2000 and tippee liability

5.16   The CJA 1993 extended the scope of tippee liability so that, unlike the Company Securities (Insider Dealing) Act 1985, the inside source need have no connection with the issuer whose securities are involved. This extension of tippee liability is also reflected under the civil liability regime for market abuse under the FSMA 2000. The FSMA 2000 civil remedy for market abuse covers insider trading (traditionally prosecuted as a criminal offence under UK law) and applies to any person whose behaviour is based on inside information. Under the FSMA 2000 market abuse regime, the FSA may impose civil sanctions on any person or firm who engages in market abuse through insider trading. The FSMA 2000 makes no distinction between primary and secondary insiders, nor requires the alleged insider to be linked directly or indirectly to the company whose securities are traded. Thus, under both the CJA 1993 and the FSMA 2000, where the person disclosing the information has access to it through their employment, it is not necessary to show that the person was in a position (eg employment, office or profession) which might reasonably be expected to give him access to such inside information.

Practical applications of tippee liability under UK law

Involuntary recipients

5.17   An issue related to those discussed above is the abuse of unpublished price-sensitive information by those who acquire it casually without any design on their part. For example, the proverbial taxi driver who overhears a conversation taking place in the rear of his cab. He might well appreciate that the information he overhears is very price sensitive, but he may have no idea of who his unintentional informant is and the standing of the knowledge that he has now acquired. It can be argued that if he does not appreciate that the information in question could only have come from an insider, then it is unobjectionable for him to utilise it. Of course, in practice, unless there is a relationship which is susceptible to proof between the person who seeks to exploit an informational advantage and his source, then it is highly unlikely that he would be identified or his trading impeached.

5.18   A more problematic situation arises when inside information is dumped on an individual or organisation and who is also made aware or cannot but be cognisant of the fact that the information is from an insider source. It may be impossible both in legal and practical terms for that person publicly to disclose the information in question. Consequently, their possession of the information in question may well serve to prevent them from trading in the relevant securities. There have been examples where information has been strategically placed so as to prevent further acquisitions in particular securities that may have resulted in a change of control of the relevant issuer. To disable a potential offeror company in this manner is both undesirable and unfair. On the other hand, that person is in possession of price-sensitive information which, for whatever reason, cannot be brought into the market. The approach to this problem in some jurisdictions is to allow the person who has been given the information to proceed with the transactions that he had already planned or at least already initiated. Of course, the best solution in such cases is to require disclosure of the information, but, as we have already pointed out, this may not always be feasible.

Eavesdropping

5.19   Another scenario that has led to some uncertainty is where inside information is deliberately acquired by those who have no relationship with the source of the information. For example, highly price-sensitive information may be obtained through an electronic eavesdropping device or simple burglary. There can be no doubt that those who obtain the information appreciate its sensitivity and its source. On the other hand, is it appropriate to regard them as falling within the scope of anti-insider dealing laws? Of course, it may well be the case that their conduct will constitute some other criminal offence or tort. In some jurisdictions, before liability for insider dealing can be imposed, it must be proved where that person is not a primary insider, that he knows the specific identity of his informant. It is not sufficient merely to prove that the information clearly came from an inside source. In the case of electronic eavesdropping and no doubt other forms of espionage, it is quite possible that the recipients of the relevant information would not be aware of the specific source, although they would, of course, be aware that the person in question was an insider. In the UK, as we shall see, it would be sufficient for the prosecution to prove that those seeking to utilise the relevant information appreciated it was from an inside source.

The insider's family and associates

5.20   Before leaving our discussion as to whom it may be appropriate to regard as being insiders, it is appropriate to address whether the spouses, children and associates of those in an access relationship should be presumed to hold the information in question. Indeed, it might be justifiable to regard the close associates and members of any person whose own dealing would be considered to be objectionable as subject to the same restrictions. In many jurisdictions, such as the UK, in which directors are under a legal duty to disclose their interests and dealings in the securities of their company, this obligation is extended to the director's spouse and infant children. It is also often extended to the interests of any company that the director owns or controls or, in some instances, in which he has a significant interest. In the UK, the specific prohibitions on directors engaging in practices such as option dealings in the securities of their companies are extended to those with whom the director is intimately and closely associated. In practice, in many of the cases that have come to light, the director or other insider has traded in the name of, or for the benefit of, a close relative or associate. The traditional civil law, which is based on the personal obligation of stewardship, may not extend to impose liability on the insider himself in such cases or, for that matter, the beneficiary of the abuse. A similar problem arises when the dealing is by a company with which the insider is associated because, in law, the company is an entirely separate legal person. While in many legal systems it is possible to 'lift the veil of incorporation', in certain circumstances such as where the company is incorporated for the purpose of evading the law or is an 'engine for fraud', the courts are cautious. They are aware of the importance of the 'corporate personality' principle in the commercial world and will therefore only seek to penetrate it where the public interest clearly mandates it. These issues involve a number of complex and difficult problems. It would not be acceptable to impose liability on an insider merely because a close family member or business with which he is associated happens to engage in a transaction while he is in possession of the relevant information. Indeed, in some countries, specific legislation has been introduced, or at least canvassed, to protect trustees who may find themselves, quite innocently, in a similar situation vis-à-vis unconnected dealings by those who manage the trust fund or by its beneficiaries. On the other hand, given the difficulties of proving to the satisfaction of the law that actual communications have occurred in the privacy of a bedroom, it may well be appropriate to resort to common sense inferences, if not presumptions. The attribution of knowledge between separate legal persons or within the structure of a body corporate are complex legal issues in all legal systems.

Conclusion

5.21   Tippee liability under the CJA 1993 has been simplified and extended under the FSMA 2000 market abuse regime to apply to a broad category of behaviour that constitutes misuse of information that is price sensitive and non-public. For example, a person who obtains inside information that was passed bona fide by another person during negotiations will incur civil liability under the FSMA 2000 and criminal liability under the CJA 1993 if that person deals on the basis of such inside information. Thus, a person who overhears inside information will have that information as an insider if he knows it is inside information and possesses it in the knowledge that it derives from an inside source. Similarly, a person who takes inside information knowing it is from an inside source will incur tippee liability under both the FSMA 2000 and the CJA 1993. Chapter 6 will consider the market abuse offence in more detail and, in particular, the offence of misuse of information.

Misuse of information

The market abuse regime – an introduction

6.1 The Financial Services and Markets Act 2000 ('FSMA 2000') introduces the 'market abuse' regime to this jurisdiction. The new provisions introduce a new layer of civil enforcement procedures that may be exercised by the FSA to address the offences of market manipulation and misuse of information by both authorised and unauthorised persons[1]. The detail of the offence of misuse of information will be considered in this chapter (see paras **[6.34]–[6.64]**), together with the provisions common to both types of offence (see paras **[6.9]–[6.33]**). Market manipulation is addressed in Chapter 7.

1 FSMA 2000, s 118.

6.2 Currently, unauthorised persons are only subject to the criminal law in respect of this type of behaviour: the Financial Services Act 1986, s 47 (which will be superseded by the FSMA 2000, s 397) prohibits misleading statements and practices and the Criminal Justice Act 1993, Pt V makes insider dealing illegal. The inadequacies of the criminal law in addressing the majority of cases of market abuse, save in the most serious cases, had been criticised for a long time. However, the government rejected previous recommendations to employ the civil law to address this issue, on the basis that such offences were 'public wrongs' and therefore were best addressed by the criminal law[1]. The criminal law, at least in respect of insider dealing, is narrowly defined and requires the state of mind of the offender to be addressed. As an approach common to all cases of market abuse, it is submitted that such inquiry fails to address the impact of the offender's actions upon the reputation of the financial markets. The market abuse regime shifts the emphasis to the effect of the offender's actions upon the market and is therefore more likely effectively to maintain the objective of maintaining the reputation of the financial markets of the United Kingdom 'as a fair and clean place to do business'[2].

1 White Paper 'Company Investigations' (1990) Cm 1149 at 18.
2 CP 59, para 1.1.

6.3 The new regime will complement rather than supersede the existing provisions of the criminal law of insider dealing and misleading statements and practices. Additionally, the regime will operate in tandem with rules applying to authorised persons whether pursuant to rules made by the FSA[1] as well as any other legal or regulatory requirements such as the provisions in the Companies Act 1985, the rules of Recognised Investment Exchanges, the provisions of the City Code on Takeovers and Mergers and overseas rules and regulatory requirements[2].

1   Eg Principle for Businesses 5 and the Conduct of Business Sourcebook.
2   MAR 1.9.

6.4 The new civil enforcement powers conferred upon the FSA to address market abuse are amongst the most radical innovations of the FSMA 2000. The primary sanction for market abuse is the imposition of an unlimited penalty by the FSA[1]. This power has provoked concerns by reason of the administrative manner in which it may be exercised by the FSA, subject to the right of an alleged offender to refer the matter to the newly formed Financial Services and Markets Tribunal[2]. In fact, the recent draft European directive on market abuse (2001/118 (COD)) makes administrative sanctions for market abuse mandatory because the proceedings are faster than criminal ones[3]. In addition, the FSA has power to apply to the court for injunctions and restitution orders, together with a penalty in either case[4]. The orders that the court may make pursuant to applications under these powers are broad ranging and include the making of 'freezing orders'[5]. These powers of course resemble those that have been conferred upon the Securities and Exchange Commission in the USA for many years. Enforcement powers are considered in detail in Chapter 11.

1   FSMA 2000, s 123(1).
2   FSMA 2000, s 127.
3   See art 14.
4   FSMA 2000, ss 381 and 383.
5   The formerly called 'Mareva injunction' in which a person's assets are frozen: see further CPR, r 25.1(1)(f).

6.5 The new enforcement powers, however, should not be overstated as in many ways the tenor of the new regime is first and foremost about setting standards. This is seen not only by the emphasis placed by the FSA upon education and giving guidance to market users[1] in respect of market abuse, but also upon the framework and text of the new provisions. In particular, central to all of the offences are the standards expected of the 'regular user'[2]. The 'regular user' is not however an actual user, but a hypothetical user[3]. In addition, the focus has moved away from the state of mind of the alleged offender to the effects of the behaviour in question upon the market[4] under the market abuse regime.

1   To which the FSA has given its commitment, see particularly CP 59, para 6.11, Chapters 10 and 11 and Policy Statement, para 4.6.
2   FSMA 2000, s 118(1)(c).
3   MAR 1.2.2.
4   For instance, in the 'misuse of information' offence, it is no longer a condition that the offender has knowledge; compare the insider dealing legislation.

6.6 Further, the Code of Market Conduct often employs standards already established in the regulatory field. For instance, the Code provides that information must be of a type 'which a regular user would reasonably expect to be disclosed to users of the particular prescribed market'[1]. The types of information that fall into this category are (a) information which has to be disclosed in accordance with any legal or regulatory requirement or (b) information which is routinely the subject of a public announcement, although not subject to any formal disclosure requirement[2].

1   MAR 1.4.4(4).
2   MAR 1.4.12.

Misuse of information – an introduction

6.7 It will already be apparent that the misuse of information category of market abuse goes beyond the criminal offence of insider dealing[1]. The break from 'knowledge' and the introduction of the touchstone of 'disclosable' and 'announceable' information are two of these factors. However, equally important is the move away from a requirement of a nexus to 'the insider' in order to make information illegitimate. Instead, information is made illegitimate if a regular user 'would or would be likely to [regard the information] as relevant when deciding the terms on which transactions in investments of the kind in question should be effected'[2]. This move is in keeping with the concern of the regime to set standards.

1   The FSA has stressed that this category is not, and is not intended to be, identical to the existing criminal provision of insider dealing: CP 59, para 6.18.
2   FSMA 2000, s 118(2)(a).

6.8 In addition, insider dealing only applies to corporate securities and derivatives. Market abuse applies to a broader range of markets and by virtue of the Financial Services and Markets Act 2000 (Prescribed Markets and Qualifying Investments) Order 2001, SI 2001/996 will apply to markets in commodity derivatives and financial futures.

The offence of market abuse

6.9 The FSMA 2000, Pt VIII and the Code of Market Conduct set out the offence of market abuse. The Code of Market Conduct has been produced by the FSA pursuant to its obligation in the FSMA 2000, s 119 in order 'to give appropriate guidance to those determining whether or not behaviour amounts to market abuse'. The FSA received its legislative powers as defined by the FSMA 2000, Sch 1, para 1(2) on 18 June 2001 by the Financial Services and Markets Act 2000 (Commencement No 3) Order 2001, SI 2001/1820. The FSA has now issued a final text of the Code of Market Conduct pursuant to these powers.

6.10 Notwithstanding the detail of the Code, it only determines behaviour that 'does not amount to market abuse', described in the Code as 'safe harbours'[1]. Otherwise, the Code in force at the time when particular behaviour occurs 'may be relied on' so far as it indicates whether or not that behaviour should be taken to amount to market abuse[2]. Thus, the Code is only of evidential value in respect of conduct amounting to market abuse. In practice, it is submitted that the Code will have high evidential value. It has been persuasively argued that this approach in defining the offence of market abuse may subject the market abuse regime to challenge by reason of the failure to define the offence clearly, a point considered in greater detail in Chapter 9. However, it is submitted that the chosen approach to market abuse is equally supportable by reason of the particular difficulties in precisely defining market abuse.

1   FSMA 2000, s 122(1).
2   FSMA 2000, s 122(2).

6.11 The preliminary triggers for market abuse are that (a) the 'behaviour occurs in relation to qualifying investments'[1] (see paras **[6.24]–[6.28]**), (b) 'traded on a market to which [s 118] applies'[2] (see paras **[6.20]–[6.23]**), (c) 'which is likely to be regarded by a regular user of the market [see paras **[6.12]–[6.16]** and **[6.18]**] who is aware of the behaviour as a failure on the part of the person or persons concerned to observe the standard of behaviour reasonably expected of a person in his or their position in relation to the market'[3] and (d) it is within the territorial scope of the Act[4] (see para **[6.33]**).

1   FSMA 2000, s 118(1)(a).
2   FSMA 2000, s 118(1)(a).
3   FSMA 2000, s 118(1)(c).
4   FSMA 2000, s 118(5).

The regular user

6.12 The standards expected by 'the regular user' are central to the market abuse regime. 'The regular user' is defined as 'a reasonable person who regularly deals on that market in investments of the kind in question'[1] and further guidance is given by MAR 1.2. The 'regular user' is not an actual regular user, but a hypothetical reasonable person familiar with the market in question[2]. The Economic Secretary described 'the regular user' as 'the cousin of the courts' reasonable man'[3].

1   FSMA 2000, s 118(10).
2   MAR 1.2.2.
3   Standing Committee A, 2 November 1999 at column 655.

6.13 The FSA has maintained that standards of accepted behaviour in the market will not always correspond to behaviour acceptable to the 'regular user'[1]. After all, institutional investors may tolerate practices that a less sophisticated user would not. The Code emphasises the regular user's concern that 'market users conduct their affairs in a manner that does not compromise the fair and efficient operation of the market as a whole or unfairly damage the interests of the investors'[2]. However, the accepted standards of a market will be relevant to the 'regular user', although not determinative[3], as will the prevailing market mechanisms and practices[4]. However, the FSA has made clear from the outset of consultation that it would not expect accepted practices frequently to diverge from the standards expected by the 'regular user'[5]. Further, the FSA has indicated that where there is a discrepancy between accepted and acceptable practice, it will usually issue guidance pursuant to its powers in the FSMA 2000, s 157 unless enforcement action is appropriate[6]. The FSA has referred to its practice in the past on issues such as insider dealing and equity derivatives on this point[7].

1   MAR 1.2.4.
2   MAR 1.2.3(5).
3   MAR 1.2.4.
4   MAR 1.2.3(3).
5   FSA Policy Statement, para 5.5 and MAR 1.2.11.
6   MAR 1.2.11 and Policy Statement, para 5.6.
7   Eg SIB Guidance Release 4/96.

6.14   The Code also makes clear that the standards expected will vary from market to market depending upon the characteristics of such market, the investments traded on the market, the users of the market[1] and from user to user depending upon their experience, level of skill and knowledge[2]. By way of guidance, the FSA has indicated that when assessing the standards to be expected of public sector bodies, it is likely that it will be relevant to take into account their statutory and other official functions[3]. Similarly, the FSA has indicated that it will take into account the different disclosure standards in equities markets and commodities markets[4].

1   MAR 1.2.3(1).
2   MAR 1.2.3(4).
3   MAR 1.2.7.
4   MAR 1.2.7.

The relevance of state of mind to the regular user

6.15   As noted above, the FSA is primarily concerned with the effects of market abuse rather than the intent of the person engaged in market abuse[1]. The strict liability of the offence was criticised in the passage of the Financial Services and Markets Bill. However, the purpose of behaviour will be relevant to the 'regular user' in certain circumstances[2]. As will be seen in Chapter 7, state of mind and motive is particularly relevant in cases of market manipulation. Further, state of mind is also relevant on the question of enforcement[3].

1   CP 59, para 6.14.
2   MAR 1.2.5.
3   Eg ENF 14.4.2 and 14.7.4.

The regular user and RIE Rules/the City Code/SARs

6.16 Some had argued that a blanket safe harbour should be imposed in respect of compliance with RIE Rules and the City Code on Takeovers and Mergers. However, this approach has been rejected by the FSA. Instead, the FSA has retained the relevance of these provisions in the 'regular user' test and conferred safe harbours upon certain of these regulations which are considered in Chapter 9. The reasons given by the FSA are as follows: (a) this approach would amount to blanket delegation[1], (b) they would become involved in the day-to-day interpretation of the RIE rulebooks and the City Code[2] and (c) the possibility of conflicting interpretations of the same provisions would arise[3]. This approach now seems to be approved by market participants[4]. However, consultees have emphasised the need for appropriate weight to be given to the RIE Rules, the City Code and SARs. The FSA has made clear that it will look to the RIEs and Takeover Panel for their views and give them due weight and acknowledges that 'if the FSA's decisions are to have credibility, they will need to be well-informed'[5]. Therefore, the rules and regulations of the market in question are factors that the 'regular user' takes into account in considering the behaviour in question[6]. By way of guidance, the FSA has indicated that it is satisfied that the RIE rulebooks do not permit or require behaviour which amounts to market abuse[7]. The FSA may also take into account the standards in an overseas jurisdiction where a person is based overseas[8]. On this point, it is worth noting that even in the European context there are substantial differences of approach to market abuse, a point that the draft European directive on market manipulation seeks to address[9].

1 CP 59, para 8.2; see also the First Report of the Joint Committee on Financial Services and Markets, 27 April 1999 at para 271.
2 CP 76, para 3.6.
3 CP 76, para 3.6.
4 FSA Policy Statement, paras 4.8 and 4.9.
5 Policy Statement, para 4.8.
6 MAR 1.2.3(2).
7 MAR 1.2.12.
8 MAR 1.2.3(3).
9 See the discussion on the draft European directive on insider dealing and market manipulation in Chapter 13.

FSA rules

6.17 It should also be noted that behaviour that conforms with a rule made by the FSA under the FSMA 2000, which includes a provision to the effect that behaviour conforming to the rule does not amount to market abuse, will not amount to market abuse[1]. This point is considered in further detail in Chapter 9.

1 FSMA 2000, s 118(8).

Mistakes

6.18 The 'regular user' shows some compassion by confirming that it would be unlikely to consider that a mistake would amount to market abuse where the person or firm in question has taken reasonable care to prevent and detect the occurrence of such mistakes[1]. The significance of internal procedures to the enforcement action of the FSA is considered in Chapter 11.

1 MAR 1.2.6.

Innovations

6.19 The FSA has also emphasised in its policy statement that it does not wish to stifle innovative transactions through the new regime, but encourages market participants to seek guidance from the FSA on such transactions[1].

1 MAR 1.2.13.

Qualifying investments traded on a market to which s 118 applies

6.20 The Treasury has the power to prescribe the markets and investments to which the FSMA 2000, s 118 applies[1] and has done this through the Financial Services and Markets Act 2000 (Prescribed Markets and Qualifying Investments) Order 2001, SI 2001/996. This Order will come into force at the same time as the FSMA 2000, s 123[2]. Interestingly, the Treasury may prescribe such markets and investments by name or by description[3]. The order may prescribe different investments or descriptions of investment in relation to different markets or descriptions of market[4]. The government therefore has the flexibility to extend the scope of the Act and adapt to new products and markets.

1 FSMA 2000, s 118(3)(a) and (b).
2 See art 2.
3 FSMA 2000, s 118(3)(a) and (b).
4 FSMA 2000, s 118(4).

6.21 The Financial Services and Markets Act 2000 (Prescribed Markets and Qualifying Investments) Order 2001, SI 2001/996, art 4 prescribes the markets to which the FSMA 2000, s 118 applies as those which are established under the rules of a UK recognised investment exchange. This is defined in art 3 as meaning any investment exchange recognised under the FSMA 2000, s 290(1)(a). At the time the order was made, the following exchanges fell within this category: London Stock Exchange plc, LIFFE Administration and Management, the London Metal Exchange Ltd, the International Petroleum Exchange of London Ltd, OM London Exchange Ltd, COREDEAL Ltd, Jiway Ltd and virt-x plc.

6.22 The Financial Services and Markets Act 2000 (Prescribed Markets and Qualifying Investments) Order 2001, SI 2001/996, art 5 prescribes the qualifying investments in relation to such markets as all investments specified for the purposes of the FSMA 2000, s 22. At the time of making the order, the relevant investments are those set out in the Financial Services and Markets Act 2000 (Regulated Activities) Order 2001, SI 2001/544, Pt III, which includes a wide range of financial instruments. However, the regime is not limited to these particular products as explained in paras **[6.27]–[6.28]**.

6.23 The final version of the Code develops the phrase 'qualifying investments traded on a market' to which the FSMA 2000, s 118(1)(a) applies at MAR 1.11.3–1.11.5. The FSA decided against producing lists of products traded on prescribed markets[1] and instead has given guidance on this point in the Code. The first point to note is that the FSA's view is that investments which have been traded on a prescribed market in the past and can still be traded subject to the rules of a prescribed market would be 'traded on' a prescribed market[2]. However, the FSA continues by noting that where there is no ongoing market in the investment, it would be unlikely that behaviour would amount to market abuse as the conditions in s 118(2) would be unlikely to be satisfied[3].

1   Policy Statement, para 11.4.
2   MAR 1.11.3.
3   MAR 1.11.4 and 1.11.5.

Behaviour

6.24 'Behaviour' includes both action and inaction[1]. The specific example of inaction given by the Code is a failure to comply with a legal or regulatory obligation of disclosure[2]. Behaviour is expanded upon in MAR 1.3.1, which provides that the types of behaviour which come within the scope of the market abuse regime include, but are not limited to:

• dealing in 'qualifying investments';
• dealing in commodities or investments which are the subject matter of, or whose price or value is determined by reference to, a 'qualifying investment';
• acting as an arranger in respect of 'qualifying investments';
• causing or procuring or advising others to deal in 'qualifying investments';
• making statements or representations or otherwise disseminating information which is likely reasonably to be regarded by the regular user as relevant to determining the terms on which transactions in qualifying investments should be effected;
• providing corporate finance advice and conducting corporate finance activities in 'qualifying investments'; and
• managing qualifying investments belonging to another.

1   FSMA 2000, s 118(10).
2   MAR 1.3.2.

6.25   The express inclusion of those involved in corporate finance and those managing qualifying investments is notable, particularly when one considers the provisions of the criminal law of insider dealing[1]. The market abuse regime is more express in its intent and targets than such legislation, in accordance with the FSA's objective of providing clarity and transparency in respect of standards within the market.

1   CJA 1993, Pt V.

6.26   Similarly, a person may engage in market abuse 'whether alone or with one or more other persons'[1]. Further, the market abuse provisions apply irrespective of whether a person acts alone or jointly or in concert[2]. In addition, where an offence under the Act is shown to have been committed by a body corporate, an officer of such body corporate may also be guilty of an offence if certain conditions are satisfied[3]. These are (a) that the offence was committed with the consent or connivance of an officer or (b) such offence is attributable to neglect on the part of such officer. Similar provisions apply to partnerships and unincorporated associations[4]. The section entitled 'requiring or encouraging' at paras **[6.29]–[6.30]** should also be considered.

1   FSMA 2000, s 118(9).
2   FSMA 2000, s 118(1).
3   FSMA 2000, s 400(1).
4   FSMA 2000, s 400.

Occurs in relation to qualifying investments

6.27   The Act does not limit the instances when behaviour will be regarded as occurring in relation to qualifying investments. Instead, it provides that 'behaviour which is to be regarded as occurring in relation to qualifying investments includes behaviour which' occurs in relation to '(a) anything which is the subject matter, or whose price or value is expressed by reference to the price or value, of those qualifying investments; or (b) investments (whether qualifying or not) whose subject matter is those qualifying investments'[1]. These expressions are explained in the Code at MAR 1.11.6–1.11.11.

1   FSMA 2000, s 118(6).

6.28   The Act is therefore of broad scope and is not limited to 'qualifying investments'. For instance, behaviour in relation to a gilt which is the subject matter of a gilt futures contract traded on LIFFE will be caught by the FSMA 2000, s 118(6)[1]. Similarly, a spread bet in relation to a basket of UK shares traded on a prescribed market will be caught where it is expressed by reference to the price of the shares[2].

1   MAR 1.11.10.
2   MAR 1.11.11.

Requiring or encouraging behaviour

6.29   The power of the FSA to impose a penalty upon a person who has 'required or encouraged' another to engage in market abuse 'by taking or refraining from taking any action, a person has required or encouraged another person or persons to engage in behaviour which if the person themselves engaged in such behaviour would amount to market abuse'[1] is a residual power designed to cover a potential loophole. 'Requiring or encouraging' is considered at MAR 1.8, although this guidance does not legally form part of the Code under the FSMA 2000, s 119. It should also be noted that the 'regular user' test is not part of 'requiring or encouraging', although the FSA will take into account factors similar to that relevant to the 'regular user' test such as acceptable market practices, the level of skill and standard of knowledge of the person concerned[2]. Further, the FSA has noted that a person need not have benefited from a transaction for it to fall foul of 'requiring or encouraging' another[3]. Benefit is not, however, an express requirement of the market abuse offence itself, although it may be relevant to the enforcement action taken by the FSA.

1   FSMA 2000, s 123(1).
2   MAR 1.8.4.
3   MAR 1.8.2.

6.30   Examples of requiring or encouraging are given at MAR 1.8.3. However, the FSA's comments in CP 76, Chapter 2 should be noted on this point. The FSA expressed the view at CP 76, para 2.6 that in many instances what was previously thought to be 'requiring or encouraging' could instead be treated as market abuse, depending upon the circumstances.

Intermediaries

6.31   Intermediaries received particular attention in CP 76. The final text of the Code considers the position of intermediaries at MAR 1.8.8. The FSA's view is that the behaviour of an intermediary who acts on behalf of a person who appears to have engaged in market abuse will not amount to either 'requiring or encouraging' or 'market abuse' unless the intermediary knew or ought reasonably to have known that the originator was engaging in market abuse. There is a subtle change from CP 76 MAR 1.8A2. The earlier draft made clear that an intermediary would be liable as a primary market abuser in these circumstances, whereas the final form of the Code leaves open the option of accessory liability. This may be due to concerns raised in the process of consultation.

6.32   It should be noted that in the policy statement the FSA has acknowledged that there are differences between electronic brokers and voice brokers[1]. The argument that there was a risk of competitive distortion between such brokers may have led to the deletion of the reference to the mere execution of an order not of itself constituting the intermediary as 'requiring or encouraging' the customer to engage in behaviour which amounts to market abuse from the final text of the Code[2].

1   At para 10.2.
2   Compare CP 76 MAR 1.8A1.

The territorial scope of the Act

6.33   Behaviour is to be 'disregarded' for the purposes of the FSMA 2000 unless it occurs (a) in the United Kingdom or (b) in relation to qualifying investments traded on a market to which the FSMA 2000, s 118 applies which is situated in the United Kingdom or which is accessible electronically in the United Kingdom[1]. The subsection may only be read sensibly if one accepts that markets that are not situated in the United Kingdom, but which may be 'accessible electronically in the United Kingdom', may eventually become 'prescribed markets'. Effective global co-operation has been identified as a key factor in combating market abuse, particularly where the Internet is involved. The draft European directive on market abuse that seeks to harmonise the European financial markets should be noted in this context.

1   FSMA 2000, s 118(5).

Misuse of information

6.34   Market abuse of this type comprises behaviour based on information (see para **[6.35]**) which is not generally available to those using the market (see paras **[6.36]–[6.44]**), but which, if available to a regular user of the market, would or would be likely to be regarded by him as relevant (see paras **[6.45]–[6.57]**) when deciding the terms on which transactions in investments of the kind in question should be effected[1]. This section is further qualified by MAR 1.4.4(4) that in itself elaborates upon these conditions and adds a further important condition that must be satisfied before conduct 'will amount to market abuse'. The information must also relate to matters which a 'regular user' would reasonably expect to be disclosed to users of the particular prescribed market. This includes both matters which give rise to such an expectation of disclosure or are likely to do so either at the time in question or in the future[2]. This is a key factor indicating the type of information that will be regarded as illegitimate for the purposes of the market abuse regime.

1   FSMA 2000, s 118(2).
2   See MAR 1.4.4(4).

Behaviour based on information

6.35 'Behaviour based on information' in the FSMA 2000, s 118(2)(a) is narrowed to 'dealing or arranging deals in any qualifying investment or relevant product' by MAR 1.4.4. This provision further states: (a) the person must be in possession of information, (b) the information must have a material influence on the decision to engage in the dealing or arranging and (c) the information must be one of the reasons for the dealing or arranging, but need not be the only one. It is submitted that the arguments on this condition are likely to concentrate upon the extent to which a person would have acted as he did in any event and thus resemble the defence conferred upon alleged insider dealers by the Criminal Justice Act 1993, s 53(1)(c) and (2)(c). Circumstantial evidence is likely to be crucial in this respect, given that the evidence of the alleged offender will be self-serving. Some guidance may be derived from the case law relating to misrepresentation in considering the requirements of this condition[1].

1 See, eg, *Chitty on Contracts* (28th edn) at paras 6–034 and 6–039.

Information which is not generally available to those using the market

6.36 The market abuse regime does not seek to achieve complete equality of information between market participants. Indeed, such a notion would probably bring the markets to a standstill. Instead, the market abuse regime acknowledges that there will always be those who are 'one step ahead' by reason of research, resources or other legitimate means.

Research

6.37 The FSMA 2000, s 118(7) qualifies sub-s (1). It provides that information will be regarded as being generally available to the users of the market if it can be 'obtained by research or analysis conducted' by or on their behalf. MAR 1.4.6 adds that limitations of resources, expertise or competence of other market users are irrelevant to the research defence. The FSA has clarified that this defence will protect a firm which trades ahead of the publication of its own research report[1]. However, such firm would still be subject to complying with disclosure to its clients pursuant to the conduct of business requirements[2].

1 CP 59, para 6.38.
2 Conduct of Business Sourcebook, rule 7.3.

The factors

6.38 The Code of Market Conduct provides that information is to be regarded as generally available where one or more of the following is satisfied:

- the information has been disclosed to a prescribed market through an accepted channel for dissemination of information or otherwise under the rules of that market; or
- the information is contained in records which are open to inspection by the public; or
- the information has otherwise been made public, including through the Internet, or some other publication or is derived from information which has been made public; or
- the information can be obtained by observation[1].

The Code emphasises that, in relation to all these factors, the fact that users of the market cannot obtain the information because of limitations in their resources, expertise or competence does not mean that the information cannot legitimately be obtained[2].

1   MAR 1.4.5.
2   MAR 1.4.6.

6.39   It will be noted that the Code of Market Conduct has employed many of the guidelines set out in the Criminal Justice Act 1993, s 58 as to when information has been 'made public' for the purposes of the Criminal Justice Act 1993, s 56(1)(c) and employs the same flexibility as such section. However, the use of the term 'generally available' as distinct from 'made public' emphasises that the concern is more upon the availability to market users rather than the public at large.

Accepted channel for dissemination of information

6.40   The somewhat Orwellian term 'accepted channel for dissemination of information' is further defined as the formal dissemination of information to other market users through an approved channel of communication on 'a structured and equitable basis'[1]. This would presumably include disclosure through the Regulatory News Service or in documents released or made available through the UKLA.

1   See the definitions section of the Code of Market Conduct at Annex C of the Policy Statement.

Information in records open to inspection by the public

6.41   Information in registers set up under statute such as companies', patent and land registers are legitimate sources of information. The definition finally employed in the Code has moved further from that used in the CJA 1993 by dropping the requirement that records are available to the public by virtue of any enactment[1], notwithstanding that it appeared in earlier drafts. It is unclear why this step has been taken and which further records are contemplated.

1   Compare the CJA 1993, s 58(2).

Information that has otherwise been made public or is derived from information which has been made public

6.42   Information that is in the public domain or deductions from information in the public domain are also included. Examples are likely to include planning decisions, court proceedings (including patent decisions) and proceedings in the House of Commons and the House of Lords. This is particularly relevant given the very limited circumstances in which proceedings may now be heard in private[1]. The final text of the Code now includes information which has been made public through the Internet 'or some other publication', text that did not appear in the previous drafts. 'Publications' are not limited to those that have been published in, or otherwise made available to the public in, the United Kingdom, in keeping with the FSA's view that limitation of resources does not make information illegitimate[2].

1   CPR, r 39.2.
2   MAR 1.4.6.

Observation

6.43   This is potentially one of the most difficult questions of degree in determining when information is legitimate. The clarification given in the final text of the Code goes beyond the previous drafts. In particular, the Code specifically addresses borderline situations of observation – overhearing information discussed in public or observing such information in public is legitimate provided rights of privacy, property and confidentiality are observed[1]. The example of observation employed by previous drafts is retained, namely the person who sells shares in the holding company of a burning factory which he observes from a train[2]. This example may already be archaic given the speed with which information now travels over the Internet. In theory, another passenger on the train could have posted the information on the web from his laptop even before the other passenger has sold his shares!

1   MAR 1.4.6.
2   MAR 1.4.8.

Examples

6.44   It should be noted that the further definitions of information which is 'generally available' based on those in the CJA 1993, s 58[1] have been relegated to examples in the final text of the Code and indeed one (communication to a section of the public) has been deleted altogether.

1   Namely, information which is only available overseas and has not been published or otherwise been made available to the public in the United Kingdom and information which is only available on payment of a fee.

Relevant information

6.45 The Code of Market Conduct develops the concept of 'relevant information' at MAR 1.4.9–1.4.11, while emphasising that whether information is 'relevant information' depends upon the circumstances of the case. Accordingly, the Code gives a provisional framework in which to consider information. The factors that the 'regular user' is likely to consider are the extent to which:

- the information is specific and precise;
- the information is material;
- the information is current;
- the information is reliable, including how near the person providing the information is, or appears to be, to the original source of that information and the reliability of that source;
- there is other material information which is already generally available to inform users of the market; and
- the extent to which information differs from information which is generally available and can therefore be said to be new or fresh information[1].

1   MAR 1.4.9.

6.46 In the case of information relating to possible future developments which do not currently give rise to an expectation of disclosure, the Code of Market Conduct states that the following factors are to be taken into account when determining the relevance of the information:

- whether the information provides, with reasonable certainty, grounds to conclude that the possible future developments will, in fact, occur; and
- the significance those developments would assume for market users given their occurrence[1].

1   MAR 1.4.10.

6.47 It should be noted that the Code of Market Conduct does not specifically require information to have a 'significant effect on the price of any securities' by contrast with the CJA 1993[1]. However, in practice, many of the features of 'relevant information' acknowledge the value of certain information. Further, the nexus of information to an inside source is not required for information to be caught by the market abuse regime, as it would under the insider dealing legislation.

1   See the CJA 1993, s 56(1)(d).

Specific and precise information

6.48 The concept of 'precision' of information was first introduced into the law relating to insider dealing in this jurisdiction by the CJA 1993. Under the earlier legislation, information was only required to be specific, but the European directive co-ordinating regulations on insider dealing defined inside information as including 'information of a precise nature'. In fact, the concept of 'precision' of information is retained in the draft European directive on market abuse.

6.49 'Specific' information retains a certain general quality. For instance, in *Public Prosecutor v Choudhury*[1] information that a company was having a financial crisis was held to be specific. Further, in *Green v Charterhouse Group of Canada*[2] information that a company was subject to a takeover was held to be specific. However, 'precise' information is information that is strictly correct. Thus, it would be necessary to know why the company was having a financial crisis in order for information to be precise.

1   [1980] 1 MLJ 76 at 78.
2   (1976) 12 OR (2d) 280.

6.50 It is arguable that the definition employed in the CJA 1993 has been narrowed under the market abuse regime by the argument that information must be both 'precise' and 'specific'. A very tight definition results. For instance, when dealing on the basis of advance information concerning an adverse announcement of annual profits by a company, the insider would have to know both that profits would be lower than expected and by how much. However, given that the test is qualified by reference to 'the circumstances of the case', it is submitted that it is unlikely that this argument would succeed. In any event, the FSA has stated that there may be information which is not 'wholly specific or precise', but is nevertheless 'relevant'[1].

1   CP 59, para 6.22.

Material information

6.51 To some extent, there is an overlap between this requirement and 'behaviour based on information' (see para **[6.35]**). The requirement that information be 'material' reflects the view in *Chitty on Contracts* (28th edn) at para 6–040, n 86 that materiality is a necessary part of a rule requiring disclosure, but is not a necessary part of a rule affording relief for active misrepresentation.

Current information

6.52 Clearly, the more current information is, the more value it will have 'when deciding the terms on which transactions in investments of the kind in question should be effected'.

Reliable information

6.53   The reliability of information in practice raises the issue of the risk taken by the investor. Any investor would analyse how reliable the information that he receives is in determining whether to deal. The closer the source to the heart of the company affected by such information, logically the more reliable the information. To this end, the final version of the Code also expressly includes the 'reliability of the source', a factor that did not appear in previous drafts.

Other available material information

6.54   It is necessary to consider whether there is other material information which is already generally available to inform other users of the market.

Fresh or new information

6.55   Similarly, this suggests that one must first consider the extent to which the information in question is already 'generally available'.

Possible future developments

6.56   The significance of this paragraph relates to the category of information that includes discussions as to mergers or takeovers or similar business ventures affecting the price of 'qualifying investments'. Once again, this factor may be considered by examining the extent of risk to the alleged insider. The investor who invests on the basis of information that company A has entered into discussions with company B and deals on the basis of such information takes a risk that these discussions may never in fact lead to a finalised agreement. However, obviously as time passes, more senior personnel and professional advisors become involved, the likelihood of an eventual deal becomes ever more certain and the risk to the investor ever more reduced.

Examples of relevant information

6.57   The examples of relevant information given by the Code of Market Conduct are:

- information concerning the business affairs or prospects of a company or a related company where the qualifying investment in question is issued by a company or is a derivative relating to a qualifying investment issued by a company;
- information relating to the deliverable supply of a commodity, such as the business operations of major suppliers in relation to a derivative instrument relating to a commodity that is a qualifying investment; and

- information as to official statistics and fiscal and monetary policy announcements before they are announced[1].

Those who have followed the insider dealing legislation will recognise these examples and their significance. The first example is in almost identical terms to the CJA 1993, s 60(4) that clarifies the CJA 1993, s 55(1)(a). At the time of passage of such legislation, the government clarified that such subsection was included to ensure that events affecting a company indirectly were included as well as those that affected it directly[2]. The example of suppliers was in fact given by the minister when illustrating the CJA 1993, s 60(4). The final version of the Code has clarified that information as to official statistics and monetary policy announcements are only relevant before they are announced. Clearly, after announcement, such information would be legitimate information.

1　MAR 1.4.11.
2　Parliamentary Debates, House of Lords, 3 December 1992, column 1495.

Disclosure of information to other users of the market

6.58　A further circumstance which must be present in order to amount to market abuse is that: 'the information must relate to matters which the regular user would reasonably expect to be disclosed to users of the particular prescribed market in question'[1]. This includes both matters which give rise to such an expectation of disclosure or are likely to do so either at the time in question or in the future. This is an extremely important provision for understanding the parameters of the new regime, relating as it does to established standards. This emphasis upon disclosure is in keeping with the approach of the SEC, which adopted Regulation FD in 2000 and the draft European directive on market abuse, which imposes similar disclosure obligations to Regulation FD. Disclosure obligations are discussed in Chapter 2. It should also be noted that the FSA has removed the previous reference to disclosure of information 'on an equal basis' in response to concerns voiced in consultation that such definition was at odds with information described as 'generally available'[2].

1　MAR 1.4.4(4).
2　Policy Statement, para 6.2.

6.59　The FSA has introduced this requirement in order to reflect 'the view that there will always be times when certain market users have access to information that is not generally available to others'[1]. In doing so, the FSA has acknowledged that the regular user does not take issue with the reality that there will always be those who possess information in advance of others.

1　CP 59, para 6.24.

6.60　The Code identifies two categories of information that will fall within the market abuse regime: 'disclosable information' and 'announceable information'[1]. Broadly, 'disclosable information' is information which has to be disclosed to the market in accordance with any legal or regulatory requirement[2]. 'Announceable information' is information which is usually the subject of a public announcement, although not subject to any formal disclosure requirement[3]. The FSA has emphasised that this section should not be read as imposing any *greater* requirements of disclosure or announcement than presently exist[4].

1   MAR 1.4.12.
2   MAR 1.4.12(1).
3   MAR 1.4.12(2).
4   CP 59, para 6.27.

Disclosable information

6.61   The examples of disclosable information given in the Code of Market Conduct include:

- information which is required to be disseminated under the Takeover Code or SARs on, or in relation to, qualifying investments traded on a prescribed market;
- information relating to officially listed securities which is required to be disclosed under the Listing Rules; and
- information required to be disclosed to a prescribed market by the rules of an RIE[1].

Legal and regulatory disclosure requirements are considered in greater detail in Chapter 2.

1   MAR 1.4.14.

Announceable information

6.62   The particular examples of 'announceable information' which may also be 'relevant information' according to the Code of Market Conduct are:

- information which is to be the subject of official announcement by governments, central monetary or fiscal authorities or regulatory authorities;
- changes to published credit ratings of companies whose securities are 'qualifying investments' or 'relevant products'; and
- changes to the constituents of a securities index where the securities are 'qualifying investments' or 'relevant products'[1].

1   MAR 1.4.15.

Possible future developments

6.63   The Code provides that an additional factor to be taken into account in determining whether information as to possible future developments is to be treated as 'disclosable' or 'announceable' information is whether the information provides with reasonable certainty grounds to conclude that the possible future developments will in fact occur and that, accordingly, a disclosure or announcement will in fact be made[1].

1   MAR 1.4.13.

Commodity derivative markets

6.64   One of the areas of continuing concern to market users has been the inter-relation between the disclosure obligations of commodity derivative markets and other markets. These have been evident throughout consultation[1] and continue[2]. The FSA has sought to address this issue by including an example on the point at MAR 1.4.17, whilst continuing to discuss this aspect of market behaviour[3].

1   CP 59, para 6.28.
2   Policy Statement, paras 6.8–6.13.
3   Policy Statement, para 6.13.

CHAPTER 7

Market manipulation

Introduction

7.1 The Financial Services and Markets Act 2000 ('FSMA 2000') introduces two new civil offences of market manipulation: false or misleading impressions and distortion of the market. These broadly reflect the two types of market manipulation identified at art 1 of the draft European directive on market abuse. The general provisions for market abuse have been considered in Chapter 6. The FSMA 2000, s 118(2)(b)(c) provides the particular conditions that must be satisfied in respect of market manipulation. These are that the 'behaviour' in question 'is likely to give a regular user of the market a false or misleading impression as to the supply of, or demand for, or as to the price or value of, investments of the kind in question' and/or 'a regular user of the market would, or would be likely to, regard the behaviour as behaviour which would, or would be likely to, distort the market in investments of the kind in question'. The Code of Market Conduct notes at MAR 1.5.6 and 1.6.7 that behaviour may satisfy both these conditions.

7.2 The civil offences will run in parallel to the statutory criminal offences of misleading statements and practices and the common law criminal offence of conspiracy to defraud[1]. The statutory offences were previously contained in the Financial Services Act 1986, s 47, but have been re-enacted in the FSMA 2000, s 397.

1   *R v De Berenger* (1814) 105 ER 536 and *Scott v Brown* [1892] 2 QB 724.

7.3 The Code of Market Conduct explains that these prohibitions seek to ensure that genuine forces of supply and demand drive the markets so that the confidence of market users is maintained[1]. The Code gives particular examples of common types of manipulative behaviour (including disseminating information, artificial transactions, abusive squeezes and price positioning, each of which are considered in greater detail below), rather than seeking to define market manipulation. This approach is similar to that of securities law in the USA where the Securities Exchange Act 1934 does not define manipulation or manipulative behaviour. Instead, the various rules made by the Securities Exchange Commission relate to specific acts or activities that are proscribed as manipulative behaviour[2].

1   MAR 1.5.3 and MAR 1.6.3.
2   See 'Manipulation', a paper presented by Marvin G Pickholz at the 18th Cambridge International Symposium on Economic Crime.

7.4   A particular tool for market manipulation in recent years is the Internet[1]. There are a number of ways in which the Internet is being used in market manipulation, including through bulletin boards, chat rooms and e-mail. These afford a wide range of opportunities to reach a significant number of potential investors at very little cost. Accordingly, the application of the Code of Market Conduct to unauthorised persons is likely to be of particular significance in market manipulation.

1   See, eg, Toross, 'Double-Click on This: Keeping Pace with On-line Market Manipulation' Loyola of Los Angeles Law Review at 1399.

7.5   The Internet also raises peculiar problems of jurisdiction, making international co-operation very important in effective prosecution. To this end, the International Organisation of Securities Commissions recently produced a report on 'Investigating and Prosecuting Market Manipulation'. Similarly, the European Commission has recently produced a draft directive on market manipulation[1]. This directive is introduced as part of the drive towards a single financial market. One of the particular aims of this directive is to introduce common provisions against market manipulation in member states.

1   2001/118 (COD).

7.6   One area of particular concern considered in the course of consultation on the Code of Market Conduct has been the position of journalists who deal ahead of publication of a tip on shares. The FSA has considered journalists engaging in this type of activity under the heading of misuse of information, although the draft European directive on market abuse addresses it in connection with market manipulation[1]. The FSA has concluded in CP 59 that this situation is not best addressed through the market abuse regime[2]; the 'journalist's tip' does not in fact fit easily into any of the types of market abuse set out in the FSMA 2000. Following consultation between the FSA and the Press Complaints Commission and the Editors' Code Practice Committee, changes including enhanced disclosure have recently been made by the publication of the Press Complaints Commission Best Practice Guidelines with a view to addressing this issue. The FSA has indicated in its policy statement at para 6.19 that it believes that the combination of enhanced disclosure obligations and public awareness of consumers dealing on journalists' tips are currently the most appropriate and proportionate response to this issue. In other situations, the FSA considers that journalists are essentially the same as any other market user.

1   See art 6.
2   CP 59, para 6.43.

False or misleading impressions

FSMA 2000

7.7   The FSMA 2000, s 118(2)(b) provides that behaviour is market abuse if it is 'likely to give a regular user of the market a false or misleading impression as to the supply of, or demand for, or as to the price or value of, investments of the kind in question'. Further guidance as to when behaviour fulfils this condition is found not in the FSMA 2000, but rather in the Code of Market Conduct. It should be recalled that the Code of Market Conduct is only of evidential value on this point[1].

1   FSMA 2000, s 122(2).

The Code of Market Conduct

The elements

7.8   The Code of Market Conduct embellishes the FSMA 2000 by seeking to provide further elements of the offence of 'false and misleading impressions'. The challenges that may be made to this approach by reason of the status of the Code are considered in Chapter 9.

7.9   The Code provides that 'in order to fall within the false or misleading impressions test':

- the behaviour must be likely to give a regular user a false or misleading impression;
- the behaviour must be likely to give rise to, or give an impression of, a price or value or volume trading;
- the impression in question must be materially false or misleading;
- in order to be likely, there must be a real and not fanciful likelihood that the behaviour will have such an effect, although the effect need not be more likely than not; and
- the behaviour may, or may be likely to, give rise to more than one effect, including the effect in question[1].

1   MAR 1.5.4.

7.10   It is suggested that the Code in fact clouds the statutory definition and underestimates the significance of the 'regular user'. For instance, it is suggested that it is unlikely that it would be supposed that an impression which was not material would give a regular user a false or misleading impression as to the supply of, or demand for, investments.

The general factors

7.11 The Code sets out general factors that 'the regular user' would be likely to take into account in considering whether a false or misleading impression has been given as to the supply of, or demand for, or as to the price of, or value of, a qualifying investment or relevant product. These factors are consistent with those found elsewhere in the Code in that the regular user will take into account: (a) 'the identity and position of the person responsible for the action which has been observed (if known)', (b) 'the experience and knowledge of the users of the market in question', (c) 'the structure of the market, including its reporting, notification and transparency requirements' and (d) 'the extent and nature of the visibility or disclosure of the person's activity'[1]. Therefore, the standards set by the market abuse regime will not be universal, but will be tailored to particular markets and circumstances. The insertion of the identity and person 'if known' may at first seem otiose. However, it is likely that it has been inserted to cover the situation where a person disguises their identity while engaging in market abuse.

1   MAR 1.5.5.

7.12 The 'regular user' test in the Code of Market Conduct makes clear that it is concerned with determining acceptable standards of behaviour[1]. Accepted behaviour may not always correspond to the acceptable standards of behaviour expected by a regular user. However, 'accepted' behaviour is a matter that is relevant, but not determinative[2]. MAR 1.5.5 adds that 'the regular user' will take into account 'the legal and regulatory requirements of the market concerned and accepted market practices' in the context of false or misleading impressions.

1   MAR 1.2.4.
2   MAR 1.2.4.

Behaviour amounting to market abuse

7.13 The Code identifies four particular types of market abuse that give rise to or are likely to give rise to false or misleading impressions. These are:

- artificial transactions;
- disseminating information;
- dissemination of information through an accepted channel; and
- course of conduct[1].

1   MAR 1.5.8–1.5.22.

Artificial transactions

7.14 The Code provides that behaviour will amount to market abuse where:

- a person enters into a transaction or series of transactions in a 'qualifying investment' or 'relevant product'; and
- such person knows (or could reasonably be expected to know) that the principal effect of the transaction or transactions on the market will be or will be likely to be to inflate, maintain or depress the apparent supply of or the apparent demand for, or the apparent price or value of, a 'qualifying investment' or 'relevant product' such that a false or misleading impression is likely to be given to the regular user;
- *unless* the 'regular user' would regard the principal rationale for the transaction as a legitimate commercial rationale and the way in which the transaction is to be executed as proper[1].

1   MAR 1.5.8.

7.15   The above is particularly interesting in that it introduces a subjective element by having regard to whether a person 'knows' the effect of the transactions. This is particularly striking given that market abuse is a strict liability statutory offence[1]. Under the FSMA 2000, the state of mind of the offender is only relevant to the imposition of a penalty[2]. In fact, the Law Society Committee considering the Financial Services and Markets Bill advocated the introduction of a mental element, but such suggestion was rejected[3]. This part of the Code apparently re-introduces such mental element into liability, while having regard to an objective standard (whether a person 'could reasonably be expected to know').

1   FSMA 2000, s 118.
2   FSMA 2000, s 123.
3   Joint Committee on Financial Services and Markets First Report, para 264.

7.16   The additional requirement that the regular user regards the behaviour as engaged in a 'proper way' addresses concerns that false or misleading impressions risked catching legitimate behaviour. At MAR 1.5.10, the Code clarifies that a transaction will be considered to be exercised in a proper way where it is executed in a manner that takes into account the need for the market as a whole to operate fairly and efficiently. MAR 1.5.10 also makes clear that where trades are carried out in accordance with the rules of prescribed markets, these will mostly be carried out in a proper way, notwithstanding that the way in which they are executed does not disclose the firm's intentions to the market.

'Legitimate commercial rationale'

7.17   Clearly, it is important for any alleged offender to understand the parameters of 'legitimate commercial rationale'. The concept of 'legitimate commercial rationale' is elaborated at some length within the Code.

7.18   The Code makes clear that transactions whose purpose is to 'induce others to trade in a "qualifying investment" or "relevant product" or to position or move the "price" of a "qualifying investment" or "relevant product"' will not normally be considered to have a 'legitimate commercial rationale'[1]. Further, a transaction will not automatically be considered to have a legitimate commercial rationale simply because the intention behind the transaction was to make a profit or avoid a loss (whether directly or indirectly)[2]. However, it will become apparent in Chapter 9 that the safe harbours do contemplate circumstances in which making a profit or avoiding a loss is legitimate.

1 MAR 1.5.9.
2 MAR 1.5.9.

7.19 The Code sets out examples in respect of which the principal rationale 'may not' be a legitimate commercial rationale, including:

- fictitious transactions;
- arrangements for the sale or purchase of a 'qualifying investment' or 'relevant product' (other than on 'repo' or 'stocklending' or borrowing terms) where there is no change in beneficial interests or market risk or the transfer or beneficial interest or market risk is only between persons who are acting in concert or collusion; or
- a transaction or series of transactions that are designed to conceal the true ownership of a 'qualifying investment' or 'relevant product' and which circumvent disclosure requirements[1].

1 MAR 1.5.14.

7.20 In addition, the Code sets out a number of factors at MAR 1.5.11 that will tend to suggest that the behaviour in question is an artificial transaction and amounts to market abuse.

7.21 Further, MAR 1.5.12 specifically provides that the extent to which a transaction generally either opens a new position, thereby creating an exposure to market risk, or closes out a position, thereby removing market risk, is a factor that tends to suggest that the transaction is likely to have a legitimate commercial rationale and is not an artificial transaction.

Disseminating information

7.22 The impact of the Internet as a medium for market manipulation cannot be overstated as experience from the USA illustrates. The posting of false or misleading information about a company on an Internet bulletin board or chat room is specifically contemplated by the Code. MAR 1.5.17 gives posting false or misleading statements regarding the takeover of a company whose shares are qualifying investments on the Internet as an example of disseminating false or misleading information.

7.23 From the point of view of 'protection of the consumer', this is arguably one of the most important areas of market manipulation as it may be the type of information most readily available to a non-professional market user. Consequently, the SEC has made this area of securities fraud a priority[1].

1   See, eg, the brochure released by the SEC: 'Pump&Dump.con: Tips for Avoiding Stock Scams on the Internet' at www.sec.gov/investor/online/pump.htm

7.24   There have been instances in the USA where the SEC alleges that an alias was used to convey information purporting to come from a company insider. This in turn allegedly triggered a press release stating that the company's accounting practices were under investigation and that its Chief Executive Officer had resigned, which was then released on the Internet. The press release was apparently picked up by a news service that published a headline containing the false information. In the case in question, the release was alleged to have had the effect of wiping $2.2 billion in market value from a high-tech company in 16 minutes[1]. This scenario highlights the particular dangers of the Internet – the alleged offender is able to change his identity and convince respected parties of the reliability of false information, who in turn carry such information to a wide audience.

1   SEC Litigation Release No 16671/31 August 2000.

7.25   Disseminating information includes the so-called 'pump and dump' schemes where false or misleading information is disseminated to potential investors with a view to raising the price of shares. Those involved in the scheme later sell when the price of shares has dramatically risen, thus realising their profits. Smaller companies' stocks are often particularly vulnerable to such schemes[1].

1   See generally 'Background Information on Microcap Fraud' at www.sec.gov/divisions/enforce/microcap.htm

The Code of Market Conduct

7.26   MAR 1.5.15 provides that behaviour will constitute market abuse where a person:
- disseminates information which is, or if true would be, 'relevant information';
- the person knows or could reasonably be expected to know that the information disseminated is false or misleading; and
- the person disseminates the information in order to create a false or misleading impression. This need not be the sole purpose for disseminating the information, but must be an actuating purpose, defined in the Code as a purpose which motivates or incites a person to act.

Relevant information

7.27   'Relevant information' for these purposes is 'in relation to an investment, information which would be likely to be regarded by a regular user of the market in question as relevant when deciding the terms on which transactions in the investment should be effected' and in the REC as information which is relevant to determining the current value of that investment[1]. It is clear from CP 59, para 6.64 that 'relevant information' has the same characteristics as for the purposes of misuse of information, which has been considered in detail in Chapter 6.

1 Definitions section of the Code of Market Conduct.

7.28 In consultation, a number of concerns were expressed as to the extent to which market rumours would be included within this definition[1]. The FSA acknowledges that it cannot restrict the flow of market rumours[2]. The FSA believes that the specific and precise nature of information introduced in the Code of Market Conduct meets this concern[3]. However, it is submitted that the more material part of 'relevant information' in excluding market rumours is likely to be the 'reliability' of information, depending as it does upon the closeness of the source of information to such information. After all, a market rumour may be both precise and specific, albeit that it may in itself be distorted in its passage from its source by 'Chinese whispers'.

1 CP 59, para 6.63.
2 CP 59, para 6.63.
3 CP 59, para 6.64.

'Knows or could reasonably be expected to know that the information is false or misleading' and 'disseminates the information in order to create a false or misleading impression'

7.29 The FSA substituted a partly subjective and partly objective test together with a consideration of the purpose of the alleged offender for the original obligation 'to take reasonable care to ensure the accuracy of the relevant information'[1]. The final wording targets the source of a rumour and those who may be expected to know that a rumour is false as distinct from imposing a general obligation upon the market not to gossip, which would probably prove unenforceable!

1 CP 59, para 6.64.

7.30 Despite the emphasis on setting standards and introducing a strict liability offence[1], the Code of Market Conduct introduces questions of subjectivity and purpose, which may be construed as 'intent'. Therefore, it may be argued that the FSA's approach departs from the scheme of the statute. The Code in part seeks to mitigate this point by providing that the 'purpose' will be to create a false or misleading impression in certain circumstances.

1 See, eg, Joint Committee on the Financial Services and Markets First Report, para 264.

7.31 The FSA may have adopted this less severe approach in relation to liability in order to appease market users. For instance, in the context of disseminating information, it may be argued that consideration of the purpose of dissemination excludes wholly innocent and inadvertent dissemination of information. This view is bolstered by MAR 1.2.6 that provides that where the person or firm has taken reasonable care to detect mistakes, it is unlikely that the regular user would consider that a mistake would amount to market abuse.

7.32   The Code as originally drafted required a person to have a material interest in an investment in order to be subject to this part of the Code[1]. This is now only a factor that will 'tend to suggest that the person had disseminated the information in order to create a false or misleading impression'[2]. The need for such amendment was twofold: (a) a person might disseminate false or misleading information in order to depress the price of shares and then buy them at that price and (b) the person who used the Internet in market manipulation, but did not receive any personal gain, would not be caught[3].

1   CP 59, para 6.65.
2   MAR 1.5.16.
3   CP 59, para 6.66.

7.33   The Code itself gives an extremely wide definition of 'an interest in a qualifying investment' or 'relevant product' for these purposes. A person has such an interest where:

● he may directly (including by holding a short position) or indirectly benefit from alterations in its market price; or
● he may be rewarded by, or is otherwise in collusion with or connected with, persons who may benefit from alterations in the market price of the 'qualifying investment'[1].

The first of these is self-explanatory. The second is consistent with the broad reach of the FSMA 2000 and references to collusion may be found elsewhere in the regime. 'Reward' is a sufficiently wide term to include all manner of gifts that a person may receive. The range of 'connected persons' is far reaching and is set out in detail in the definitions in the annex to the Code of Market Conduct.

1   MAR 1.5.13.

Dissemination of information through an accepted channel

7.34   The significance of the 'accepted channels for the dissemination of information' such as the Regulatory News Service has been underlined by the emphasis upon legal and regulatory obligations of disclosure in 'misuse of information'[1]. This aspect of 'false and misleading impressions' underpins the importance of preserving the accuracy and reliability of the formal channels used for disseminating information to market users and encourages the responsible use of these services by company insiders and their advisers[2].

1   See Chapter 6.
2   CP 59, para 6.67 and MAR 1.5.20.

7.35 The standards set for those using the 'accepted channels' is prima facie more rigorous than in 'disseminating information', in keeping with the integral role of such channels in the fair functioning of the markets. The Code adds the following to the statutory requirements of market abuse in this context:

- the information is, or if true would be, 'relevant information'; and
- the person responsible for the submission of the information to the accepted channel for dissemination of information has not taken reasonable care to ensure it is not false or misleading[1].

1   MAR 1.5.18.

7.36 It is clear from the above that while there is some room for error, reasonable care must be exercised when using the 'accepted channels' to distribute information. The requirement for reasonable care is reinforced by the regular user's approach to mistakes[1].

1   MAR 1.2.6.

Course of conduct

7.37 The Code recognises that a false or misleading impression may be conveyed equally by conduct as by statements. In practice, this provision will be of particular relevance to the commodity derivative markets as is demonstrated by the examples given in the Code[1]. The particular examples are moving an empty cargo ship or physical commodity stocks. Such movement might create a false or misleading impression as to the supply of, or demand for, a commodity or the deliverable into a commodity futures contract[2]. Given that these would be public events based on observation for the purposes of the Code, it follows that market users may base their decisions to deal upon such events.

1   CP 59, para 6.68.
2   MAR 1.5.22.

7.38 Behaviour will constitute market abuse according to the Code where a person engages in a course of conduct if:

- the person knows or could reasonably be expected to know that a principal effect of the course of conduct on the market will be, or is likely to be, to give a false or misleading impression to a 'regular user' as to the supply of, or demand for, or as to the price or value of, a 'qualifying investment' or 'relevant product';
- unless the regular user would regard the principal rationale for the conduct in question as a legitimate commercial rationale and the way in which the conduct is engaged in as proper[1].

1   MAR 1.5.21.

7.39 The factors to be taken into account in considering 'legitimate commercial rationale' and a proper way are the same as those for artificial transactions[1].

1 MAR 1.5.21.

Distortion of the market

7.40 The FSMA 2000, s 118(2)(c) provides that behaviour is caught by this category of market abuse if:

'a regular user of the market would, or would be likely to, regard the behaviour as behaviour which would, or would be likely to, distort the market in investments of the kind in question'.

There are two particular types of market distortion identified by the Code as amounting to market abuse: price positioning and abusive squeezes. Although the statutory condition relating to distortion of the market does not specifically refer to supply and demand, MAR 1.6.3 makes clear that these matters apply with equal force to this aspect of market abuse.

7.41 The Code adds to the Act at MAR 1.6.4 by providing that:

- behaviour will amount to market abuse if the behaviour engaged in interferes with the proper operation of market forces with the purpose of positioning prices at a distorted level. This need not be the sole purpose of entering into the transaction or transactions, but must be an actuating purpose; and
- in order to be likely, there must be a real and not fanciful likelihood that the behaviour will have such an effect, although the effect need not be more likely than not. The 'behaviour' may, or may be likely to, give rise to more than one effect, including the effect in question.

7.42 The FSA acknowledges that it is an 'intrinsic characteristic of a market that prices move in response to individual transactions' and that there is a 'spectrum of views as to what distortion means'[1]. The FSA itself believes that a price is likely to be distorted when price movements deviate from the norms expected by a regular user of the market[2]. The policy statement of the FSA notes at para 8.1 that the section on distortion remains the most controversial in the Code. This controversy arises because of the concerns that legitimate behaviour was apparently caught by the Code. The Code has therefore changed significantly from CP 76. First, the Code acknowledges at MAR 1.6.5 that market users will legitimately trade at times and in sizes most beneficial to them in maximising profit. Similarly, MAR 1.6.6 accepts that where prices are trading outside their normal range, this will not necessarily indicate that they are trading at a distorted level. As will be seen, a person's 'purpose' is particularly significant to distortion of the market, given that market transactions inherently affect the price of the market.

1   CP 59, para 6.72.
2   CP 59, para 6.72.

Price positioning

7.43   Behaviour will constitute market abuse according to MAR 1.6.9 where:

- a person enters into a transaction or series of transactions;
- with the purpose of positioning the price of a 'qualifying investment' or 'relevant product' at a distorted level;
- which need not be the sole purpose for entering into the transaction or transactions, but must be an 'actuating purpose', defined as a purpose which motivates or incites a person to act.

7.44   The Code now also relies upon legitimate commercial rationale and executing the transaction in a proper way as part of the consideration of whether market abuse by price positioning has taken place (MAR 1.6.10). Similarly, the factors at MAR 1.6.11 that are taken into account in considering whether price positioning has taken place are much more detailed and provide more certain guidance to market users than previous drafts[1]. Specific examples of price positioning at a distorted level are now also given in the Code at MAR 1.6.12. These also improve upon the rather vague examples given in previous drafts[2].

1   Compare, eg, CP 76 at MAR 1.7.12.
2   Eg CP 76 at MAR 1.7.13.

Abusive squeezes

7.45   An abusive squeeze is behaviour amounting to market abuse[1]. An abusive squeeze is defined by the Code at MAR 1.6.13 as where a person with:
- a significant influence over the supply of or demand for, or delivery mechanisms for, a 'qualifying investment' or 'relevant product'; and
- a position (directly or indirectly) in an investment under which quantities of the 'qualifying investment' or 'relevant product' in question are deliverable

engages in behaviour with the purpose of positioning at a distorted level the price at which others have to deliver, take delivery or defer delivery to satisfy their obligations (the purpose need not be the sole purpose for such conduct, but must be an actuating purpose).

1   MAR 1.6.13.

7.46 The Code emphasises that a significant influence over supply, for instance where there is market tightness, is not in itself abusive[1]. The Code sets out a number of factors at MAR 1.6.16 that will be taken into account when considering whether a person has engaged in an abusive squeeze. The Code has taken those factors that are specific to abusive squeezes from the list of factors that were previously included in the Code as general factors common to market distortion[2]. These include:

- the extent to which a person is willing to relax his control or other influence in order to help maintain an orderly market and the price at which he is willing to do so; and
- the extent to which the person's activity causes or risks causing settlement default by other market users on a multilateral basis and not just a bilateral basis. The more widespread the risk of multilateral settlement default, the more likely that the market has been distorted.

The Code now also gives a specific example of an abusive squeeze at MAR 1.6.18 to assist market users. It seems likely that the FSA will give specific examples of price positioning when giving guidance to market users.

1   MAR 1.6.14.
2   Compare CP 76 at MAR 1.7.5.

7.47 From the above, it will be appreciated that abusive squeezes have much in common with the prohibition under art 86 of the EC Treaty against abuse of a dominant position. It is likely that evidence relating to the 'regular user' will be particularly complex in cases of this type and will probably involve expert economic evidence.

CHAPTER 8

Fraud and sharp practice

Introduction

8.1 While it has long been recognised that one of the most important justifications for regulating conduct in the financial markets and financial services industry is the protection of investors, there has been surprisingly little discussion as to what this really means. For example, should all investors, no matter how professional or sophisticated they are, be given the same level of protection and to what type or quality of risk should this cover? In the context of our present discussion of insider dealing and market abuse, however, it is widely accepted that all investors should be protected from the risk of being defrauded. To the extent that we regard insider dealing and market abuse as a form of 'fraud', we can be reasonably confident that most would agree that it is reasonable for the law to intervene to protect investors. While some legal systems appear to be quite happy to regard those who abuse inside information as 'defrauding' at least the market, if not individual investors, in the United Kingdom, we have tended to adopt a rather different analysis. In English law, before we characterise something as 'fraudulent', we generally require some kind of knowing representation that is materially false with the intention that some identified person will rely upon to their harm. We would normally describe such conduct as 'dishonest'. While, as we have seen, in certain and generally exceptional circumstances, it is possible to regard an omission to disclose information as amounting to a form of representation, in the context of most instances of insider dealing, a failure to disclose the information in question will not be so regarded. When we consider the new offences of market abuse, in some respects we are closer to the normal conception of fraud, but in others even further away. When the market abuse involves the commission of an act intended to create a false or misleading impression or where a statement is actually made with the same intention, we are in the realm of fraud. Where, however, there is merely a taking advantage of privileged information, it is difficult to conceive this as fraud in any sense known under traditional English law.

8.2   It is obviously the case that investors' legitimate interests may be harmed by conduct which is not undertaken with the intention that it should cause harm or in circumstances where the person concerned appreciates that it could, but just does not care whether in fact it does or not. Indeed, it is probable that investors are more likely to be harmed by negligent rather than fraudulent conduct in most developed markets. While there are many laws and procedures designed to address this problem, this chapter focuses on what might be described as 'sharp practice' and not the competence of financial intermediaries. We are concerned here with what the Financial Services and Markets Act 2000 ('FSMA 2000') describes as 'financial crime'. There has been considerable concern, over many years, as to whether the law and the various agencies that are required or rather expected to enforce it, have or for that matter can, adequately police 'sharp practice' in the financial sector. Despite the early development of laws and even the recognition that specialised enforcement machinery might be necessary, the general view is that the traditional criminal justice system has not delivered. The Fraud Trial Committee, sitting under Roskill LJ, observed in 1986:

> 'the public no longer believes that the system ... is capable of bringing the perpetrators of serious fraud expeditiously and effectively to book. The overwhelming weight of evidence laid before us suggests that the public is right'[1].

1   'Report of the Fraud Trial Committee' (1986, HMSO) para 1.

8.3   While a great deal has been done since 1986 to improve the law and its enforcement, one of the driving forces behind the restructuring of the supervision of the financial sector and the FSMA 2000 was the concern to address financial crime and deal with it on a broader basis than the ordinary criminal justice system. Consequently, the FSMA 2000, s 2(2) provides that the reduction of financial crime is one of the four objectives that the Financial Services Authority should pursue to discharge its various statutory and regulatory functions. This objective is 'fleshed out' in the FSMA 2000, s 6, where it is made clear that the FSA is to be concerned with reducing the extent to which financial intermediaries are 'used for a purpose connected with financial crime'[1]. In particular, the FSA must have regard to ensuring that financial intermediaries are aware of the risks of being used in connection with financial crime and the importance of installing and adequately maintaining systems designed to prevent, detect and monitor the incidence of financial crime. The meaning of 'financial crime' is spelt out in s 6(3) as including any offence involving fraud or dishonesty, misconduct in, or misuse of information relating to, a financial market or the handling of the proceeds of crime. This is very broad and would cover most, if not all, of what we have previously labelled 'sharp practice'. It also includes 'handling the proceeds of crime', whatever that crime may be. The notion of handling is wide enough to include laundering the proceeds of crime and the FSA is given specific authority to promulgate rules on this by the FSMA 2000, s 146. It should also be noted that s 6(4) makes clear that an 'offence' includes an act or omission which would be an offence if it had taken place in the United Kingdom, even if it actually occurred overseas. It is, of course, important to appreciate that these provisions do not require the FSA to do anything other than in the exercise and discharge of its powers to pursue the reduction of crime as an objective. They do not mandate the FSA to pursue financial crime outside its limited statutory remit.

1   FSMA 2000, s 6(1).

8.4   On the other hand, it is clear that, in pursuing it objectives, the FSA is not only confined to utilising the weapons of the traditional criminal justice system. In addition to its various and many powers relating to prevention and compliance, it is now armed, as we have seen, with significant investigative and civil enforcement powers. The arming of the FSA with these powers, while long recommended by some, has raised serious issues, not least of human rights.

8.5   This chapter will now address in more detail the more important 'financial crimes' that are relevant in protecting the integrity and stability of the financial markets and the financial services industry.

The creation of false markets

8.6   The early English law recognised that certain forms of conduct could undermine the efficient and fair operation of markets and there were common law offences, such as 'forestalling, regrating and cornering', as early as the eleventh century[1]. These were later superseded by statutory offences and today survive, to some degree, within the offence of conspiracy to defraud. While scandals were certainly not unknown in the financial markets, it was not until the early part of the last century that legislation was introduced specifically to outlaw certain frauds in the context of investments. The Prevention of Fraud (Investments) Act 1939, which was replaced and slightly amended by the Prevention of Fraud (Investments) Act 1958, made it a serious offence to induce an investment transaction by making a false statement, either dishonestly or recklessly, or by dishonestly concealing a material fact. This provision was more or less re-enacted in the Financial Services Act 1986, s 47(1) and with some useful redrafting as the FSMA 2000, s 397. While few prosecutions were successfully brought under these provisions, until the Financial Services Act 1986, there was no attempt to address, through legislation, attempts to manipulate the market, other than through making false statements. Before the Financial Services Act 1986, s 47(2), creating a false market by conduct was left to the general criminal law and various self-regulatory provisions. Consequently, the statutory control of manipulative practices, as opposed to the inducement of transactions by fraudulent misrepresentation, is relatively new in the United Kingdom. It follows that English law does not have the wealth of experience in addressing the many problems that arise from attempting to curb and control the creation of false markets that, for example, US law has.

1   See W S Holdsworth, *A History of English Law* (1922–1938, Little Brown) IV, p 375.

The common law

8.7   The most significant area of law in England with regard to manipulation was, prior to the enactment of the Financial Services Act 1986, s 47(2), the common law. The judiciary have rarely shown much sympathy for those involved in manipulating public markets. For example, in *Rubery v Grant*[1], Sir Robert Malins VC considered that to allege that a person was a member of a share rigging syndicate amounted to an allegation that they were dishonest. He added:

> 'going into the market pretending to buy shares by a person whom you put forward to buy them, who is not really buying them, but only pretending to buy them, in order that they may be quoted in the public papers as bearing a premium, which premium is never paid, is one of the most dishonest practices to which men can possibly resort'.

The learned judge went on:

> 'there is a class of people who think it is a legitimate mode of making money, but if they would only examine it for a moment they would see that a more abominable fraud, and one more difficult of detection, cannot be found'.

1   (1872) 13 LR 443.

8.8   Perhaps the first English case to be decided by the English courts, or at least reported, is that of *R v De Berenger*[1]. This case involved one of the most audacious frauds ever perpetrated on a stock market. The United Kingdom had been at war with France for over two years and the price of British government stock was naturally depressed. The conspirators sought to raise the price of stock on the London Stock Exchange, enabling them to dump securities that they had already acquired, by spreading rumours that Napoleon had been killed and that peace was certain. The London Stock Exchange appointed a committee of inquiry which discovered the relevant facts. De Berenger and seven others were indicted of:

> 'unlawfully contriving by false reports, rumours, acts and contrivances, to induce the subjects of the King to believe that a peace would soon be made ... thereby to occasion without any just or true cause a great increase and rise of the public government funds and the government securities of the Kingdom ... with a wicked intention thereby to injure and aggrieve all the subjects of the King who should, on 21 February, purchase or buy any part or parts, share or shares of and in said public government funds and other government securities'[2].

The defendants contended that seeking to raise the price of securities in the market was not of itself a crime and that there was no criminal conspiracy without some allegation that they had intended to cheat certain investors or cause harm to the government. Indeed, it was argued that it was in the government's interest that the price of its securities should be kept high.

1   (1814) 105 ER 536.
2   (1814) 105 ER 536.

8.9   The court, however, had little sympathy for such arguments and held that it was not necessary for the Crown to allege, let alone prove, that anyone had in fact been misled and injured. Both the means used, along with the object of the enterprise, were unlawful. The public had the right to expect that the market had not been interfered with by wrongful means. Lord Ellenborough stated:

> 'A public mischief is stated as the object of this conspiracy; the conspiracy is by false rumours to raise the price of the public funds and securities and the crime lies in the act of conspiracy and combination to effect that purpose and would have been complete although it had not been pursued to its consequences, or the parties had not been able to carry it into effect. The purpose itself is mischievous, it strikes at the price of a vendible commodity in the market and if it gives a fictitious price, by means of false rumours, it is a fraud levelled against all the public, for it is against all such as may possibly have anything to do with the funds on that particular day. The excuse is that it was impossible that they should have known, and if it were possible, the multitude would be an excuse in point of law. But the statement is wholly unnecessary, the conspiracy being complete independently of any persons being purchasers. I have no doubt it must be so considered in law according to the cases'.

The decision in *De Berenger* does not address directly, however, the issue as to whether it is an indictable conspiracy to interfere with the proper operation of the markets, not through the circulation of false rumours and information, but by a course of dealing. Under the ordinary law, it is possible to make a statement by word or by conduct, so as a matter of principle manipulative conduct could be regarded as constituting a false and misleading representation. Nonetheless, in *De Berenger*, one of the learned judges said:

> ' ... the raising or lowering the price of the public funds is not per se a crime. A man may have occasion to sell out a large sum, which may have the effect of depressing the price of stocks, or may buy in a large sum, and thereby raise the price on a particular day, and yet he will be guilty of no offence. But if a number of persons conspire by false rumours to raise the funds on a particular day, that is an offence and the offence is, not in raising the funds simply, but in conspiring by false rumours to raise them on that particular day'.

8.10 In a subsequent civil case involving an action for rescission against a stockbroker who had agreed to purchase shares on the Stock Exchange on behalf of the plaintiff for the sole purpose of creating trading on the market at a premium in order to create the impression that there was a thriving market and thereby induce other investors to purchase, in denying rescission, the court expressed the view that the relevant agreement amounted to a criminal conspiracy to defraud the public[1]. The view was expressed by Lopes LJ that there is 'no substantial distinction between false rumours and false and fictitious acts'.

1 *Scott v Brown, Doering, McNab & Co* [1892] 2 QB 724.

The fair price

8.11 On the other hand, it is also clear that not every concerted intervention into the market to hold a price will be considered manipulative. In *Sanderson and Levi v British Westralian Mine and Share Corpn*[1], a contract was enforced pursuant to which a jobber on the Stock Exchange had made a market at a fair price, while the defendant distributed a substantial block of shares. In the rather less authoritative decision in *Landon v Beiorly*[2], where a new trial was ordered[3], the court also denied rescission of an allotment on the basis that the pegging of share prices during the launch of the company was to prevent 'undue depreciation below their actual worth'.

1 (1898) 43 Sol Jo 45.
2 (1849) 10 LTOS 505.
3 (1849) 13 LTOS 122.

8.12 Thus, it is clear on the English authorities that there is a distinction between manipulation and what we describe today as stabilisation. It is not without interest, however, that the courts of other jurisdictions have not always been prepared to accept such a distinction. For example, in *Harper v Crenshaw*[1], the US Court of Appeals for the District of Columbia went further than the English Court of Appeal in *Scott v Brown*[2] and held that an agreement to stabilise the price of shares, while a large block of shares was brought onto the market, was illegal and unenforceable. There was no evidence that the agreement sought to create a fictitious price for the securities in question or to raise the price higher than the real value of the relevant securities. In *Bigelow v Oglesby*[3], an Illinois appellate court declined to enforce a syndicate agreement among underwriters because it contained what was then a standard clause for stabilisation. The court distinguished the English case of *Sanderson & Levi* on the basis that in the present case the agreement was to stabilise the price of the relevant shares at a level which had not already been determined by the market itself.

1 82 F 2d 845 (DC Cir, 1936).
2 [1892] QB 724.
3 303 Ill App 27, 36, 23 NE 2d 382 (1939).

Conspiracy

8.13   It is important to remember when considering these authorities that the law might not necessarily be the same in the case of a criminal and a civil conspiracy and different considerations apply as to whether the persons concerned are being prosecuted for a criminal offence, are seeking to enforce an agreement inter-party or are being sued before the civil courts by an innocent third party. Unfortunately, the judges, in categorising certain conduct as illegal, do not always observe these distinctions. It would seem that a conspiracy to influence the price of shares or other securities on a market by making false statements or by engaging in purposeful conduct, such as a series of transactions with the intention of misleading the market, will be a conspiracy at criminal law. Conspiracy to create a public mischief no longer exists, but the facts in the relevant cases would fall within the scope of conspiracy to defraud today. Generally speaking, however, it would be appropriate for the prosecution to allege a statutory conspiracy to breach the FSMA 2000, s 397(1)(a), (b) or (c)[1].

1   See *R v Cooke* [1986] AC 909 modifying the strict rule in *R v Ayres* [1984] AC 447 to the effect that a conspiracy to defraud could not be charged where a substantive offence could be made out.

8.14   Considerable discussion has taken place over the years as to the proper scope of conspiracy in the criminal law. The Law Commission's working party published a consultation document in 1973[1] in which it concluded that the crime of conspiracy should be confined to an agreement to commit a specific offence. In other words, the mere agreement to engage in a course of conduct, no matter how malicious, should not of itself constitute a crime, unless the conduct in question was itself a specific offence. The Law Commission took the view, however, that there were situations covered by the crime of conspiracy to defraud which might not be susceptible to this approach[2].

1   Working Paper 50, 'Inchoate Offences'.
2   Working Paper 56, 'Conspiracy to Defraud'.

8.15   The Criminal Law Act 1977, s 1 enacted a statutory offence of conspiracy to replace the common law offence of conspiracy. This reflected the Law Commission's view that the crime of conspiracy should be limited to circumstances where the object of the agreement is to commit an act which would itself be a substantive offence already known to the criminal law. However, the Criminal Law Act 1977, s 5(2) excepted the common law offence of conspiracy to defraud which remains outside s 1. Discussion has taken place as to whether conspiracy to defraud should remain an exception to the general rule. The Law Commission report 'Criminal Law: Conspiracy to Defraud'[1] takes the view that it still has a role to play. This is illustrated in *Adams v R*[2]. The Privy Council was of the opinion that an agreement to conceal transactions with regard to which there was a fiduciary duty of disclosure, so that those responsible might avoid being called to account for their unauthorised profits, amounted to an indictable conspiracy to defraud.

1   1994, HMSO.
2   [1995] 1 WLR 52.

Enforcing the bargain

8.16   The agreement between the parties to the conspiracy would generally be unenforceable before the civil courts as being contrary to public policy. Indeed, Sir Frederick Pollack[1] referred to *Scott v Brown*[2] in which an attempt was made to enforce such an agreement, describing it as reminiscent of the 'well-known legal legend ... of a highwayman coming into equity for an account against his partner'. Indeed, some US courts have taken this approach quite far and refused to enforce agreements involving the touting of shares, such as *Ridgely v Keene*[3]. In England, the courts have certainly declined to allow a wrongdoer to enforce such a transaction against the other party when that party is innocent and where both parties are involved in the wrongdoing. The general rule is that the courts should remain aloof. Losses and profits remain where they fall.

1   In an article published in the Law Quarterly Review in 1893 (9 LQR 105).
2   [1892] 2 QB 724.
3   134 AD 647, 119 NYS 451 (2nd dept, 1875).

8.17   In a case involving insider dealing, Knox J, despite a statutory provision to the effect that breach of the then insider dealing law did not make the relevant contract void or voidable, declined to lend the court's support to the enforcement of a partially completed transaction[1]. It has long been the English law that an innocent party can seek rescission or cancellation of a fraudulent transaction and the courts will not be keen to allow formalities or technical arguments to stand in the victim's path[2]. It is rather less likely that the courts would be prepared to see such an agreement enforced rather than rescinded by an innocent party. This is particularly so when the purpose of the agreement is to achieve something which is contrary to the public interest. In such circumstances, an innocent party would generally have other remedies than those based on the relevant agreement.

1   *Chase Manhattan Equities Ltd v Goodman* [1991] BCLC 897.
2   See *Gillett v Peppercorne* (1840) 3 Beav 78.

8.18   It is unclear to what extent a 'third party' such as an investor in the market, who claims to have been harmed by the manipulation, can pursue those responsible in the civil courts for deceit. In *Bedford v Bagshaw*, Pollock CB, stated:

'all persons buying shares upon the Stock Exchange must be considered as persons to whom it was contemplated the representations would be made ... I am not prepared to lay down a general rule, that if a person makes a false representation, everyone to whom it is repeated and who acts upon it may sue him. But it is a different thing where a director of a company procures an artificial and false value to be given to shares which he professes to offer to the public'[1].

1   (1859) 4 H & N 538.

8.19   The Chief Baron thought that where the person responsible contemplated that the plaintiff was 'one of the persons' to whom the representation could be made or 'ought to have been aware he was injuring or might injure', a cause of action might be found. Of course, in this case, the defendant had effectively procured a false value for stock by fraudulently securing a quotation and settling date. The plaintiff reasonably assumed that the sufficient shares had been taken up to justify the quotation. In *Barry v Croskey*[1], while agreeing with Pollock CB's comments, Page Wood VC, referring to the contention that 'every person, who in consequence of (the defendant's) frauds on the Stock Exchange, was induced to purchase stock at an advanced price in reliance on the false rumour he had circulated, was entitled to maintain an action against (the defendant)' questioned whether 'such consequences' would not be too remote to form ground for action. In *Peek v Gurney*[2], Lord Chelmsford also thought it highly dubious that those who had made an assumption on the basis that, according to the rules and practices of the market, certain underlying facts must exist or have been represented to exist had a viable complaint. In *Salaman v Warner*[3], a remedy was denied to a jobber who had acted on his 'own judgment' as to a presumed state of affairs, rather than on a direct representation to himself. Of course, these cases are primarily concerned with false representations made to the market authorities, which result in securities being traded at an inflated price. Where there is a direct representation, such as the issue of a false statement directly to the market, then it is not unlikely, at least in the case of fraud, that all those who can establish direct loss will be able to sue for the full extent of that loss.

1   (1861) 2 John & H 1.
2   (1871) LR 13 Eq 79.
3   (1891) 7 TLR 484, CA.

8.20   The real problem in cases of manipulation by conduct in particular, is whether it is possible to contend that the market price is itself a representation of, for example, compliance with all the rules and procedures which contribute to the availability of the market and, thus, price. Where a market has been manipulated and a 'false price' achieved, all those who come to the market or rely upon the market, at the relevant time, are harmed. In the leading US case of *US v Brown*[1], Woolsey J, at first instance, referring to some of the English decisions, observed:

'when an outsider, a member of the public, reads the price quotations of a stock listed on an exchange, he is justified in supposing that the quoted price is an appraisal of the value of the stock due to a series of actual sales between various persons dealing at arm's length in a free and open market on the exchange'.

In other words, the investor is entitled to assume that the price is a true reflection of the proper interaction of supply and demand. While similar sentiments can be found in cases such as *Scott v Brown*[2], it is questionable whether an English court would, on the basis of the common law, find liability to market participants for their loss. The twin hurdles of reliance and causation are likely to prove insurmountable.

1   5 F Supp 81 (SDNY, 1933).
2   [1892] 2 QB 724.

8.21   To what extent it may be possible to base an action for manipulation on some other cause of action than fraud is debatable. The courts have not been particularly sympathetic to arguments that seek to invoke allegations of conspiracy. At the end of the day, for a civil claim based on this particular tort, it is necessary to show that the plaintiff's legitimate interest has been harmed. In the context of our present discussion, this would be problematic to say the least. While it may well be appropriate to frame an action in the tort of negligence, the courts are notoriously reluctant to contemplate open-ended liability and in most cases that can reasonably be conceived of as manipulation, it is most unlikely the courts would find sufficient proximity between the wrongdoer and a person who simply comes into the market. The most likely civil claim for manipulative conduct that violates the FSA's rules and, in particular, the market abuse provisions is under the FSMA 2000, s 150. This creates a right of action for 'private persons' who suffer loss as a result of such a contravention by an authorised person. A plaintiff may recover simply by showing a breach of the rules which has resulted in him suffering loss. Of course, as with the Financial Services Act 1986, ss 62 and 62A, it has to be shown that the loss in question occurred as a result of the violation. This was and remains a major stumbling block. It is, however, important to remember that the cause of action under s 150 is in addition to any rights that may exist at common law.

Misleading regulators

8.22   From our discussion above, it is clear that a number of abuses have occurred as a result of the 'crooks' misleading the market authorities and other regulators into permitting a state of affairs to come about or continue, which of itself creates an impression that certain underlying and justifying events have satisfactorily taken place. In *R v Aspinall*[1], it was held that it is an indictable conspiracy at common law to obtain a listing of securities on the Stock Exchange by falsely representing that the required number of shares have been allotted and paid for. In this case, it was emphasised that it was enough for the prosecution to show that the defendants' purpose was to mislead the Stock Exchange's officials; it was not necessary to prove that the defendants intended to injure investors by securing a higher price for the shares they were floating than would otherwise have been obtainable. It might also amount to the crime of conspiracy to defraud, to agree with others to induce, by false statements, made by word or conduct, a public official to do, or not to do, an act in the course of his official duties. For example, it has been argued that furnishing the executive of the City Panel on Takeovers and Mergers with false information designed to mislead it in exercising its responsibilities under the Code might well fall within the scope of this offence. The FSMA 2000, s 398 makes it a criminal offence for a person knowingly or recklessly to give 'in purported compliance with any requirement imposed by or under this Act' false or misleading information to the Authority or, under the FSMA 2000, s 399, to the Director-General of Fair Trading. This provision is somewhat narrower than the offence which was created under the Financial Services Act 1986, s 200 and which was not confined to misleading officials of the Securities and Investments Board.

1   (1876) 1 QBD 730; affd (1876) 2 QBD 48, CA.

Concert parties and nominees

8.23   Transparency in the sense of requiring disclosure of transactions and dealings which lend themselves to possible abuse has long been a characteristic of commercial and corporate legislation in the United Kingdom. Thus, there are statutory provisions in the Companies Act 1985 requiring directors to disclose their dealings in the shares and other securities of their company and related companies on their own behalf or that of their spouses and infant children[1]. There are also provisions requiring substantial shareholders and those who, acting together in concert, have a substantial interest in a particular company to disclose their holdings and report subsequent transactions. Under the Companies Act 1985, s 199, a person has a notifiable interest when he is interested in shares in the relevant share capital of a public company, whether listed or not, of an aggregate value equal to, or more than 3% of, the nominal value of that share capital. Relevant share capital is defined in the Act as meaning the company's issued share capital of a class carrying rights to vote in all circumstances in general meetings of the company. Furthermore, a person will be deemed to be so interested in such shares held by a spouse, infant child or trusts and companies which he controls. To address the practice of 'warehousing', there are 'concert party' provisions in the Companies Act 1985, s 204. Under this section, persons will be regarded as acting in concert if there is an agreement or arrangement between them for the acquisition by any one or more of them of interest in shares of a particular public company. To activate the section, the agreement must impose obligations or restrictions on any one or more of the parties concerning the use, retention or disposal of an interest in shares of the relevant company, acquired in pursuance of the agreement and an interest being in fact acquired by any one or more of those persons. In such cases, the holdings of each member of the concert party are aggregated and the obligation to report the total holding is placed on each individual member of the party.

1 Companies Act 1985, ss 324–329.

8.24 Although the Companies Act 1985 makes non-compliance with these reporting obligations a criminal offence and there are wide ranging investigatory powers[1], in practical terms, an individual who is prepared to engage in manipulative conduct is unlikely to be overly concerned about the prospect of a derisory fine. In practice, there have been virtually no prosecutions under these provisions[2] and relatively few examples of action by issuers and the Department of Trade, under these statutory powers, to freeze interests in shares the beneficial ownership of which is uncertain. The obligation to disclose dealings and interests imposed under the Companies Acts are mirrored and to some extent extended by various regulatory disclosure obligations set out in the FSA Listing Rules and the City Takeover Code[3].

1 Companies Act 1985, ss 212–219 and 442–446.
2 See *Meridian Global Funds Management Asia Ltd v New Zealand Securities Commission* [1995] 2 BCLC 116 with regard to a prosecution under the differently worded New Zealand provisions where the Privy Council emphasised the importance of effective timely disclosure of substantial acquisitions.
3 See the discussion in Chapter 10.

8.25 There are other provisions in the Companies Act 1985 relating to disclosure of directors and certain other insiders' interests (Companies Act 1985, s 137) controlling such persons' involvement with substantial property transactions with the company and related companies[1] and regulating the circumstances when they might receive loans and other financial facilities[2]. There are also provisions regulating the circumstances in which companies can become involved directly and otherwise in providing financial assistance in the purchase of their own securities and in buying their own shares and in reducing capital[3]. All these provisions, together with the general law relating to directors' duties, are more or less relevant to controlling abuses on the market.

1 Companies Act 1985, ss 320–322.
2 Companies Act 1985, ss 330–344.
3 Companies Act 1985, ss 151–169.

False statements

8.26 Mention has already been made of the outlawing of false statements that are made for the purpose of inducing investment transactions. The law has long recognised that those responsible for promoting new issues of stock have a special responsibility to ensure that those who are likely to subscribe are given all the information that they need to make an informed decision. In addition to requiring full disclosure of material facts, there are statutory obligations on those responsible for promoting new issues and placing securities in the market to ensure that due care is exercised in complying with the relevant disclosure requirements. For example, under the FSMA 2000, s 90, persons responsible for a false or misleading statement or omission in listing particulars will be liable to compensate any person who has acquired the securities in question for any loss that they have suffered unless it can be proved by them that they had reasonable grounds for believing what was said was not false or misleading. Indeed, under the FSMA 2000, s 91, the FSA can impose financial penalties on the issuer or its directors if they were 'knowingly concerned' in the breach.

8.27 The history of specific provisions directed at the fraudulent inducement of investment transactions within the market is more recent, as we have seen. The relevant provision is the FSMA 2000, s 397(1). This is more or less identical, although somewhat better drafted, than the former provision, the Financial Services Act 1986, s 47(1). Under s 397(1), the offence may be committed in one of three ways: (a) the making of a statement, promise or forecast knowing it to be misleading, false or deceptive in a material particular, (b) dishonestly concealing any material facts whether in connection with a statement, promise or forecast made by the person in question or otherwise and (c) recklessly making, dishonestly or otherwise, a statement, promise or forecast which is misleading, false or deceptive in a material particular. An offence will be committed under s 397(2) when a person acts in such a manner, for the purpose of inducing, or is reckless as to whether it may induce, another person, whether or not the person to whom the statement is made to enter into, or offer to enter into, or refrain from so doing, with regard to a 'relevant' agreement or exercising or refraining from exercising any rights conferred by a 'relevant' investment. We will examine this offence in more detail as it is the main weapon in the criminal justice system's armoury for dealing with the fraudulent inducement of investment transactions.

8.28 The making of a statement, promise or forecast may take two forms: first, the making of a statement which the defendant knows to be misleading, false or deceptive, or dishonestly concealing a material fact and, secondly, the reckless making, dishonestly or otherwise, of a statement which is in fact misleading, false or deceptive. In the first situation, the prosecution must prove that the person making the statement or concealing the relevant material fact did so dishonestly and was therefore essentially fraudulent. On the other hand, in the second situation, dishonesty is not required. Recklessness will be sufficient for criminal liability. Recklessness in this context may mean 'a high degree of negligence without dishonesty'[1] or a rash statement without any real basis of facts[2]. In *Metropolitan Police Comr v Caldwell*[3], it was said that if a person fails to address his mind to the possibility that there is an obvious risk that a statement might not be true, he may be considered reckless.

1   *R v Bates* [1952] 2 All ER 842.
2   *R v Grunwald* [1963] 1 QB 935.
3   [1982] AC 341.

8.29 There has been some debate as to what 'dishonest concealment of a material fact' means. It would seem to be the better view that before the defendant can be said to have concealed a fact, there must be an independent duty upon him to disclose it. Generally speaking, the law of contract does not impose an obligation on one party to a transaction to disclose facts to the other, no matter how material those facts may be, even when it is clear that the other party does not have access to the information in question. There are certain exceptions to the general rule of *caveat emptor*, such as where there is a pre-existing fiduciary relationship, but these are narrow and would not normally be present in the context of investment transactions. It has been argued that in cases of extreme self-interest where the circumstances indicate obvious dishonesty on the part of the defendant, a duty of disclosure should arise. There is no authority, however, for such a view. It has also been argued that it cannot be dishonest for a person to refrain from disclosing information which may be confidential to another person. This argument is misconceived as the issue of dishonesty is one of fact for the jury. Nonetheless, unless the defendant can be proved to have been under a duty to disclose the information in question, and few in the market will be under such a duty, then it cannot be said that mere non-disclosure amounts to concealment. It should be noted in this context that it will be rare for an insider to be under any duty to disclose the facts which constitute his inside information. The issuer may be under a duty of timely disclosure, but such duties would hardly ever apply to individuals. Where what is said by what is omitted creates a false impression, the law imposes a duty to correct the half truth. By the same token, if later events falsify what has innocently been said before, the law expects the statement to be corrected. In such cases, a dishonest failure to correct what has been said might well constitute concealment for the purposes of the FSMA 2000, s 397(2).

8.30 It should be noted that unlike, for example, the provisions outlawing insider dealing in the Company Securities (Insider Dealing) Act 1986, the offence in the FSMA 2000, s 397(2) may be committed on or off the markets. It might well be relevant in a face to face transaction not involving intermediaries, whether authorised or not. However, its scope is confined to inducing 'relevant agreements'. These are agreements which will be specified by the Treasury. In practice, virtually all agreements pertaining to investment contracts will be covered. The same broad approach applies to the term 'relevant investment' with regard to the exercise of rights. It is also important to note the wide jurisdictional scope of the offence. Although framed in restrictive language, s 397(6) makes it clear that conduct or results in the UK are sufficient for jurisdiction. Therefore, if the statement is made from, or the facts are concealed in, the UK, or the person affected is in the UK or the relevant rights are or would be exercised in the UK, there will be sufficient jurisdiction for an English court.

8.31 There are circumstances where the Theft Act 1968, s 19 might also prove to be a useful weapon against fraudulent misstatements. This provision makes it a serious offence for a person who is or who purports to be an officer of a company to publish, cause to be published or connives in the publication of a statement or account which he knows to be misleading, false or deceptive in a material particular. While it is not necessary for the prosecution to prove dishonesty, it must be established that the person concerned had the intention of deceiving the existing shareholders or creditors of his company as to its affairs. This offence, it should be noted, does not extend to oral statements.

Manipulation

8.32   When discussing the common law's stand against the deliberate creation of false markets, mention was made of the fact that, apart from some very ancient statutes relating to the integrity of markets, it was not until the enactment of the Financial Services Act 1986, s 47(2) that there were UK statutory provisions specifically designed to outlaw the manipulation of markets other than by the making of false statements. It is possible, of course, to make a representation by conduct, but in the context of the financial markets, seeking to establish a charge or claim on such a basis would in practice be exceedingly difficult, albeit not impossible. Section 47(2) has been re-enacted as the FSMA 2000, s 397(3).

8.33   The provision makes it a serious offence deliberately to undertake an act or course of conduct which gives a false or misleading impression as to the price or value of an investment if that is done for the purpose of creating that impression and thereby inducing other persons to deal in investments. It also applies to misleading investors as to the size or liquidity of a market for the investment in question.

8.34   The subsection applies to any person, whether they be a body corporate or a natural person. As in the case of the FSMA 2000, s 397(2), it applies whether the dealings take place on or off the market. The main thrust of the offence is to penalise an act or course of conduct which creates a false or misleading impression as to the market in or the price of an investment. It is not entirely clear as to whom the misleading impression must be directed. If the conduct in question is directed at a particular type of investor, such as professional investors or institutional investors, it is arguable that the issue is whether such persons and not the general market would have been given the relevant impression. The use of the word 'impression' is also worthy of note. It would seem to mean that the conduct in question must be directed towards creating a perception in the minds of those concerned. It is a rather different test from that, for example, in determining whether there has been a sufficient inducement to contract in the law of misrepresentation.

8.35   The impression that is conveyed, or that it is intended should be given, must be directed at either the state of the market or the value of the investment. Thus, acts or conduct which create a false impression as to the state of the market in terms of activity, depth or, indeed, any other relevant characteristic would be within the scope of the offence. It should be noted that not only artificial transactions, in the sense of washed transactions, may give rise to liability. Transactions which actually do involve independent consideration and result in proper execution, but which are inherently misleading because they are, for example, matched or pool operations, would also be caught. Indeed, the scope of the offence would be wide enough to catch conduct which would not necessarily be considered to involve manipulative trading. Thus, if an underwriter who is left with a large inventory of shares that are not taken up in a new issue made additional market purchases in the expectation of teasing the market into action, he might well be guilty of an offence under the FSMA 2000, s 397(3).

8.36 It is also an offence, as we have seen, where the misleading impression is as to the price or value of the investment in question. The problem with this and similarly worded offences in other jurisdictions is that it presupposes the existence of a fair price or real value. In the case of securities that are listed on a stock exchange, the correct value is the market price which is arrived at by the consensus of the bona fide purchasers and sellers. This principle has been regularly applied by the courts not only in relation to securities, but to commodities and land. It follows that any attempt to interfere with this market equilibrium is potentially unlawful under the FSMA 2000, s 397(3). Thus, many forms of share support and market making may, at least in theory, be caught by this provision. Wherever there is an attempt to influence the price of a security to a level above or below that which the market has or would set if unimpeded by the conduct in question, there should be at least prima facie evidence of the commission of a criminal offence. Both the courts and those charged with bringing prosecutions may be expected to have regard to commercial and market regularity and provided what is done comports with generally accepted practices, then it remains unlikely that the sledgehammer of the criminal law will come crushing down.

8.37 Nonetheless, it cannot be assumed that the mere fact that what has been done is a reasonably widespread practice and something to which most people would not take exception will discourage a prosecution and/or a conviction. It must be remembered that in the Blue Arrow prosecutions the defendants maintained that what they had done in attempting to support the price of shares in the market at the time of a sensitive rights issue was common practice[1]. This did not prevent their conduct being characterised by the Serious Fraud Office as manipulative and fraudulent. Of course, in the result, the jury took a rather different view. As long ago as 1840, Lord Langdale MR in *Gillett v Peppercorne*[2] observed 'it is said that this conduct is every day's practice in the City. I certainly should be very sorry to have it proved that such sort of dealing is usual; for nothing can be open to the commission of fraud than transactions of this nature'. Of course, in criminal prosecutions, the tribunal of fact, usually the jury, will have to be satisfied beyond a reasonable doubt that the defendant has acted dishonestly in the case of fraud and with the appropriate degree of intent in relation to the FSMA 2000, s 397.

1   See generally G Gilligan, *Regulating the Financial Services Sector* (1999, Kluwer) p 107 et seq.
2   (1840) 3 Beav 78.

8.38   The intent of state of mind (mens rea) that must be proved in the case of the FSMA 2000, s 397(2) is that the defendant had an intention to create an impression as to the market in or the price or value of a security and that he intended to induce another person to deal in the relevant security. It is very important to note that the prosecution does not need to establish that he intended to create a false or misleading impression as such. It is enough that he intended to create an impression as to the value or price of the investments. The implication is then fairly raised that he intended to create a false and misleading impression. This much is clear from the relationship of the statutory defence in s 397(5) to the offence. Section 397(5) provides a defence to a charge under s 397(3) if the defendant reasonably believed that his conduct would not create an impression that was false or misleading. Thus, if s 397(3) could not be breached unless the purpose of the conduct was to create a false or misleading impression, s 397(5) would be unnecessary. It must also be proved that what has been done has been to induce others to deal in the relevant securities. Therefore, no offence would be committed if the defendant could establish that he shuffled his investments for tax or, for that matter, any other reason than to induce a transaction. Mason J stated in the Australian case *North v Marra Developments Ltd*[1], 'purchases or sales are not often made for indirect or collateral motives ... plainly enough, it is not the object of the section (ie the equivalent of provision) to outlaw all such transactions'.

1   (1982) 56 LJR 106.

8.39   In a criminal prosecution, of course, it is for the prosecution to prove all the elements of the offence beyond a reasonable doubt. Where, however, a statute places an evidential burden on the defendant, it is generally speaking necessary for him to establish the relevant facts to the standard of the civil law, ie a balance of probabilities. The prosecution will, however, be able to rely on proper inferences from evidence, circumstantial and otherwise. Thus, in the Canadian case *R v Lampard*[1], in a prosecution of a stockbroker for manipulative practices, McLennan JA observed, with regard to the defendant's intent:

'he had been in the brokerage business for many years and must be taken in the absence of evidence from which some other reasonable explanation may be inferred, not only to have foreseen that each wash trade would create a false appearance of active public trading, but to have intended that result'.

In the leading Canadian case *R v Macmillan*[2], the court, in dismissing the defendant's appeal, stated:

'in the absence of any explanation ... and in the absence of evidence of circumstances which might reasonably lead to another conclusion, the only logical inference to be drawn from her conduct is that her real and dominant intention was to create a false or misleading appearance of active public trading in the shares of Golden Arrow (ie the manipulated stock). The suggested intent to benefit friends could amount to no more than a mere subsidiary consideration'.

1   (1968) 2 OR 470.
2   (1968) 66 DLR (2d) 680.

8.40   As has already been pointed out, under the common law, in a charge of conspiracy to defraud, it is not necessary to establish that the defendant intended to defraud a specific individual. It is enough that his statements are directed at the market and those who happen to be on the market on the particular day. It is not entirely clear from the wording of the FSMA 2000, s 397(3) whether the same rule would apply in a prosecution under this provision. It does refer to the conduct in question 'thereby inducing another person'. Therefore, need the prosecution prove that a manipulator had the intention to induce a transaction with a particular and ascertained person? To require so would be to restrict the scope of this offence unduly and it is probable that the court would not require such a narrow interpretation. It should be sufficient for an offence to have been committed under this provision that the defendant intended to affect investors generally or a class thereof.

8.41   As in the case of offences under the FSMA 2000, s 397(2), the offence of 'conduct manipulation' is both a conduct and result crime in terms of jurisdiction. Section 397(7) provides that a British court will have jurisdiction provided the act is done, or the course of conduct is engaged in, within the UK or the false or misleading impression is created in the UK.

8.42   Mention has already been made of the possible 'inter-play' between the FSMA 2000, s 397(2) in so far as it outlaws the dishonest concealment of material facts and the law relating to the abuse of inside information. It must not be forgotten that s 397(3) also covers at least some of the conduct addressed in the market abuse provisions discussed. The important point to note, however, with regard to s 397, is that it creates a series of quite serious criminal offences carrying a maximum penalty of seven years' imprisonment and an unlimited fine. The market abuse provisions, on their own, are outside the traditional criminal justice system.

Civil consequences

8.43   It would seem that the commission of an offence under the FSMA 2000, s 397(2) or (3) does not give rise to a civil claim under the Act. While an offence might well amount to a breach of one of the rules covered by the FSMA 2000, s 150 and thereby provide a private person with a cause of action for compensation, by its wording, it does not extend to violation of s 397 as such. Of course, the FSA's various enforcement powers, including seeking an injunction and restitution orders, are available on the same basis. In relation to the predecessors of s 397, it has been argued that an aggrieved party might be able to mount a statutory tort action for breach of the relevant provisions, but the better view is that such a cause of action is unlikely to be recognised by the courts. Surely, if Parliament had intended to provide investors with such a cause of action, it would have done so, specifically in the FSMA 2000. As we have seen, the common law might provide a remedy in conspiracy or for deceit in appropriate cases.

High pressure selling

8.44   The high pressure selling of securities at a greater price than they are worth has long been identified as a major issue in investor protection. High pressure selling operations, some times referred to as 'boiler room' operations, are often associated with other fraudulent schemes and this form of crime has attracted organised criminals. As early as 1936, the government established a committee under Sir Archibald Bodkin 'to consider operations commonly known as share pushing and share hawking and similar activities'. The result of the committee's recommendations was the enactment of the Prevention of Fraud (Investments) Act 1939 which, in addition to addressing fraudulent statements, as we have seen, regulated the selling practices of share dealers and the dissemination of investment related information and, in particular, advertisements. The Financial Services Act 1986, s 56 went somewhat further than this and in effect made it a 'civil offence' to make unsolicited calls to procure an investment agreement, to or from the UK, unless such were made in conformity with rules drawn up by the Securities and Investments Board. In *Alpine Investments BV v Minister van Financien*[1], the European Court accepted that while such rules curbing 'cold calling' were a restriction on a person's freedom to offer cross-border services, they could be justified on the basis that a member state had the right to ensure the protection of investors and the integrity of its markets.

1   Case C-384/93: [1995] All ER (EC) 543.

8.45   The Financial Services Act 1986, s 56 has been replaced by the FSMA 2000, s 30. At the cornerstone of the new regulatory regime is the FSMA 2000, s 21 which prohibits a person, in the course of business, communicating an invitation or inducement to engage in investment activity unless that person is an authorised person or the communication is approved by an authorised person. The rules promulgated by the FSA on financial promotion by authorised persons achieve more or less the same result as the earlier regime. If a person enters into 'controlled agreement' (that is one within the purview of s 21) as a result of an 'unlawful communication', then, subject to the discretion of the court, the customer is entitled to compensation for any loss or restitution of any moneys or property transferred and the agreement is unenforceable against him. Where the other party to the claimant is not the communicator, that person will be liable for any losses, subject to the discretion of the court. It must also be remembered that activity in breach of the prohibition in s 21, in addition to amounting to a criminal offence, will also bring into play the full enforcement powers of the FSA under the FSMA 2000, s 25.

Insolvency offences

8.46 It is sadly too often the case that a fraud will only be discovered once an insolvency occurs. While to some the insolvency provisions in the general law and the FSMA 2000 may appear to be 'shutting the stable door after the horse has bolted', they have an important role in attributing responsibility, tracing misappropriated funds and facilitating compensation and restitution. The procedures provided for by these laws also assist in attempting to resolve the conflicts which inevitably arise between various parties when there is not enough money to meet every obligation. Perhaps the most important in the control of fraud and sharp practice are those provisions which address misconduct on the part of those who manage insolvent enterprises and which enable the authorities to intervene. For example, under the FSMA 2000, s 367, the FSA may petition the court for a winding up, not only of an authorised person, but also any unauthorised person which is engaged in activity in contravention of the general prohibition on conducting unauthorised investment business. Of course, these statutory provisions are in addition to those in the general law relating to companies and insolvency.

8.47 There are a number of specific offences relating to malpractice and abuses before and during liquidation. The Insolvency Act 1986, s 206 provides that a present or former officer of a company in liquidation who, within the previous year, conceals, fraudulently removes or pawns any of the company's property or conceals or falsifies any records relating to the company's property, will be deemed to have committed an offence. By the same token, an officer or former officer who is privy to any of these actions will also be deemed to have committed an offence. It should be noted that the term 'officer' includes shadow directors. Section 206 not only applies to things done prior to and in anticipation of a liquidation, but also to things done during a winding up. The defendant is entitled to a defence if he can establish that he had no intent to defraud, conceal information from the company or defeat the law.

8.48   The Insolvency Act 1986, s 207 provides when a company is being wound up, a person is deemed to have committed an offence if he, being at the time an officer of the company, has made or caused to be made any gift or transfer of, or charge on, or has caused or connived at the levying of any execution against, the company's property, unless the transaction in question took place more than five years before the commencement of winding up or if he proves that, at the time of the conduct constituting the offence, he had no intent to defraud the company's creditors. There are further offences[1] relating to the conduct of officers during the winding up which place an obligation on such persons to co-operate fully with the liquidator in identifying the company's property and require accurate statements and records to be made. Perhaps the most important provision is, however, the Insolvency Act 1986, s 213 which relates to fraudulent trading.

1   Insolvency Act 1986, ss 208–211.

8.49   In addition to these offences, there are provisions facilitating contribution and restitution. The Insolvency Act 1986, s 212 provides for summary proceedings in cases of misfeasance. Where, in a winding up, it appears that a person involved in the management or promotion of the company has misapplied or retained, or become accountable for, any money or other property of the company, or been guilty of any misfeasance or breach of any fiduciary or other duty in relation to the company, the court may, on the application of the liquidator or a creditor, examine the person concerned and make an order requiring restoration or contribution. The Insolvency Act 1986, s 213 is concerned with fraudulent trading and empowers the court, again on application, to make orders with regard to a person who it appears has carried on a business with intent to defraud the company's creditors. Given the requirement of intent to defraud, as in the case of a prosecution brought under the Insolvency Act 1986, s 206[1], it is necessary to prove 'actual dishonesty, involving real moral blame'. Consequently, the provision is of limited use and proceedings for wrongful trading under the Insolvency Act 1986, s 214 are usually far more efficacious.

1   See *Re Patrick and Lyon Ltd* [1933] Ch 786.

Money laundering

8.50   Money laundering is the process by which the proceeds of criminal activity are 'divorced' from the criminal enterprise from which they are derived. Of course, there are many reasons, some lawful, why it might be desirable to 'hide' wealth or sever it from its source. However, in the context of the proceeds of crime, criminals may well find it desirable to adopt such procedures to prevent attention being drawn to what might otherwise appear to be 'unaccountable wealth' or to evade the various laws allowing the courts to seize and confiscate the proceeds of crime. It is generally accepted that one of the best strategies in combating highly profitable crimes, such as illicit trafficking in drugs or arms, and crimes that are motivated by economic gain, such as fraud and corruption, is to attack the proceeds and attempt to make the crime 'unprofitable'. It is also the case that many criminal enterprises require the re-investment of the proceeds of crime back into the business. By disrupting the flow of such wealth through the 'criminal pipeline', law enforcement agencies may impede the criminal enterprise. Consequently, most legal systems have an arsenal of laws allowing for the investigation and tracking of the proceeds of crime, their freezing and seizure and then, usually after conviction, their forfeiture or the confiscation of the value of the proceeds. In the United Kingdom, the amounts of money and the value of property actually confiscated has not been impressive[1]. Consequently, the government intends to introduce legislation that will allow property to be seized even without a conviction where it can be established, in a civil claim brought by the Criminal Assets Recovery Agency, that the wealth in question is on a balance of probabilities derived from serious crime[2]. It must also be remembered that the tax law also plays an important role in depriving criminals of their illicit profits and the new legislation will greatly facilitate the role of the authorities in taxing the proceeds of crime.

1   See 'Recovering the Proceeds of Crime' (2000, HMSO) PIU.
2   See Cm 5066 'Proceeds of Crime, Consultation on Draft Legislation' (2001, HMSO).

8.51   While those concerned with maintaining the integrity of the financial services industry and confidence in the capital markets have long recognised the dangers presented by money laundering, until the FSMA 2000 there were no special provisions in the law relating to those operating in the industry. Mention has already been made of the FSMA 2000, s 2(2)(d) which places an obligation on the FSA to pursue the reduction of financial crime as one of its four regulatory objectives. The FSMA 2000, s 6(3)(c) makes it clear that financial crime includes 'any offence involving handling the proceeds of crime'. As 'offence' is defined to include an act or omission which would be an offence if it had taken place in the United Kingdom and the United Kingdom provisions on money laundering extend to the proceeds of conduct, which, had it taken place in the United Kingdom, would amount to a serious offence, the FSA's concern to reduce financial crime is, indeed, set widely. In addition to its general objective to reduce financial crime, the FSA is empowered by the FSMA 2000, s 146 to make rules for the prevention and detection of money laundering in connection with the carrying on of regulated financial activity by authorised persons. The FSA has now published a comprehensive set of rules imposing on those engaged in the financial services industry specific obligations relating to the identification of customers, the recording of transactions, training and the compliance role of money laundering reporting officers. The full disciplinary and enforcement powers of the FSA are applicable to these rules, as are the provisions for civil liability under the FSMA 2000, s 150. It is important to appreciate that this regime is parallel and separate from the general criminal law and the Money Laundering Regulations 1993. However, it should be noted that, pursuant to the FSMA 2000, s 402(1)(b), the FSA has authority to prosecute for violations of the Money Laundering Regulations 1993 as well as enforce its own rules.

8.52 It is beyond the scope of this book to discuss in detail the provisions for pursuing the proceeds of crime, although it should be noted that the law does impose obligations, reinforced by the criminal law, on those who handle or advise on the handling of the property in question. Perhaps the most significant of these relate to laundering. These offences will be codified and refined in the promised legislation to which reference has been made. At present, there are a number of offences which differ to some degree as to whether the proceeds in question are derived from a drug related crime, are terrorist funds or the proceeds of some other serious crime. It should, however, be noted that all the offences and those relating to the tracking and seizure of the proceeds of crime extend to property derived from an activity, even conducted outside the United Kingdom, which, had it occurred within the United Kingdom, would have amounted to a serious crime. The wide implications of the anti-money laundering regime for those engaged in the financial services industry need to be carefully considered.

8.53 The provisions relating to the laundering of the proceeds of drug trafficking have been consolidated and re-enacted in the Drug Trafficking Act 1994. The Drug Trafficking Act 1994, s 50 provides that it is an offence for anyone to assist a drug trafficker to launder money by assisting them to retain or control the benefits of their criminal activity, even if this merely amounts to providing advice. It is necessary for the prosecution to prove that the accused knew or suspected that the other person is, or was, engaged in drug trafficking or has benefited from the drug trafficking activities of another person. The accused is entitled to a defence if he can prove that he did not know or suspect that this was the case or that he would have informed the authorities, but for a factor which reasonably prevented him from so doing. If a person does make disclosure of his suspicions to the proper authorities, which include, in the case of employees of banks and financial intermediaries, the relevant compliance officer, they do not commit an offence even if they subsequently, at the request of the authorities, provide assistance that would otherwise be in the scope of the offence. The Drug Trafficking Act 1994, s 52, in an attempt further to encourage reporting of suspicious transactions, provides that it is an offence to fail to disclose knowledge of suspicion of money laundering activity to the authorities provided this is acquired in the course of certain professional duties or certain types of employment. It is a defence, however, to prove that the person concerned had a reasonable excuse for not passing on the information in question or that it was passed to a designated compliance officer within the relevant business or organisation. With regard to disclosure under both the Drug Trafficking Act 1994, ss 50 and 52, there is immunity from the consequences of what might amount to a breach of contract or confidence. However, this does not extend to, for example, liability for defamation, although there is likely to be a defence of qualified privilege.

8.54 The Drug Trafficking Act 1994, s 53 makes it an offence to 'tip off' another person that an investigation into money laundering is in progress or is about to be commenced, which is likely to be prejudicial to the investigation. This is a widely drawn provision, although the accused is entitled to a defence if he can prove that he did not know or suspect that the disclosure was likely to prejudice any money laundering investigation. Legal advisers are given specific protection from this offence, but on condition that the information in question is not communicated in the furtherance of a criminal offence. Finally, with regard to the proceeds of drug trafficking, it should be noted that the offences relate to the proceeds of such activity wherever it takes place. It is not necessary that the proceeds in question have to be a result of activity which is an offence under United Kingdom law, although it must be such as would have been an offence had it occurred within the jurisdiction.

8.55 The atrocities that occurred on 11 September 2001 in the USA and the subsequent declaration of a 'war on terrorism' have lead to a number of important initiatives against the funds of terrorist organisations. It is probable that over the next year or so many countries will take powers to interdict assets that are suspected to belong to, or be at the disposal of, terrorist organisations. The US government has utilised its powers under its national security legislation[1] to freeze the funds and control the accounts and financial facilities of a number of individuals and organisations that are suspected of being involved in, or associated with, terrorist activity. Other jurisdictions have followed suit. Of course, similar orders have been made in the USA with regard to organised crime and, in particular, those suspected of involvement in drug trafficking. Indeed, the use of such devices has a long history with regard to those who support or are associated with enemy states. Economic sanctions have also been used to some effect both at a national and international level with regard to, for example, the regime in Iraq and South Africa in the days of apartheid.

1   Executive Order, Bulletin of the Office of Foreign Assets Control, 24 September 2001 pursuant to the International Emergency Economic Power Act (50 USC, s 1701 et seq) and the National Emergencies Act (50 USC, s 1601 et seq).

8.56 Governments have long recognised the significance of interrupting the flow of funds to terrorist and subversive organisations. In Northern Ireland, specific legislation was enacted to address the funding of terror[1] and the Northern Ireland Office had considerable success in disrupting the financial and business activities of several well-known terrorist organisations. The Prevention of Terrorism (Temporary Provisions) Act 1989 also outlawed the provision of financial support for those engaged in terror and introduced specific provisions relating to the laundering of assets associated with terrorist organisations. Although there were exceedingly few prosecutions, these offences provided a useful backdrop for the authorities' relatively successful strategy of disruption. Lord Lloyd of Berwick was appointed in December 1995 to consider what provisions were necessary to counter the threat of terrorism with the development of the peace process in Northern Ireland and the perception, which proved all too right, that there was an increasing risk from international terrorism. His report, which was published in October 1996[2], provided the basis for the Terrorism Act 2000, which has armed the UK with laws which go considerably further than most other countries in enabling the authorities to address the threat of both domestic and international terrorism. It is probable, however, that even more far-reaching powers will be introduced to freeze wealth associated with those who are suspected of supporting terrorist activity, in the proposed Proceeds of Crime Bill, to which reference has already been made[3].

1   See the Northern Ireland (Emergency Provisions) Acts 1991 and 1996.
2   Cm 3420 and see also 'Legislation Against Terrorism, a Consultation Paper', Cm 4178 (1998, HMSO).
3   See para **[8.50]** and the statement of Gordon Brown, Chancellor of the Exchequer, on 25 September 2001.

8.57   This is not the place to enter into a detailed discussion of the provisions of the Terrorism Act 2000, which will have an increasingly significant impact on the operation of the financial sector both in the UK and elsewhere after the attacks on New York and Washington. It is important to appreciate that its provisions, in the main, extend to terrorist activity against governments anywhere in the world. In addition to wide-ranging powers for investigation and control, the Terrorism Act 2000, Pt III introduces much-strengthened provisions relating to terrorist property. The Terrorism Act 2000, s 14 defines terrorist property as 'money or other property which is likely to be used for the purpose of terrorism and the proceeds of commission of acts of terrorism or carried out for the purposes of terrorism'. This definition also includes the resources of terrorist organisations. When the definition of terrorism itself is considered, the notion of terrorist property is very wide. The Terrorism Act 2000, s 1 provides that terrorism means the use or threat of action designed to influence the government or intimidate the public, or a section of it, for the purpose of advancing a political, religious or ideological cause. The action in question must involve serious violence, serious damage to property, a serious risk to the life of another person or to the health and safety of the public, or is designed seriously to disrupt an 'electronic system'. Where firearms or explosives are used, it will be taken that the action was done with the intention of influencing the government or public. Section 1(4) makes it clear that terrorist action anywhere, against any person or property, threatening any government or society, is within the scope of the Act.

8.58   The Terrorism Act 2000, s 15(1) makes it a criminal offence to invite another to provide money or property intending that it will be used, or having reasonable cause to suspect that it may be used, for the purposes of terrorism. Section 15(2) makes it an offence for a person to receive property intending that it will be used for terrorism or having reasonable cause to suspect that it may be so used. The person who provides such property with a similar intent or suspicion will also be guilty of an offence pursuant to s 15(3). It is made clear that the provision of property falls within these offences even if it is merely lent or given without consideration. Indeed, it is an offence simply to make such resources available for terrorism or a terrorist organisation[1].

1   See the Terrorism Act 2000, Pt II.

8.59   The Terrorism Act 2000, s 16 provides that a person commits an offence if he uses money or other property for the purposes of terrorism. Furthermore, an offence will also be committed by a person who possesses money or other property who intends that it will be used for the purposes of terrorism or who has a reasonable suspicion that it might. A similarly broad offence is also provided for in the Terrorism Act 2000, s 17, which makes it a crime if a person enters into, or becomes concerned in, an arrangement as a result of which property is made available or is to be made available to another and he knows or has reasonable cause to suspect that it will be or may be used for terrorism. The objective standard should be noted with regard to these offences. To be convicted, it is necessary for the prosecution to prove only that the accused knew facts which would have given a reasonable person cause to suspect. Of course, in most cases, the circumstances will be such that the accused could not credibly contend that he was unaware of the facts upon which a reasonable suspicion would arise.

8.60   The anti-money laundering offence is found in the Terrorism Act 2000, s 18. This provides that an offence will be committed if a person enters into, or becomes concerned in, an arrangement which facilitates the retention or control, by or on behalf of another, of terrorist property. It is made clear that this can be achieved by any process, although concealment and transfer to nominees are specifically mentioned. The accused is entitled to a defence if he can prove on a balance of probabilities that he did not know and had no reasonable cause to suspect that the arrangement related to terrorist property. Of course, it must always be remembered that in some cases there will be an overlap with the offences relating to the laundering of the proceeds of drug-related crime and other serious crimes. Under the anti-terrorism provisions, however, the onus on the accused to prove that he had no reasonable suspicion is, of course, more onerous.

8.61   The Terrorism Act 2000, s 19 makes it a criminal offence for a person who becomes suspicious in the course of their employment, trade or business and does not report his suspicion to the authorities or, where appropriate, a compliance officer. It is important to appreciate that the duty to report a suspicion arises even with regard to activity that, had it taken place within the UK, would have been an offence under the Terrorism Act 2000, ss 15–18 even though what was done took place overseas. In large measure, this provision mirrors the Drug Trafficking Act 1994, s 52 discussed in para **[8.53]**. It is provided in the Terrorism Act 2000, s 21 that a person does not commit an offence with regard to anything that he may do if he does it with the express consent of the authorities, or after he has made known to the authorities, or his compliance officer, his suspicions and the facts upon which his suspicion is based. The Terrorism Act 2000, s 39 is similar to the Drug Trafficking Act 1994, s 53 in that it makes it a criminal offence to 'tip off' another that an investigation is in progress or about to be initiated.

8.62 The Terrorism Act 2000, Pt III also contains a number of provisions allowing the authorities to seize and even forfeit property. There are specific provisions in the Terrorism Act 2000, s 23 allowing courts to forfeit terrorist property consequent upon a conviction under the offences that have been discussed above. However, there is a more far-reaching regime for the seizure and detention of property that the authorities have reasonable grounds for suspecting is terrorist property under the Terrorism Act 2000, ss 25–27. Indeed, an application may be made to the court for a forfeiture order of seized property, notwithstanding the absence of any conviction, provided the authorities can show on a balance of probabilities that the property in question is terrorist property. As has already been pointed out in para **[8.50]**, the British government has already proposed adopting similar provisions with regard to other forms of serious criminal activity.

8.63 The provisions in the Drug Trafficking Offences Act 1986 relating to money laundering were extended by the Criminal Justice (International Co-operation) Act 1990. These additional and important provisions have been codified in the Drug Trafficking Act 1994. The Drug Trafficking Act 1994, s 49(1) provides that it is an offence for a person to conceal or disguise any property which, wholly or partly, directly or indirectly, represents his own proceeds of drug trafficking. It is also an offence if the trafficker converts or transfers the property or removes it from the jurisdiction of the courts. This provision is aimed at the drug trafficker himself attempting to launder the proceeds of his crime, whereas s 49(2) makes it a crime for another person to engage in such acts for the purpose of assisting any person to avoid prosecution for a drug trafficking offence or the making of a confiscation order, knowing or having reasonable grounds to suspect that the property in question is derived from the proceeds of drug trafficking. Obviously, there is some overlap with the Drug Trafficking Act 1994, s 50 which, as we have seen, makes it an offence to assist another to retain the benefits of his illicit trafficking.

8.64 The Drug Trafficking Act 1994, s 51 is a particularly significant provision as it makes it an offence to acquire, possess or use property knowing that it directly or indirectly represents another person's proceeds of drug trafficking. It is important to note that before the offence can be committed the person concerned must actually know that the property in question is derived from drug trafficking, mere suspicion is not sufficient. Whilst the section will not apply to property transferred under a legitimate contract, where the consideration is unreal, wholly inadequate or illegal, there may well be an offence under this provision provided there is the requisite degree of knowledge. Statutory protection is afforded to those who legitimately provide goods and services provided that this does not assist in the drug trafficking activities of the recipient, even if the provider of the relevant services is aware that payment is from the proceeds of a drug related offence. Thus, a lawyer receiving payment for defending a drug trafficker would not commit an offence under this provision. It is also a defence to a charge under this section that proper disclosure has been made to the authorities, or where appropriate to a compliance officer or that the person concerned would have made due disclosure, but delayed in so doing for a reasonable cause.

8.65 Prior to the Criminal Justice Act 1993, attempts to launder the proceeds of crimes other than those relating to drug trafficking and terrorism did not amount to a specific criminal offence. Where a freezing or confiscation order had been made under the Criminal Justice Act 1993, an attempt to evade it might constitute contempt of court. There are also a variety of disparate provisions such as those in the Companies Act 1985 relating to the freezing of rights attaching to shares in certain circumstances, which, in particular circumstances, might have relevance in preventing activity which resembles laundering. Furthermore, the handling of the proceeds of a theft or deception is a specific offence under the Theft Act 1968, s 22. The Criminal Justice Act 1993 extends most of the provisions relating to money laundering to property derived from such criminal activity as is susceptible to the making of a confiscature order, after conviction, under the Criminal Justice Act 1988.

8.66 Section 93A, which has been added to the Criminal Justice Act 1988, makes it an offence for a person knowing or suspecting that another is, or has been, engaged in, or has benefited from criminal conduct, to enter into an arrangement, or be otherwise concerned with, in facilitation of the retention or control by or on behalf of another's proceeds of criminal conduct, whether by concealment, removal from the jurisdiction of the courts or transfer to nominees or otherwise. It is also an offence to enter into an arrangement or be otherwise concerned with, whereby the proceeds of a person's criminal conduct are used to secure funds that are placed at his disposal or are used to acquire property by way of investment for that person's benefit. As in the case of the drug related offences, an accused is entitled to a defence if he proves that his acts were done after proper disclosure to the authorities and with their approval or that he reported what had happened as soon as reasonable. Protection is also provided for those who disclose in breach of contract or an obligation of confidentiality. An accused will also be entitled to a defence if he can prove that he neither knew nor suspected that any arrangement related to the proceeds of criminal conduct or that the arrangement involved facilitating the laundering of such proceeds. Section 93B mirrors the Drug Trafficking Act

1994, s 51 in that it makes it an offence to acquire, use or possess property knowing that it is in whole or part directly or indirectly derived from the proceeds of criminal conduct. As in the case of s 51, it is necessary that the prosecution establishes actual knowledge, mere suspicion not being sufficient for liability. The same defences are also available, namely the payment of adequate consideration, provision of goods and services in the ordinary course of business and 'whistle blowing'. By s 93C(1), it is an offence to conceal, disguise, convert, transfer or remove from the jurisdiction of the courts any property which is directly or indirectly, in whole or part, the proceeds of criminal conduct. Section 93C(2) makes it a crime for anyone else to assist another to do this, provided they have knowledge or reasonable grounds to suspect that any of the property represents, directly or indirectly, the proceeds of criminal conduct. The objective element should be noted. Finally, s 93D makes it an offence for a person knowing or suspecting that a money laundering investigation is in progress or is about to be initiated, discloses this knowledge or suspicion to another if such is likely to prejudice the inquiry.

8.67 Reference has already been made to the Money Laundering Regulations 1993 in the context of the role of the FSA in policing money laundering. These statutory rules are concerned with the putting into place, within financial institutions and certain other intermediaries, mechanisms to ensure due compliance with the substantive provisions, to deter money laundering and facilitate detection and efficient investigation. The rules impose obligations to create, implement and operate internal procedures designed to identify and, to some extent, monitor customers, record their transactions, provide adequate training for staff and provide a regime for compliance with the law. Failure to comply with these obligations amounts to a criminal offence under reg 5(2), although it is a defence for the person or institution concerned to show that it took all reasonable steps and exercised proper due diligence in seeking to comply with the Regulations. Under reg 5(3), it is provided that a court may take into account, in deciding whether there has been due compliance with the Regulations, 'any relevant supervisory or regulatory guidance which applies to that person' or in a case where there is no specific 'official' guidance, guidance offered by a 'a body that regulates, or is representative of, any trade, profession, business or employment carried on by that person'. A number of professional bodies, such as the Law Society, have issued specific rules and guidance for their members. The Joint Money Laundering Steering Group has also published extensive Guidance Notes, compliance with which will almost inevitably be considered to meet the statutory standard of due diligence. Mention has already been made of the decision by the FSA to consider its own Money Laundering Rules as separate, albeit parallel to this regime. It has explicitly stated that its sourcebook, which contains its rules, is 'not relevant regulatory or supervisory guidance for the purposes of reg 5(3) of the Money Laundering Regulations 1993'. Of course, there is nothing at variance in the FSA's rules with the Guidance Notes and the FSA has also stated that 'in assessing a relevant firm's compliance with its duties to identify a client ... the Authority will have regard to the relevant firm's compliance with the Joint Money Laundering Steering Group's Guidance Notes'. This approach has not, however, been particularly well received by the industry and those responsible for compliance.

Other crimes

8.68 There are a number of other offences that, to a greater or lesser extent, may be relevant in controlling abusive conduct in the financial sector. It may well be possible to establish that what has occurred amounts to theft, contrary to the Theft Act 1968, s 1, although there would appear to be a reluctance on the part of prosecutors and, in particular, regulators, to label misconduct as simple theft! Apart from the more usual offences associated with forgery, uttering false documents and false accounting, it must be remembered that there are numerous offences of a more specific nature in the Companies Acts, insolvency legislation, banking laws and, of course, tax laws. Perhaps the most significant offences in practice are, however, those associated with obtaining property or services by deception. Mention has already been made of conspiracy to defraud, but it will generally be preferable to charge a conspiracy to commit a specific statutory offence and the most usual one will be that of obtaining property by deception contrary to the Theft Act 1968, s 15. The importance of this particular offence is illustrated with regard to the practice of 'stagging'. This occurs when a person, in the expectation that a particular issue is likely to be significantly over-subscribed and therefore in anticipation that his application will be 'scaled down', applies for a greater number of shares than he could in fact purchase. On notice of allotment, he will then sell in the market in the firm expectation that he will receive a premium and be able to cover the cost of subscription with the money he has obtained.

8.69 Stagging has not been considered objectionable in itself, although in recent years regulators and some judges have expressed doubts as to its propriety. In a number of the major privatisation issues, given the declared policy of the government to favour small investors and spread the issues as widely as possible, the terms of issue made it clear that allocation would be restricted to stipulated amounts and that multiple applications would not be accepted. Indeed, in one of two instances, this was provided for in the relevant legislation contemplating de-nationalisation. In such circumstances, the courts had no difficulty in regarding those who deliberately and thus, dishonestly, made multiple applications as obtaining the relevant shares by deception, contrary to the Theft Act 1968, s 15[1]. Moreover, it has been held in cases where the person engaging in stagging is aware that a cheque sent with his application, which is normally required, cannot be honoured by his bank on the first presentation, also commits a deception[2]. The fact that he expects to be in funds on the occasion of subsequent representation is irrelevant. Nor did it make any difference that what had happened was not an uncommon practice and one in which bankers had seemingly connived.

1   See, for example, *R v Best* (1987) Times, 6 October.
2   See *R v Goldstein and Green* [1976] 1 All ER 1.

Civil fraud

8.70   When examining the law relating to the manipulation of markets, reference was made to the possibility of suing in the civil courts for compensation. Mention has also been made of the statutory tort action that is expressly provided for under the FSMA 2000, s 150 in relation to violations of the various rules promulgated by the FSA. In the context of restitution and compensation, it is also important to remember the various powers that the FSA has to initiate civil actions. None of the statutory provisions, however, displaces the traditional common law remedies based on fraud. It is therefore worthwhile examining the civil law relating to fraudulent misrepresentation.

8.71   The dividing line between the criminal and civil law with regard to fraudulent conduct has never been entirely clear in English law. Indeed, one of the earliest causes of action, that of deceit, involved considerations of almost a penal nature. Given the harm that allegations of dishonesty can cause to individuals, particularly if they are in business, the courts have always been concerned by way of procedure and proof to ensure as far as is practical that such allegations are not made and pursued wantonly. Therefore, as a matter of pleading in the civil law, averments of fraud must be specially pleaded with all the relevant facts establishing the specific averment set out. While there is a difference between the standard of proof in an ordinary criminal trial and one for fraud in the civil law, judges have often emphasised that as the seriousness of the allegation increases in criminal proceedings, the standard of proof that is required to be met will be more exacting. Therefore, in practice, there may not be a great deal of difference between the standards of proof required to establish fraud in the civil and criminal law, particularly when it is remembered that in most cases considerable reliance will need to be placed on documentary evidence. Where allegations of fraud or deliberate misconduct involving moral turpitude are made and persisted with in circumstances which the court considers unjustified, there will be serious cost implications for the plaintiff and on occasion judges have expressed their disapproval of counsel.

8.72   The issue of fraud may arise in the civil law in a number of ways. However, since *Paisley v Freeman*[1], it has been the rule that if a person knowingly or recklessly, ie not caring whether it is true or false, makes a statement to another with the intention that it shall be relied upon by that person, who in fact does rely on it and as a consequence suffers harm, then an action in deceit will be available. It is the need for the plaintiff to establish that the defendant acted with actual knowledge or could not care less whether what he said was true or not, which distinguishes liability in fraud from, for example, liability in the tort of negligence[2]. In the case of negligent misstatement, the defendant will be liable if an ordinary reasonable person would have known that what was said was untrue, ie the standard is objective. Where a person has been induced to enter into a contract as a result of a fraudulent misrepresentation, the law provides remedies or rescission and damages. While rescission may be a more attractive remedy in the case of investment transactions, it will not always be available. There is a strict rule which requires full restoration of property transferred under the relevant contract, ie the parties must be restored to their original position. It follows that if the victim of the fraud, rather than run the risk of a further, perhaps unrelated, diminution in the value of his securities, disposes of them, he will have lost his right to rescind. In *Smith New Court v Scrimgeour Vickers*[3], Nourse LJ observed that, in the case of a fungible asset like quoted shares, the rule which requires restitution *in specie* is a hard one and in cases of fraud it was clear that the court had little sympathy with it, although in the circumstances it was not appropriate to depart from it. The rule works harshly, particularly in the case of an omission to disclose information which does not give rise to an independent cause of action for damages[4].

1 (1789) 3 TR 51.
2 See *Derry v Peek* (1889) 14 App Cas 337.
3 [1994] 4 All ER 225.
4 See *Banque Keysey Ullman v Skandia* [1989] 2 All ER 952.

8.73 In an action for damages, the courts have been concerned to ensure that a fraudster takes no benefit from his fraud or the false circumstances that he has created. In *Clark v Urquhart, Stracey v Urquhart*[1], Lord Aitkin emphasised that the measure of damages is the 'actual damage directly flowing from the fraudulent inducement' and this includes consequential loss[2]. On the other hand, deprecations of the value of shares by market forces operating after the date of acquisition does not flow directly from the fraudulent inducement, but from the purchaser's decision to retain the shares and accept the hazards of the market rather than sell at once[3]. The measure of damages will therefore be the difference between the price that the plaintiff paid and the 'true value' of the securities at the time he was fraudulently induced to acquire them. Valuation is always a difficult task and determination of the price depends upon a number of assumptions, one of the most important being what assumption should be made about the information which was available to the market[4]. In *Smith New Court v Scrimgeour Vickers*[5], the Court of Appeal considered that there were only two plausible possibilities in determining what assumption should be made as to information in the case of fraud. First, to assume that the market knew everything it actually did know, but was not influenced by the misrepresentation itself or, secondly, to assume that the market was omniscient. The Court of Appeal thought that the first approach was rational, but the second arbitrary and therefore disagreed with Chadwick J who at first instance appeared to have assumed that the market was omniscient. In the result, the Court of Appeal held that the correct measure of damages in a case where a person is induced to acquire shares by deceit is the difference between the price that was actually paid and the price which, in the absence of the misrepresentation, the parcel of shares would have fetched on the open market at that time.

1   [1930] AC 28 at 68.
2   See *Doyle v Olby (Ironmongers) Ltd* [1969] 2 All ER 119.
3   See *Waddell v Blockley* (1879) 4 QBD 678.
4   See *Lynall v IRC* [1971] 3 All ER 914 and with regard to insider trading.
5   [1994] 4 All ER 225.

8.74   The relationship between actions for deceit and in the tort of negligence have already been alluded to. As it is not necessary for a plaintiff in an action for damages to specify the particular tort which he is seeking to rely on for a remedy, provided he asserts and establishes the facts required for liability under at least one accepted cause of action, there may in practice be little lost in not alleging to being able to prove dishonesty, given the court's attitude to allegations of fraud. Apart from the desire to brand a person as a fraudster, it remains possible to obtain exemplary damages in cases of proven fraud and the statue of limitation may be more favourable[1], but in the majority of cases plaintiffs are well advised to refrain from specific averments of fraud. In the case of misrepresentation inducing a contract between the parties, the statutory remedies for negligent statements provided by the Misrepresentation Act 1967, s 2(1) are, in practical terms, superior to an action in tort. Under s 2(1), the person responsible for the misrepresentation has the burden of establishing that he had reasonable grounds for believing and did in fact believe what he said to be true.

1   Limitation Act 1980, s 32.

8.75   As we have seen, the issues of fraud may also be relevant in other actions such as conspiracy and under specific statutory provisions giving rise to a civil remedy. Equity follows the law and will not enforce a bargain that has been procured by fraud. Furthermore, the courts have developed a form of restitutionary liability for those who receive property transferred in breach of trust or who facilitate the laundering of such property with the requisite degree of dishonesty[1]. It must also be remembered that whilst there have been significant developments in the criminal law facilitating the taking and receipt of evidence from overseas, the civil law provides far greater weapons in obtaining evidence and discovery, in freezing funds and in enforcing orders of the court. Whilst the criminal courts possess statutory power, in certain circumstances, to order restoration and even compensation, as we have seen in the context of insider dealing, such orders are rarely appropriate in the case of securities related fraud.

1   See *Agip (Africa) Ltd v Jackson* [1992] 4 All ER 385 at 451; *El Ajou v Dollar Land Holdings plc* [1993] 3 All ER 717 and *Royal Brunei Airlines Sdn Bhd v Tan* [1995] 2 AC 378.

Disqualification procedures

8.76 While fraud does not always involve the use of a company, it often does. Consequently, it is sensible to deprive those who have committed fraud and other misconduct of the opportunity to misuse the privilege of using a company as a vehicle for their dishonesty. This is one of the justifications for disqualifying certain persons from being involved in the management of companies. Disqualification proceedings under the Company Directors Disqualification Act 1986 play an important role in preventing further abuses and constitute an additional sanction with regard to conduct that has already taken place.

8.77 It should be noted that in certain circumstances an order may be made with regard to a foreign citizen in relations to conduct taking place outside the United Kingdom. In construing the Company Directors Disqualification Act 1986, s 6, Arden J decided that the fact that modern communications enabled companies to be controlled across frontiers, given Parliament's intention to create an effective and integrated response to misconduct, justified an interpretation of the provisions which could extend to foreigners and conduct out of the jurisdiction[1]. An order made under the Act against a director or, in many cases, a shadow director makes it unlawful for him to be a director, liquidator, administrator or receiver of a company or be in any way, either directly or indirectly, concerned with the promotion, incorporation or management of a company in the United Kingdom during the currency of the order.

1   See *Re Seagull Manufacturing Co Ltd (No 2)* [1994] 1 BCLC 273.

8.78 There are a number of statutory grounds upon which an application can be made by the Secretary of State, or in some instances the liquidator or even a creditor, to the court under the Company Directors Disqualification Act 1986. Conviction for an indictable offence in connection with the promotion, formation, management or liquidation of a company is a ground under the Company Directors Disqualification Act 1986, s 2. It has been held that a conviction for insider dealing, when the conduct in question clearly had a relevant factual connection with the management of the company, was sufficient to justify a disqualification order[1]. Under the Company Directors Disqualification Act 1986, s 3, a court may make a disqualification order where there has been persistent default in making returns or delivering accounts and other documents required under the Companies Act 1985. The Company Directors Disqualification Act 1986, s 5 empowers the court to make an order on summary conviction for failing to comply with the statutory provisions relating to the filing of returns where there has been three such convictions within a period of five years.

1   See *R v Goodman* [1994] 1 BCLC 349.

8.79 The Company Directors Disqualification Act 1986, s 4 empowers the courts to make an order where it appears to the court in the course of insolvency proceedings, which need not necessarily end in a determination of insolvency, that there has been fraudulent trading or a breach of duty to the company. It should be noted that a conviction is not a prerequisite to the court exercising its powers under this section. The Company Directors Disqualification Act 1986, s 5 gives the court power to disqualify a person.

8.80   The Company Directors Disqualification Act 1986, s 6 relates to the disqualification of directors who have been associated with an insolvent company and are found to be unfit to be a director. It has been accepted by the courts that deliberately concealing transactions from the company and its shareholders is sufficient for the court to determine that a person is unfit to be a director[1].

1   See *Re Godwin Warren Control Systems plc* [1993] BCLC 80.

8.81   By the Company Directors Disqualification Act 1986, s 8, the Secretary of State is empowered to seek an order for disqualification when he has received a report from inspectors appointed under the Companies Act 1985 or the Financial Services Act 1986, or information pursuant to his own powers of investigation, indicating that it is in the public interest that an individual should be so disqualified. Before the court can make an order, it must be satisfied that the conduct in relation to the company makes the person concerned unfit to be involved in corporate management under the Company Directors Disqualification Act 1986, s 9. In determining the issue of unfitness, it is further provided that the court has regard to the matters set out in the Company Directors Disqualification Act 1986, Sch 1, Pt 1 which relates to the question of unfitness in cases brought under the Company Directors Disqualification Act 1986, s 6. Thus, a director who abuses his power in circumstances indicating a lack of commercial probity was held to be unfit[1]. The House of Common's Select Committee on Trade and Industry severely criticised the refusal of the Secretary of State to initiate such proceedings against the Fayed brothers following a recommendation by inspectors appointed to inquire into the House of Fraser affair. Although there was evidence that the Fayeds and their advisers had misled the City Panel on Takeovers and Mergers, the Department of Trade and Industry took the view that their conduct was not related to the management of a company, albeit that it is arguable that their misconduct facilitated the acquisition of the House of Fraser[2].

1   See *Re Looe Fish Ltd* [1993] BCLC 1160.
2   See 'Company Investigation', Third Report of the Trade and Industry Committee (1990, HMSO).

8.82   Finally, with regard to the grounds for disqualification, the Company Directors Disqualification Act 1986, s 10 permits a court to disqualify a person against whom it decides to make an order under either the Insolvency Act 1986, s 213 for fraudulent trading or the Insolvency Act 1986, s 214 for wrongful trading.

8.83 Breach of a disqualification order constitutes a criminal offence under the Company Directors Disqualification Act 1986, s 13, as well as contempt of court. Under the Company Directors Disqualification Act 1986, s 15, a person who is involved in the management of a company in violation of an order made under the Act, or a person who acts or is willing to act as a 'frontman' for a person whom he knows to be subject to disqualification, will be personally liable for all debts of the company. It should be noted that the same rules apply with regard to undischarged bankrupts[1].

1   See the Company Directors Disqualification Act 1986, ss 11 and 15.

8.84 Under the FSMA 2000, s 56, the FSA is empowered to issue 'a prohibition order' prohibiting an individual from performing a specified function or any function falling within a specified description if it appears to the Authority that the individual 'is not a fit and proper person to perform' the relevant functions in relation to regulated activity carried on by an authorised person. Before the Authority makes such an order, it is necessary for the individual concerned to be given a warning notice and he may request that the decision is referred to the Financial Services Tribunal. While the notion of 'fit and proper' is open textured, it is clear that fraud and many of the other forms of misconduct described in this chapter would justify the Authority in concluding that the person responsible is not a fit and proper person to be involved in investment business. The same may well also apply to those responsible for supervising that person's activities. It is a criminal offence under s 56(4) to perform or agree to perform a function in breach of a prohibition order, although it is a defence to show that the person concerned took all reasonable precautions and exercised all due diligence to avoid committing the offence. Furthermore, under s 56(6), an authorised person must take reasonable care to ensure that no function of his, in relation to the carrying on of a regulated activity, is performed by a person who is prohibited from performing that function pursuant to a prohibition order. If an authorised person violates this, any private person who suffers loss as a result has a right of action against him under the FSMA 2000, s 71.

8.85 In this context, it is also important to note the provisions in the FSMA 2000, Pt XII relating to control over authorised persons. Obviously, the safeguards that have been put in place to ensure that only fit and proper persons become authorised, or employ persons that are fit and proper, would count for very little if authorised persons could come under the control of unscrupulous individuals. The obligations to give notice and comply with orders by the FSA are reinforced by the criminal law under the FSMA 2000, s 191.

Offences by bodies corporate

8.86 Mention has already been made of the use that fraudsters make of companies as a vehicle for fraud. While the common law is well able to cut through corporate personality and fix liability directly on the individuals responsible when the corporate form is a sham or has been employed merely as an engine of fraud, the position is more difficult when a 'real' company that is not purely a device for the fraudster is involved. The law is able to attribute knowledge and even a guilty intent to a company, provided that knowledge or intent reposes in an individual who is sufficiently senior to be regarded as the company's mind or at least determinant over the function in question[1]. Indeed, in some cases, the courts have gone even further and held that the acts of an individual may be attributed to the company, even if that person is acting outside the duties of his employment and in breach of his employer's instructions, if acts are carried out in the course of his employment. In such cases, the attempts that the employer has gone to in ensuring compliance with the law are merely an issue for mitigation.

1   See generally Cheong-Ann Png, *Corporate Liability* (2001, Kluwer).

8.87   The FSMA 2000, s 400 addresses the reverse problem when it is appropriate to hold individuals responsible for offences committed by a company. Of course, it is necessary that the company be guilty and thus has the requisite state of knowledge before this issue arises. The section states that if an offence under the Act committed by a company is shown to have been committed with the consent or connivance of an officer or to be attributable to any neglect on his part, that officer, as well as the company, will be guilty of the offence in question. The concept of 'officer' is defined to include all those who have managerial responsibility, including directors and 'an individual who is a controller' of the company. Similar rules are applicable to partnerships. The exact implications of this provision are difficult to state. Provided a company could be given the requisite degree of culpability to justify a charge under the FSMA 2000, s 397(2) or (3), it is possible that charges could be brought against an 'officer' who was only guilty of 'neglect'.

Conclusion

8.88   Given the emphasis that has been placed on the protection of investors, the need to maintain confidence in the integrity of the markets and the desirability of reducing financial crime, the policing of fraud and other abuses will inevitably attract a great deal of attention. The FSA cannot complain that it has not been given the weapons to police at least those offences within its statutory purview. The civil enforcement powers that have been entrusted to it are considerable and there has been a significant 'tidying up' of the relevant legislation which will no doubt render enforcement less hazardous. On the other hand, experience has shown in the United Kingdom and elsewhere that the problems in dealing effectively with serious fraud are far ranging and intractable. Obviously, much will depend upon the level of co-operation and collaboration that the FSA is able to achieve, not only with other authorities in the United Kingdom, but also with its counterparts overseas. A great deal will also depend upon how much it can rely upon those in the industry and in particular those working in compliance to get their own houses in order and work effectively with the authorities. While civil enforcement by or through the FSA is destined to become a more significant feature of policing the markets, it remains very doubtful whether private litigants will become the champions of integrity to the extent that some think they are in the United States.

CHAPTER 9

Defences

Insider dealing and market abuse

Introduction

9.1 This chapter analyses the defences to insider dealing and market abuse. It sets out the statutory defences to each of the insider dealing offences under the Criminal Justice Act 1993 ('CJA 1993'). These defences will succeed only if, after the prosecution has proved all the ingredients of the offence, the defendant proves on a balance of probabilities that the offence was not committed[1]. This chapter also assesses possible defences under the Financial Services and Markets Act 2000 ('FSMA 2000') market abuse regime and the role of the FSA's Code of Market Conduct in determining whether particular behaviour does not amount to market abuse. The Code of Market Conduct is conclusive as to whether particular behaviour does not amount to market abuse[2]. These are described in the Code as 'safe harbours' and are considered below. Moreover, the chapter discusses the extent to which other regulatory rules, such as the City Code on Takeovers and Mergers and the Model Code, attract safe harbour status. Similarly, the European Convention on Human Rights, which has received heightened publicity recently in light of the enactment of the Human Rights Act 1998, provides a backdrop to the FSMA 2000 and it remains to be seen whether it may provide a basis for a successful challenge.

1   CJA 1993, s 53. See also *R v Cross* [1991] BCLC 125 (upholding the general principle that the burden is on the accused to raise a statutory defence).
2   FSMA 2000, s 118(8).

General defences to insider dealing under the CJA 1993

9.2 A successful prosecution of the dealing[1] or encouragement[2] offences must first allege and prove all the elements of the offence of insider dealing as set out in the CJA 1993, s 52. For example, the prosecution might prove that the defendant has possessed and used price-sensitive information in relation to publicly-traded securities with a view to the making of a profit or the avoidance of a loss. The burden then shifts to the defendant to prove, on a balance of probabilities, any defence provided in the CJA 1993, s 53. For example, a successful defence might show that, at the time the agreement to deal was entered into, the defendant did not expect the dealing to result in a profit or to avoid a loss[3] which was attributable to price-sensitive information in relation to the securities. It should be emphasised that the offence is committed at the time the agreement is made and not on completion of the transaction. Thus, the statutory language does not appear to provide a defence in the situation where the transaction, on which the agreement to deal was based, does not in fact take place. Precluding a defence on this basis in respect of the encouragement offence seems to be appropriate because the encouragement will have factually occurred, whether or not a deal takes places, so the expectation of the parties at that time is clearly important. This approach, however, has raised some concern regarding its application to the dealing offence[4], where it is argued that if the transaction does not take place, the deal itself will not have occurred so that the expectations at the contract formation stage seem less important. Prosecutions will probably be rare where completion has not taken place.

1   CJA 1993, s 53(1)(a).
2   CJA 1993, s 53(2)(a).
3   CJA 1993, s 53(2)(b).
4   See B A K Rider and M Ashe, *Insider Dealing* (1993, Jordans) p 54.

9.3   The CJA 1993, s 53(1)(c) and (2)(c) also provides defences to both the dealing offence and the encouragement offence where the defendant can show that it would have acted in the same way without the inside information. In such a case, after the prosecution has proved all the ingredients of the offence, the defendant must show that, on a balance of probabilities, its possession of inside information did not affect its decision to deal or to encourage another to deal. The policy rationale seems to be that an individual that is planning *either* to deal or to encourage someone else to deal should not be inhibited from doing so merely by being in possession of inside information. It would follow that a defence is available for an individual who has come into possession of inside information after making a decision to deal. A defence may also be available in circumstances where an investor who possesses inside information was forced to sell because of economic circumstances. For example, economic compulsion may provide a defence for a person who was forced to sell in the face of no other readily realisable property. In the above situations, some commentators note that it would seem proper and right to permit defences to prevail, but the second situation involving a defence based on economic compulsion would be more difficult to prove on a balance of probabilities[1].

1   See Rider and Ashe, *Insider Dealing*, p 54.

9.4   Moreover, it would be more difficult to prove that possession of the inside information had had no effect on a decision to deal, in the absence of any economic pressure to sell. An important factor for maintaining a defence will be the timing of the deal, unless the defendant can show that the timing of the deal was not related to the inside information. For example, a defence may be available for a trustee who, whilst possessing inside information about securities, dealt in them on the basis of independent advice and for the benefit of the trust.

9.5   The CJA 1993, s 53(1)(b) provides a defence to the dealing offence if it can be shown that the individual, at the time of dealing, believed, on reasonable grounds, that the information had been disclosed to a wide enough audience to ensure that those taking part in the dealing were not prejudiced by not having the information[1]. This defence can be raised when two parties are in contact with each other and they are in possession of inside information that can or cannot yet be made public (eg properly conducted corporate transactions). For example, this defence would cover underwriting transactions where both parties know or are aware of the information.

1   Section 53(1)(b) states in the relevant part:
 '(1) An individual is not guilty of insider dealing by virtue of dealing in securities if he shows –
  (b) that at the time he believed on reasonable grounds that the information had been disclosed widely enough to ensure that none of those taking part in the dealing would be prejudiced by not having the information'.

9.6   A similar defence is available for the encouragement offence where the defendant can show, on reasonable grounds, that it believed, before the dealing occurred, 'that the information had been or would be disclosed widely enough to ensure that none of those taking part in the dealing would be prejudiced by not having the information'[1]. In addition, there are two defences involving the disclosure offence that cover situations where no dealing was expected[2] or where the deal was not expected to lead to a profit or to avoid a loss on the basis of information that was price sensitive[3]. These defences need not cover the proper performance of professional, office or employment responsibilities because the definition of offence under the Act expressly omits 'the proper performance of the functions of [one's] employment, office, or profession'[4].

1   CJA 1993, s 53(2)(b).
2   CJA 1993, s 53(3)(a).
3   CJA 1993, s 53(3)(b).
4   CJA 1993, s 52(2)(b). This provision states in the relevant part:
 '(2) An individual who has information as an insider is also guilty of insider dealing if –
  (b) he discloses the information, otherwise than in the proper performance of the functions of his employment, office or profession, to another person'.

Special defences under the CJA 1993

9.7   The CJA 1993 provides three special defences to the dealing and encouragement offences. These defences may be described generally as 'market defences'. Two of these defences are specific, covering market makers and those involved in price stabilisation. The third defence relates to what has become known as 'market information'.

Market maker's defence

9.8 Market makers are recognised under the rules of recognised investment exchanges ('RIEs') as performing the essential function in normal times of buying or selling securities registered with a regulated market. Market makers are ordinarily required to comply with the rules of an RIE or an approved organisation and to be willing to acquire or dispose of securities according to these rules[1]. A market maker may raise a defence where it can show that it acted in good faith in the course of its business, or in its employment, as a market maker[2]. It is important to note that in the original Criminal Justice Bill this defence would have applied to *any* employee of a market maker. This was later amended so that the defence would *only* apply to an employee of a market maker who was primarily engaged in market making activity[3]. Most experts agree that it is not clear whether this defence is available to a market maker who, after becoming aware of inside information by mistake, continues to deal in the securities in question. In such circumstances, obvious difficulties would arise for a market maker who, for example, was employed by a corporate broker with responsibility for dealings in a particular share and who would arouse suspicions amongst traders if he suddenly withdraws from the market. In this situation, the insider dealing offence would appear to cover the market maker who stayed in the market and dealt.

1   CJA 1993, Sch 1, para 1(2).
2   CJA 1993, Sch 1, para 1.
3   Parliamentary Debates, House of Commons, Standing Committee B, 15 June 1993, column 216.

9.9 Accordingly, the market maker's defence in the CJA 1993, Sch 1, para 1 is much narrower than the equivalent defence that had been available under the Company Securities (Insider Dealing) Act 1985. The counterpart provision of the 1985 Act prohibited the market maker from dealing whilst in the possession of inside information if the inside information on which the market maker dealt had been obtained by the market maker in the course of its business and was of a type for which it was reasonable for the market maker to have obtained in the ordinary course of that business[1]. The CJA 1993 sought to do away with these requirements in order to impose liability on a broader basis, but does provide a defence in the CJA 1993, s 53(1)(c) for a market maker who was wrongly exposed to inside information and continues to deal[2].

1   Company Securities (Insider Dealing) Act 1985, s 3(d).
2   Section 53(1)(c) provides in the relevant part:

'(1) An individual is not guilty of insider dealing by virtue of dealing in securities if he shows –

(c) that he would have done what he did even if he had not had the information'.

Price stabilisation defence

9.10   The price stabilisation defence would be available for an individual who was dealing in securities, or encouraging another to deal in securities, on the basis of inside information if the individual can show that the dealings were in conformity with the price stabilisation rules of a recognised exchange or regulated market[1]. The price stabilisation rules are found in Pt 10 of the Conduct of Business Rules 1990 that are now enforced by the FSA[2]. The purpose of these rules is to permit a manager of an issuance of securities to enter the market (usually by purchasing shares) in order to stabilise or maintain the market price of those securities. A defence is available for price stabilisation if such activity is carried out in conformity with the rules of a regulated exchange. For example, the FSA's price stabilisation rules, adopted pursuant to the FSMA 2000, s 144(1) and (3), contain safe harbour provisions to the effect that behaviour conforming to those rules will not amount to market abuse[3]. These safe harbour provisions for price stabilising activity are available to any person, whether that person is a firm or not, who can show one of the following: they acted in conformity with the price stabilisation rules for the purposes of the CJA 1993, Sch 1, para 5(1), their conduct conformed with the price stabilising rules for the purposes of the FSMA 2000, s 397(4) or (5)(b) (misleading statements and practices) or their behaviour conforms with the rules in accordance with the FSMA 2000, s 118(8) (market abuse)[4].

1   CJA 1993, Sch 1, para 5.
2   These rules were originally adopted by the Securities and Investments Board in 1990 and, under the Financial Services Act 1986, s 48(7), conformity with these rules provided a defence against the offence of market manipulation under the Financial Services Act 1986, s 47(2).
3   Mar 1.7.2. Other FSA rules containing provisions to the effect that behaviour conforming to that rule does not amount to market abuse will be discussed below and include the rules relating to Chinese Walls, certain parts of the Listing Rules in MAR 1, Annex 1G and rule 15.1(b) of the Listing Rules.
4   See the FSA Handbook, Chapter 2, Price Stabilising Rules, MAR 2.1.2(1)(a)–(c).

9.11   The price stabilising safe harbours would cover any person concerned with an offer of securities for cash. For instance, there is no legal restriction on the appointment of stabilising managers to whom the FSMA 2000 price stabilising rules would apply. The main focus, however, is on lead managers when they are considering or undertaking an offer of securities for cash. These safe harbours could also apply to agents appointed by lead managers[1]. The safe harbours would cover both initial public offers and public offers of additional securities, along with securities already in issue[2]. The FSA observes that an offer is likely to be public in character where it is made in a prospectus[3].

1   MAR 2.1.2(2).
2   MAR 2.1.3(R).
3   Other offers may be regarded as public when they are made to a section of the public, such as distributions and placements that are not essentially private (see MAR 2.1.4), but the requirement that there must be a public announcement means that some offers for sale of securities, for example by means of block trade, would not be covered.

Market information defence

9.12 The statutory language for this defence is general in nature and provides that an individual will not be guilty of insider dealing 'by virtue of dealing in securities or encouraging another person to deal if he shows that':
- the information which he had as an insider was market information; and
- it was reasonable for an individual in his position to have acted as he did despite having that information as an insider at the time[1].

1 CJA 1993, Sch 1, para 2(1).

9.13 The CJA 1993 defines 'market information' in broad terms to be information which someone inevitably acquires as a consequence of the activities involved in the acquiring or disposing of securities. For information to qualify as 'market information', it must consist of one or more of the following facts:

- that securities of a particular kind have been or are to be acquired or disposed of or that their acquisition or disposal is under consideration or the subject of negotiation;
- that securities of a particular kind have not been or are not to be acquired or disposed of;
- the number of securities acquired or disposed of or to be acquired or disposed of or whose acquisition or disposal is under consideration or the subject of negotiation;
- the price (or range of prices) at which securities have been or are to be acquired or disposed of or the price (or range of prices) at which securities whose acquisition or disposal is under consideration or the subject of negotiation may be acquired or disposed of; or
- the identity of the persons involved or likely to be involved in any capacity in an acquisition or disposal[1].

1 CJA 1993, Sch 1, para 4(a)–(e).

9.14 The second prong of the individual's defence requires a determination that the individual had acted reasonably in his position in doing any act, despite having acquired market information as an insider prior to the act. The CJA 1993, Sch 1, para 2(2) provides criteria for determining whether the individual acted reasonably in doing any act, despite possessing market information as an insider. These criteria include: the type and content of the information, the circumstances and capacity in which the insider first acquired or had the information and the capacity in which the insider now acts. An investment practitioner should apply the reasonableness test in using market information in specific circumstances by making reference to the rules and principles of the Model Codes and the regulatory requirements of the FSA[1].

1 Parliamentary Debates, House of Commons, Standing Committee B, 15 June 1993, column 217.

9.15   In addition, a market defence exists for an individual who acted in connection with an acquisition or disposal, which was under consideration or subject to negotiation, 'with a view to facilitating the accomplishment of the acquisition or disposal'[1]. This defence would also be available for an individual who acted in connection with a series of such acquisitions or disposals or had acted with a view to facilitate a series of acquisitions or disposals.

1   CJA 1993, Sch 1, para 3(a)(i)–(iii).

9.16   This market information defence is available only for individuals in possession of market information that was obtained as an insider and for which it was reasonable, under the circumstances, for the individual to have dealt, despite possessing the information as an insider at the time. An example of market information would be when an individual sells a large block of shares and the publication of this information would impact on the share price, as would the prior knowledge that someone intended to buy or sell a large block of shares.

The City Code/RIE rules/SARs

9.17   As noted in Chapter 6, the FSA has rejected the argument that there should be a blanket exemption for compliance with the rules of RIEs or the City Code. The FSMA 2000, s 120 confers a power upon the FSA to include provision to the effect that behaviour conforming with the City Code does not amount to market abuse, provided that the Treasury's approval has been given. Certain RIE rules and provisions of the City Code have been given safe harbour status as will be seen below, but these only apply to market manipulation[1]. The rationale given by the FSA for not applying similar safe harbours to misuse of information is that the criminal offence of insider dealing has been dealt with for a number of years by other bodies, such as the London Stock Exchange and the Department for Trade and Industry, without disrupting the takeover process[2].

1   MAR 1.7.7 and 1.7.8.
2   CP 76, para 1.9.

FSA Rules

9.18   Additionally, behaviour will not be market abuse if it conforms with a rule made by the FSA under the FSMA 2000, which includes a provision to the effect that behaviour conforming to the rule does not amount to market abuse[1]. The Code of Market Conduct explains that the rule must expressly require or permit the person to engage in the behaviour in question[2]. The FSA Rules containing a provision to the effect that behaviour conforming to that rule does not amount to market abuse are the price stabilising rules[3] made under the FSMA 2000, s 144(1) and (3), the rules relating to Chinese

Walls[4] and certain parts of the Listing Rules set out in MAR 1, Annex 1G and r 15.1(b) of the Listing Rules[5].

1 FSMA 2000, s 118(8).
2 MAR 1.7.2.
3 Compare the CJA 1993, s 53(4) and Sch 1, para 5.
4 COB 2.4.
5 MAR 1.7.3.

9.19 The Model Code on directors' dealings in securities set out in the appendix to Chapter 16 of the Listing Rules benefits from these provisions, as can be seen from MAR 1, Annex 1G. This moves from the position stated in CP 76, para 4.34 where the FSA stated that it would not give the Model Code or any of its provisions safe harbour status and would provide guidance to those concerned that their actions may contravene the market abuse provisions[1].

1 CP 76, paras 4.34 and 4.40.

European Convention on Human Rights ('ECHR') and natural justice

9.20 As noted in Chapter 6, it has been argued that the FSMA 2000 is criminal in nature for the purposes of the ECHR and consequently the Human Rights Act 1998. The government has anticipated many of the arguments that may be made on the basis of the ECHR and has sought to dowse them. For instance, legal assistance is available to those referring a matter to the Financial Services and Markets Tribunal in certain circumstances[1].

1 FSMA 2000, s 134.

9.21 It is interesting to note that Morison J recently rejected the argument that disciplinary appeal tribunal proceedings of the Securities and Futures Authority involved a criminal charge within art 6, ECHR[1]. The applicant relied upon the unlimited fines and other penalties that may be imposed, a similar argument to that made in relation to the market abuse regime[2]. The core conclusion by Morison J that makes the *Fleurose* reasoning on disciplinary proceedings distinguishable from the market abuse regime lies at para 52. The learned judge concluded that because the disciplinary regime involved voluntary participation, it was not criminal in nature. By contrast, the market abuse regime applies to everyone and is mandatory.

1 *R (on the application of Fleurose) v Securities and Futures Authority Ltd* [2001] EWHC Admin 292, [2001] 2 All ER (Comm) 481.
2 See, eg, the joint opinion of Lord Lester of Herne Hill QC and Javan Herberg annexed to the First Report of the Joint Committee on Financial Services and Markets.

9.22 One of the main potential areas of challenge to the FSMA 2000 under the ECHR that remains unresolved is whether the scheme of clarifying the FSMA 2000 with the Code of Market Conduct is legitimate, where the Code is only of evidential value as to what amounts to market abuse pursuant to the FSMA 2000, s 122. Article 7(1), ECHR includes the principle that an offence must be clearly defined in law so that an individual may foresee the legal consequences of his actions: see *Kokkinakis v Greece*[1]. In fact, in the *Fleurose* case, Morison J accepted that this was an aspect of natural justice[2]. The objection under the ECHR or natural justice may therefore be the same. The FSA has focused upon this point in its policy statement[3]. Although the FSA has undoubtedly improved the clarity of the Code for market users in its final version, this cannot cure the real issue as to the paucity of definition in the FSMA 2000. The limited legal effect of the Code is acknowledged by the FSA at para 1.5 of its policy statement where it has said that 'the Code sets out the standards that the regular user is likely to expect. But the FSA's opinion is not determinative and it is ultimately for the [Financial Services and Markets] Tribunal to decide'.

1   (1993) 17 EHRR 397.
2   See para 63.
3   See, eg, para 4.2.

Misuse of information

9.23   The FSA has rejected calls that the defences to misuse of information should replicate those on insider dealing contained in the CJA 1993[1] and has maintained this view in its policy statement at para 6.22. It is suggested that this conclusion is supported by the different purposes of each regime. Accordingly, the defences to misuse of information contain some, but not all, of the defences to insider dealing. In particular, the defence to insider dealing based on the lack of expectation of a profit is irrelevant to misuse of information. This is in keeping with the focus of the latter regime upon the effects of the offender's actions upon the market as distinct from the profit or avoidance of loss to the individual offender.

1   CP 59, para 6.55.

9.24   The Code of Conduct creates four specific safe harbours for misuse of information: (a) dealing or arranging required for other reasons, (b) dealing or arranging not based on information, (c) trading information and (d) facilitation of takeover bids and other market operations[1].

1   MAR 1.4.20, 1.4.21, 1.4.26 and 1.4.28.

Dealing or arranging required for other reasons

9.25   A person who is 'required to deal in order to comply with a legal (including contractual) or regulatory obligation in circumstances where the obligation existed before the relevant information was in his possession will not be guilty of market abuse'[1]. The FSA has drawn attention to this safe harbour in the context of the listing rules[2]. Further, the FSA has indicated that this replicates in part the market maker's defence to insider dealing[3]. Similarly, this includes in part the 'would have dealt anyway' defence from the CJA 1993, s 53(1)(c).

1 MAR 1.4.20.
2 CP 76, para 4.6.
3 See the CJA 1993, s 53(4) and Sch 1, para 1 and CP 59, para 6.56.

Dealing or arranging not based on information

9.26 These defences reflect and expand upon the defences contained in the CJA 1993, s 53(1)(c). However, the defence is to some extent narrower than its counterpart under the CJA 1993 in that it is limited to 'dealing' or 'arranging' and does not extend to accessory liability[1]. This is particularly significant if the FSA maintains its view that many instances of encouraging another to deal will fall within the FSMA 2000, s 118(2)(a) by reason of being behaviour 'based on information'[2].

1 See the CJA 1993, s 53(2)(c).
2 CP 76, para 2.6.

Firm decision

9.27 Dealing or arranging to deal by a person will not amount to market abuse if the alleged offender establishes that he had taken a firm decision to deal or arrange deals before the 'relevant information' was in his possession and the terms on which he had proposed to enter into the transaction did not alter after receipt of the information[1]. 'Dealing' is defined by reference to the FSMA 2000, Sch 2, para 2[2]. This provides that dealing is 'buying, selling, subscribing for or underwriting investments or offering or agreeing to do so, either as a principal or as an agent'. Further, in the case of an investment which is a contract of insurance, carrying out the contract is included. 'Arranging' is also defined in the definitions section of the Code.

1 MAR 1.4.22.
2 Definitions section of the Code of Market Conduct.

9.28 A 'firm decision' is one that is settled or definitely established. Therefore, very good evidence is likely to be necessary in order to satisfy this defence. An assertion by the defendant that he had taken a firm decision to deal before receiving 'relevant information' that is not 'generally available' will almost always be viewed with suspicion. The need to establish a pre-existing commitment to the deal in order to come within the defence seems higher in market abuse than the defence to the criminal offence of insider dealing, which merely requires the alleged offender to establish that 'he would have done what he did even if he had not had the information'[1].

1 CJA 1993, s 53(1)(c).

Presumption of no influence

9.29   MAR 1.4.23 creates a presumption that possession of relevant information by one or more individuals within an organisation did not influence a person's decision to deal or arrange deals in certain circumstances. However, it should be noted that this presumption is given only evidential effect.

9.30   This safe harbour is significant to more complex persons caught by the market abuse regime, namely body corporates, partnerships, trusts and unincorporated associations. The Code introduces a presumption that possession of the information in question did not influence a person's decision to deal or arrange deals if none of the individuals in possession of the information (a) had any involvement in the decision to engage in dealing or arranging or (b) behaved in such a way as to influence, directly or indirectly, the decision to engage in the dealing or arranging or (c) had any contact with those who were involved in the decision to engage in the dealing or arranging whereby the information could have been transmitted[1]. The requirement that there be 'no contact' might seem extreme and the FSA has indicated that this is not an absolute requirement if firms are able to show by other methods that there was no influencing of behaviour[2]. The final text of this safe harbour has been slightly modified from earlier drafts of the Code, which required (a) to be satisfied in all cases.

1   MAR 1.4.23.
2   CP 59, para 6.37.

Chinese Walls

9.31   The Code makes the establishment of effective Chinese Wall arrangements in compliance with COB 2.4 important in relation to establishing the protection of this safe harbour. MAR 1.4.24 provides that 'relevant information' does not influence the decision to deal or arrange deals if (a) the information in question was held behind an effective Chinese Wall and the individual or individuals who dealt or arranged deals was or were on the other side of the wall or (b) arrangements equivalent to Chinese Walls had been established and maintained in respect of the information and the individuals who dealt or arranged deals did not therefore have access to the relevant information. The Code makes MAR 1.4.24 conclusive.

Trading information

9.32   The defence of 'trading information' may be compared with the special defence to insider dealing of market information[1]. A typical example of trading information is knowledge that an individual has sold shares or that someone intends to sell a block of shares[2]. This is another area in which the FSA acknowledges that true equality cannot be achieved and is not expected by the regular user of the market[3].

1   CJA 1993, s 53(4) and Sch 1, para 2.
2   Compare the comments of the Economic Secretary, Parliamentary Debates, House of Commons, Standing Committee B, 15 June 1993, column 216 in respect of the defence of market information under the CJA 1993.
3   See CP 59, para 6.50.

9.33   The safe harbour afforded by the Code of Market Conduct is that 'dealing' or arranging deals will not amount to misuse of information solely because it is based on information as to that person's intention or any other person's intention to deal or arrange deals in relation to any 'qualifying investment' or information concerning transactions that have taken place[1]. However, behaviour based on information as to a possible takeover bid or relating to new offers, issues, placements or other primary market activity is excluded from this defence[2].

1   MAR 1.4.26.
2   MAR 1.4.26.

9.34   From the outset, the FSA has emphasised that the free use of trading information was without prejudice to any other regulatory or legal obligations governing the use of such information[1]. The FSA has in this context emphasised the importance of obligations of confidentiality to customers by authorised firms and the threat of disciplinary action to firms improperly transmitting information under all or any of the FSA's Principles for Businesses 1 (integrity), 2 (skill, care and diligence) and 6 (customers' interests)[2]. Further, the FSA has made clear that MAR 1.4.26 does not legitimise the 'front running' of customer orders[3].

1   See CP 10 and 59, para 6.49.
2   CP 59, para 6.54.
3   MAR 1.4.27.

9.35   One of the areas of consultation in respect of this safe harbour has been whether the defence should be restricted by reference to a person's own or his customer's intentions to deal[1]. The FSA retained the broader definition of 'any other person's intention' following representations from practitioners. The persuasive argument seems to have been the expectation of market users to take advantage of their ability to understand, analyse and assess the implication of transaction flows through the market in reaching this conclusion[2]. Once again, one sees the FSA responding to the practice of the market in endeavouring to create a workable Code of Market Conduct.

1   CP 59, para 6.51.
2   CP 59, para 6.54.

Facilitation of takeover bids and other market operations

9.36   Without further clarification, a person building a stake in a takeover bid would be caught by the market abuse regime since the knowledge that he was pursuing a takeover bid would be 'relevant knowledge' that is not 'generally available'. Accordingly, a tightly worded safe harbour has been created in respect of the facilitation of takeover bids 'and other market operations'. The clarity of this safe harbour in its final form[1] improves upon earlier versions[2].

1 MAR 1.4.28–1.4.30.
2 Eg CP 76 at MAR 1.5.28–1.5.29.

9.37 The safe harbour sets out first the circumstances in which the dealing or arranging deals must take place at MAR 1.4.28(1). These are:

- in connection with the acquisition or disposal of an equity or non-equity stake in a company;
- engaged in for the sole purpose of making the acquisition or disposal (this is illustrated by MAR 1.4.30 considered below); and
- engaged in for the sole benefit of the person making the acquisition or disposal.

9.38 MAR 1.4.28(2) then sets out the information that benefits from this safe harbour. This includes the identity of the persons involved or likely to be involved in any capacity in an acquisition or disposal and the price (or range of prices) at which investments have been or are to be acquired or disposed of or may be acquired or disposed of.

9.39 The FSA give examples of the type of behaviour that it believes are within the safe harbour, although it should be noted that these are merely of evidential value. The examples given include seeking from holders of securities irrevocable undertakings or expressions of support to accept an offer to acquire those securities[1]. The FSA also makes clear that while building or assisting in building a stake or other market operations are within the safe harbour, a bidder who enters into transactions that afford him economic exposure are outside the safe harbour[2]. Similarly, a person who acts for a bidder cannot deal for their own benefit in 'qualifying investments' or 'relevant products' in respect of information concerning the bid which is 'relevant information'[3].

1 MAR 1.4.29.
2 MAR 1.4.30.
3 MAR 1.4.30.

9.40 The FSA's guidance on 'requiring or encouraging' at MAR 1.8.6 should also be noted in this context. The FSA acknowledges that a person making a takeover bid must pass information that is relevant information that is not generally available to certain parties, such as professional advisors, and confirms that this will not amount to 'requiring or encouraging'. The Listing Rules and the Model Code (see, eg, Listing Rules 9.4, 9.5 and 9.15 and Model Code, paras 11 and 12) should also be noted in this context[1]. The final version of the Code of Market Conduct has been streamlined on the latter provisions[2].

1 MAR 1.7.3.
2 Compare, eg, CP 76 at MAR 1.9.5 and 1.9.9.

9.41 Similarly, MAR 1.8.7 should be mentioned. This provides that a person ('A') will not be regarded as having required or encouraged another person ('B') to engage in behaviour amounting to market abuse in circumstances where (a) A is an advisor to B and B is considering the acquisition or disposal of an equity or non-equity stake and (b) A advises B to acquire or dispose of an equity or non-equity stake in the target company for the purposes and in the manner specified in the safe harbour in MAR 1.4.28. However, clearly if A were then to proceed to deal in qualifying investments affected by such information, A would himself be committing market abuse.

9.42 Given the substantial opportunity for market abuse in the context of a takeover bid both in terms of variety of offenders and the seismic effect that a takeover may have on a wide range of products, the clarity with which the FSA has expressed itself on the facilitation of takeover bids is to be commended. Those representing someone who has succumbed to the temptation of dealing on the basis of this type of information for personal gain are left with little room for imaginative argument. The narrowly drafted defence allows little manoeuvre, by contrast with the more loosely worded counterpart defence in the CJA 1993[1].

1 CJA 1993, s 53(4) and Sch 1, para 3.

Other lines of defence

9.43 The safe harbours are more concerned with the character of behaviour rather than the character of information. However, consideration should also be given to whether the information in question was itself 'relevant' and 'generally available'. For instance, could the information be obtained by research or analysis or observation?[1] Does the information concern future developments, which at the time of dealing were not yet certain?[2] Would a 'regular user' expect such information to be disclosed or announced to other market users?[3] These and other aspects of the information relevant to market abuse were considered in more detail in Chapter 6.

1 FSMA 2000, s 118(7) and MAR 1.4.5.
2 MAR 1.4.10.
3 MAR 1.4.12.

9.44 Further, the alleged offender may argue that he has not fallen below the standards expected of him by the regular user, for instance by reason of his knowledge, skill and experience. Alternatively, it may be argued that the behaviour in question is in accordance with the standards expected by the 'regular user'. With regard to the latter, it must be remembered that the 'regular user' is not an actual user, but a hypothetical user who is only persuaded, but not convinced, by the actual practice of a market place. The 'regular user' test was considered in greater detail in Chapter 6.

Market manipulation

False or misleading impressions

Permitted transactions

9.45   MAR 1.5.24 provides that behaviour which satisfies the legitimate commercial rationale and executed in a proper way tests in MAR 1.5.8 will not amount to market abuse even though the conditions described in relation to artificial transactions are satisfied where the following conditions are also satisfied:

- transactions which effect the taking of a position, or the unwinding of a position taken, so as to take legitimate advantage of:
  - (a) differences in the taxation of income or capital returns generated by 'investments' or 'commodities' (whether such differences arise solely because of the identity of the person entitled to receive such income or capital or otherwise); or
  - (b) differences in the 'prices' of 'investments' or 'commodities' as traded in different locations; or
- transactions which effect the lending or borrowing of 'qualifying investments' or 'commodities' so as to meet an underlying commercial demand for the 'investment' or 'commodity'.

Required reporting or disclosure of transactions

9.46   MAR 1.5.25 makes clear that making a report or disclosure will not of itself give rise to a false or misleading impression if made in accordance with the way specified by any applicable legal or regulatory requirement and the report or disclosure was expressly required or expressly permitted by the FSA Rules or the rules of a prescribed market or the rules of the Takeover Code or SARs or by any other applicable statute or regulation or the rules of any competent statutory, governmental or regulatory authority. This safe harbour has been slightly modified in the final text[1]. The final text isolates the manner of disclosure from what is in fact disclosed. This approach now makes superfluous the previous paragraphs devoted to the Listing Rules and reporting cross-trades. The Code now also gives specific examples of required disclosure and reporting at MAR 1.5.26.

1   Compare CP 76 at MAR 1.5.25.

Chinese Walls

9.47   Given that the knowledge of employees is likely to be imputed to their employer, an organisation could find itself in a position where an individual for whom it is responsible should have known that information he is disseminating is false or misleading by reason of information held by another section of the organisation. The FSA has responded to such concerns by creating a new safe harbour concerned with Chinese Walls in the final text of the Code at MAR 1.5.27. In summary, where effective Chinese Walls are established or there are similar effective arrangements and there was nothing which was known or ought reasonably to have been known to the individual who disseminated the information which should have led him to conclude it was false or misleading, the organisation will not be attributed with both pieces of conflicting information. MAR 1.5.28 and 1.5.29 expand upon these factors. This safe harbour does seem superfluous when one considers the 'regular user' test set down by the Act. Would a 'regular user' really have the concerns raised in these circumstances?

Distortion of the market

9.48 Behaviour which complies with London Metal Exchange rules contained in 'Market Aberrations: the Way Forward' published in October 1998, which govern the 'behaviour' expected of long position holders, will not amount to market abuse in that the behaviour will not amount to distortion[1].

1   MAR 1.6.19.

City Code

9.49 The FSA has exercised the powers conferred by the FSMA 2000, s 120 with the approval of HM Treasury in MAR 1.7.7–1.7.8[1]. The safe harbours created are conclusive that behaviour does not amount to market abuse. These powers have been exercised in relation to market manipulation only and not in relation to misuse of information[2]. The FSA has clarified in the final text of the Code at MAR 1.7.6 that it is of the view that the other provisions of the Takeover Code and SARs do not permit or require behaviour which amounts to market abuse.

1   MAR 1.7.4.
2   MAR 1.7.5.

9.50 First, behaviour conforming with any of the rules of the City Code or SARs in relation to the timing, dissemination or availability, content and standard of care applicable to a disclosure, announcement, communication or release of information and which are specified in MAR 1, Annex 2G, does not of itself amount to market abuse in that the behaviour does not give rise to a false or misleading impression or distortion in so far as the behaviour is expressly required or permitted by the rule in question[1]. Further, behaviour conforming with Rule 4.2 of the City Code (in relation to restrictions on dealings by offeror and concert parties) does not of itself amount to market abuse in that the behaviour does not give rise to a false or misleading impression or distortion in so far as behaviour is expressly required or expressly permitted by that rule[2].

1   MAR 1.7.7.
2   MAR 1.7.8.

9.51   These safe harbours are subject to MAR 1.7.10 which provides that these provisions do not apply where behaviour which conforms with the particular rule of the City Code is nonetheless in breach of any general principle set out at section B of the City Code which is relevant to that rule.

9.52   MAR 1.7.11–1.7.13 expand upon these provisions. MAR 1.7.13 makes clear that where MAR 1.7.7 and 1.7.8 do not apply, mere compliance with the City Code or the SARs does not absolve behaviour that is otherwise market abuse in some other respect. The example given is where a person complies with Rule 1 of the SARs in relation to building a stake, but his decision to build a stake is based on relevant information that is not generally available and is outside any of the safe harbours relating to misuse of information. In these circumstances, the behaviour would be likely to amount to market abuse.

Other lines of defence

9.53   It will be recalled that within false or misleading impressions there are a number of different types of defence, depending on which particular type of market abuse is alleged. For instance, in 'artificial transactions' and 'course of conduct' cases, the defence will seek to establish that the behaviour in question was motivated by a legitimate commercial rationale and executed in a proper way. Similarly, where disseminating information is alleged, the defence will be particularly concerned to convince the Financial Services and Markets Tribunal in relation to the motive of the person making disclosure and when it became clear that the information in question was false or misleading. Finally, where the FSA alleges that false or misleading information has been disseminated through an accepted channel, the defence will be concerned to establish reasonable care on the part of the person submitting such information to the channel in question.

One of the main areas of dispute in relation to distortion of the market is likely to be whether a person had the motive to distort the market. It is suggested that this requirement is likely to be most easily satisfied by the FSA where there is a scheme between a number of parties and sales of artificially inflated stocks to customers of one of the parties[1].

1   Compare the allegations made by the SEC in *SEC v Leonard B Greer and Judah Wernick* Civil Action No 97, Civ 7267, Litigation Release No 17026/5 June 2001.

Conclusion

9.54   The CJA 1993 provides a series of defences to deal with what may be broadly described as 'motive' and also with particular market situations. The Code of Market Conduct explains that behaviour in conformity with any FSA rule will not amount to market abuse *only* if the rule expressly requires or permits the person to engage in the behaviour in question. The FSA Rules containing a provision to the effect that behaviour conforming to that rule does not amount to market abuse are the price stabilisation rules, the rules relating to Chinese Walls and certain parts of the Listing Rules in MAR 1, Annex 1G. Further, this chapter addressed the extent to which other regulatory rules, such as the City Code, the Model Code and the rules of RIEs, attract safe harbour status and thus provide a defence to market abuse under the FSMA 2000. The FSA has rejected the argument that there should be a blanket exemption for behaviour in compliance with the rules of RIEs or the City Code. The FSA, acting pursuant to the FSMA 2000, s 120, has decided to provide safe harbour status for certain rules of the RIEs and provisions of the Takeover Code.

CHAPTER 10

Model codes

Introduction

10.1 As discussed in previous chapters, the freedom of directors and other insiders of listed companies to deal in their company's securities is restricted in a number of ways – namely, by statute, common law and regulation. In addition to these legal and regulatory requirements, there have been further extra-legal restrictions on the disclosure of price-sensitive information and in dealing on the basis of inside information that derives from the standards and codes of the self-regulatory organisations ('SROs') that were in effect under the Financial Services Act 1986 and which have been reincorporated, with some modification, under the Financial Services and Markets Act 2000 ('FSMA 2000'). Indeed, the FSMA 2000 contains the legal definition of market abuse and requires the FSA to produce a Code of Market Conduct that sets out detailed standards to be observed by everyone who uses the UK markets. Moreover, extra-legal codes and rules for disclosure of share dealing on the basis of inside information can also be found in the City Code on Takeovers and Mergers ('City Code')[1], which is administered by the City Takeover Panel.

1 See *Gore-Browne on Companies* (2000), ss 29.1–29.6.

10.2 This chapter describes the role of the Code of Market Conduct and analyses some of the reporting requirements of the FSA Rules, such as the Listing Rules and Model Code[1]. The chapter also discusses the disclosure requirements of the City Code and how its restrictions on disclosure during takeovers may be treated as a safe harbour under the FSA regime. The City Code and the Listing Rules, along with the Model Code, have long contained provisions designed to discourage insider dealing and market abuse[2] by relying on the principle of timely disclosure as a means to promote fair, transparent and efficient markets. Effective disclosure means that information must be disclosed in a timely manner, which will reduce the opportunities for insiders to take advantage of information asymmetries in the market place. Moreover, the City Code, Listing Rules and Model Code contain procedures for the handling of price-sensitive information which requires that such information be kept confidential until the appropriate time to disclose it[3]. The Listing Rules, Model Code and City Code all denounce insider dealing and thereby provide a basis for disciplinary action under the FSMA 2000 market abuse regime[4].

1   Formerly known as the Listing Rules of the London Stock Exchange. See *Gore-Browne on Companies*, Appendix A, the Listing Rules, A.001–A.017.
2   See B A K Rider at al, *Guide to Financial Services Regulation* (1997, CCH) p 218.
3   *Guide to Financial Services Regulation*, p 218.
4   See B A K Rider and M Ashe, *Insider Crime* (1993, Jordans) p 79.

Background to self-regulation and compliance

10.3   As discussed in Chapter 1, the first substantive provisions that were aimed at insider dealing were introduced in the Companies Act 1967, which prohibited directors, their spouses and infant children from purchasing options in the securities of their company or a related company[1]. These prohibitions applied regardless of whether there had been any allegations of insider dealing amongst the insiders. An important rationale of these provisions was to prevent insider speculation and not insider dealing per se, although it was recognised that the acquisition of options by insiders enabled them to take advantage of insider information. The difficulty in proving these offences resulted in few prosecutions.

1   See the Companies Act 1985, ss 323–327.

10.4   Notwithstanding the legal restrictions of the Companies Act, however, the system of control and supervision of financial markets prior to 1986 was, by and large, self-regulatory in character in which non-statutory rules regulated the behaviour of those conducting investment business[1]. Substantial reliance was placed on the efficacy of self-regulatory procedures with respect to insider dealing through a range of institutions, the most prominent of which were the Panel on Takeovers and Mergers and its City Code and the London Stock Exchange's Model Code[2]. Although these bodies were well placed to make self-regulation serve the needs of market participants by controlling access to the privileges of the market, insider dealing was a practice that pervaded the UK market. By 1973, however, self-regulatory bodies such as the Panel on Takeovers and Mergers and the Stock Exchange recognised that legislation was required to make insider dealing a criminal offence[3].

1   See B A K Rider (ed), *The Regulation of the British Securities Industry* (1979, Oyez) at Chapters 1 and 2.
2   Before the FSMA 2000, the Model Code appeared in the Appendix to Chapter 16 of the Listing Rules.
3   See Rider and Ashe, *Insider Crime – the New Law* (1993) p 79.

10.5   After the 1980 companies legislation criminalised insider dealing, the burden of enforcement shifted from the City bodies to government.

Although self-regulatory bodies continued to discourage and detect market abuse, the government took the lead in enforcing the criminal prohibition on insider dealing. Later, the Financial Services Act 1986, whilst maintaining self-regulation as an essential element of the overall regulatory regime, returned the primary responsibility for policing insider dealing and market abuse to the self-regulatory bodies. The Financial Services Act 1986 authorised the designated SROs to ensure that their members complied with the law on insider dealing and with the relevant conduct of business standard set by the Securities and Investments Board ('SIB') for the conduct of investment business[1]. Although many of the standards adopted by the SROs had a bearing on fair dealing and probity, the SIB had always required compliance with the law prohibiting insider dealing. For instance, Core Rule 28(2) imposed an obligation on firms to use their best efforts to ensure that they do not knowingly effect, either in the course of regulated business or otherwise, a transaction for a customer which it knows is prohibited by the CJA 1993, s 51. This type of facilitative liability places an obligation on a firm to use reasonable care not to facilitate the execution of transactions for their customers which would constitute insider dealing. In other words, firms are under a positive duty not to transact business for persons whom they know are relying on the transaction in question to commit an offence. If members of a firm facilitate an insider dealing transaction and are not aware of having done so, they will not have breached the Core Rule, so long as the Chinese Wall defence operates in such cases. Under the Core Rules, the firm was not under an obligation to question their clients in order to determine whether a transaction was objectionable. The Rule would only apply when the firm had actual knowledge that the transaction was objectionable. This actual knowledge standard was to be judged on a subjective basis and most experts agreed that to 'know', in this context, would have included deliberately closing one's eyes[2], but it was still necessary to prove that those who were responsible did actually know the facts. Although it was true that knowledge based on a reasonable person test would raise an inference against the alleged facilitator, that would not, in itself, constitute knowledge. Professor David Hayton has referred to this standard of knowledge as 'Nelsonian knowledge', ie knowledge that was obtainable, but for deliberately shutting one's eyes to the obvious[3].

1   Rider and Ashe, *Insider Crime – the New Law* citing J Suter, *The Regulation of Insider Dealing in Britain* (1989, Butterworths) Chapter 2 and B Rider, C Abrams and E Ferran, *CCH Guide to the Financial Services Act 1986* (2nd edn, CCH) Chapter 3.
2   See Rider and Ashe, p 80.
3   David J Hayton, *The Law of Trusts* (3rd edn, 1996, Sweet & Maxwell) p 22.

10.6   Under Core Rule 29(1) and (2), however, a firm would not have incurred liability where the inside information is the firm's own intentions to take a particular position in the market. Core Rule 28(3)(b) also excluded from the application of the obligations under Core Rule 29(1) and (2) a firm which is a recognised market maker which is under an obligation to deal in the relevant securities. This allowed a market maker which has been duly recognised by an investment exchange to maintain its proper function in the market by ensuring stability and liquidity. Moreover, Core Rule 29(c) excluded a firm if it served as a trustee or personal representative, provided that it acted on the advice of a third party appearing to be an appropriate adviser who was not prohibited from dealing under the CJA 1993.

10.7 The SIB and each SRO and recognised professional body had its own rule book, but there was a certain cohesion that existed because of what was described as the 'new settlement', which was brought about by amendments introduced by the Companies Act 1989[1]. The new settlement provided for three tiers of Conduct of Business Rules that applied to all those who conducted investment business in the UK, which included all those who were directly authorised by the SIB or by one of the SROs or to any person who had not sought authorisation. The first tier consisted of ten general principles that had very little to do with insider dealing or market abuse. The second tier was the most significant tier and it consisted of a series of Core Rules promulgated by the SIB for general application throughout the industry. The third tier consisted of rules and codes that provided a more detailed understanding of how the Core Rules would apply to the relevant areas of industry activity[2]. For purposes of this discussion, it is necessary to focus on the Core Rules and in particular the Rule that addressed insider dealing, Rule 28(1).

1   See J Pritchard, 'Investor Protection Sacrificed: the new Settlement' (1992) 13 Company Lawyer 171.
2   There was some variation in the rules of the SROs in this third tier and even some so-called 'derogations' in regard to the Core Rules themselves. See Rider and Ashe, p 80.

10.8   Core Rule 28(1) provided that 'a firm must not effect (either in the UK or elsewhere) an own account transaction when it knows of circumstances when one of its associates, or an employee, is prohibited from effecting that transaction by the statutory restrictions on insider dealing'. Most experts viewed this Rule as providing a civil remedy to supplement the criminal provisions against insider dealing because it expressly provides that a firm can be liable, whereas the criminal offences only apply to individuals[1], but it should be noted that a firm will only be liable for a breach of Core Rule 28(1) if it was aware that someone connected with it cannot deal by virtue of the CJA 1993, s 51. Core Rule 36(3) provided that a firm will only be taken to have acted knowingly if the individuals who had acted on behalf of the firm act with knowledge. Thus, a firm would not violate Core Rule 28(1) if it had had an effective Chinese Wall, so that those who had dealt in the relevant securities were not aware that their colleagues were prohibited from so dealing. In the absence of a Chinese Wall, Core Rule 36(3) resulted in civil liability for the firm when one of its associates, the firm itself or an employee of either is actually within the scope of the CJA 1993, s 51[2].

1   See Rider and Ashe, p 81. Moreover, before the FSMA 2000, it was true that a breach of the Core Rules could give rise to civil liability under the FSA 1986, ss 61 and 62.

2   In this context, associates include individuals who were appointed as representatives of the firm or any other person whose business or domestic relationships with the firm or, for that matter, another associate, could reasonably be expected to give rise to a community of interest between them which may involve a conflict of interest in dealings with third parties. See Rider and Ashe, p 81.

10.9   Civil liability could also arise for the firm when conduct was outside the scope of a Core Rule, such as Core Rule 28, through what was formerly the SIB's General Principles. Specifically, General Principle 1 stated that a 'firm should observe high standards of integrity and fair dealing'. Moreover, General Principle 3 created an obligation for firms to comply with good market practices and with such codes and other standards which had been endorsed by the SIB (today the FSA). This meant that the City Code and the Model Code would have been considered binding on firms. However, failure to comply with what was formerly the SIB's General Principles did not result in civil liability under the Financial Services Act 1986, ss 61 and 62[1].

1   See Rider and Ashe, p 81.

The London Stock Exchange's Listing Rules

10.10   The London Stock Exchange first published the Model Code in 1977[1]. This established minimum standards of good practice as a guide for listed companies to measure and improve their own internal compliance procedures. The Stock Exchange's Listing Rules imposed a contractual obligation on listed issuers that they must operate rules no less demanding than those contained in the Model Code. Knox J expressed this view in *Chase Manhattan Equities Ltd v Goodman*[2] that the obligation to operate such procedures is placed on the company and not on individual company directors. In this case, the failure of a director of a company to report dealings to his company in violation of the Model Code was held not to have been a misrepresentation to third persons with whom he had transacted. Knox J recognised that a duty to speak to one person, here the company, might give rise to liability to a third person, but in this case the contention that breach of the Code constituted a misrepresentation to the market was held to be untenable[3]. It should be emphasised, however, that Knox J viewed the director in question to be under an obligation to comply with the Model Code, as he was aware of its terms, even though there was no evidence that his company had incorporated the Model Code into any contract with him. According to this view, it could also be argued that a breach of the terms of the Model Code, even if it has not been incorporated into the contract, would give rise to a claim in damages, though some experts observe that it would justify dismissal[4].

1   See M Ashe and L Counsell, *Insider Trading* (1994, Tolley).
2   [1991] BCLC 897 at 924.
3   [1991] BCLC 897 at 929.
4   See Rider and Ashe, p 83.

10.11   The Model Code provides guidance in this area by emphasising that there is no objection to a director investing in the securities of his own company. Model Code Rule 4, however, requires that any insider dealing in the shares of a company must comply with the law restricting insider dealing. For example, before a director purchases shares in its company, he must notify an appointed director or the board of directors prior to any dealings in the securities of the company[1]. The Model Code applies to dealings by or on behalf of a director's spouse or infant child. The Model Code also applies in full force to investments of a director that have been placed under discretionary management. Whilst the Model Code only applies to directors and their families, boards are encouraged to apply the same standards to relevant employees.

1   Model Code, Rule 6.

10.12   Unlike the CJA 1993, the Model Code is not applicable to non-UK listed companies operating in the UK. The prohibitions on insider dealing contained in the CJA 1993 are extended by the Model Code to transactions called 'closed periods' where, although not a criminal offence, a director of a listed company is not permitted to deal. Model Code Rule 3 prohibits a director who is in the possession of price-sensitive information from dealing in the securities of his own company or in the securities of another UK listed company. It should be emphasised that restrictions on a director's dealings in its own company will apply irrespective of how the director came into possession of the information. The Stock Exchange adopted Rule 1(f) of the Model Code which defined price-sensitive information to be any information regarding transactions that are required to be notified to the Company Announcements Office according to Chapters 10 and 11 of the Listing Rules[1]. The FSA has now adopted this definition for the UK Listing Rules.

1   Model Code, Rule 1(f). This was taken from the definition of price-sensitive information under the Company Securities (Insider Dealing) Act 1985, s 10.

10.13   In May 2000, the supervisory authority exercised by the London Stock Exchange over the Listing Rules and Model Code was transferred to the FSA, as required by the FSMA 2000. In regard to insider dealing, the FSA has incorporated the standards and rules of disclosure as provided in the Listing Rules and Model Code into the new market abuse regime.

The Code on Takeovers and Mergers

10.14   Traditionally, a significant area of regulation in the area of insider dealing and market abuse derives from non-statutory regulation. This section is concerned principally with the conduct of transactions. This involves the non-statutory model codes that are applied in the securities markets to such transactions where there is a change in control of a publicly-listed company resident in the UK or of certain types of private companies. The City Code and the Rules Governing Substantial Acquisition in Shares ('SARs') contain legally non-binding principles regarding disclosure of information and other procedures that govern matters related to takeovers and mergers. The City Code provides an institutional framework of norms and rules within which takeovers are conducted.

10.15   The Panel on Takeovers and Mergers ('the Panel') operates and applies the Code and SARs to ensure fair and equal treatment of all shareholders in relation to takeovers. The Panel has existing responsibilities to ensure the fair and equitable treatment of all shareholders in regard to takeovers and mergers.

The Code

10.16   The Code's responsibilities apply to those who are actively engaged in the securities markets and to the directors of companies which are subject to the Code and the new FSA regime. It also applies to any person seeking to gain or consolidate effective control of such companies or to any person who is knowingly concerned in such transactions to which the Code applies and includes professional advisers to the extent that they advise on such transactions. The principle of Rule 3 exhorts all persons (whether acting on behalf of offeror or offeree) to be aware of the provisions of the Code and to comply with its standards and rules.

10.17   The Code consists of ten General Principles and 30 Rules[1]. General Principle 6 addresses the issue of market manipulation of the shares of a company by directors or others in control of the company. It states:

> 'All parties to an offer must use every endeavour to prevent the creation of a false market in the securities of an offeror or offeree company. Parties involved in such transactions must take care that statements are not made which may mislead shareholders or the market'.

1   The Code also provides explanatory notes for many of the Rules, which explain how the Panel will interpret most aspects of the Rules and appendices that provide guidance on the application of several of the Rules to actual takeover situations. See the discussion in *Gore-Browne on Companies*, s 29.4.

10.18   General Principle 9 requires directors to give regard to the interests of the company and shareholders when deciding what course of action to advise for shareholders[1].

1   It states that directors of an offeror or offeree company must always, in advising their shareholders, act only in their capacity as directors and not have regard to their personal or family shareholdings or to their personal relationships with the companies.

Dealings and restrictions on the acquisition of shares and rights over shares

10.19 Rules 4–8 apply to transactions in the context of takeover or merger transactions. These rules establish standards and rules for certain circumstances which apply to a broader range of activity than does the CJA 1993, Pt V. The Panel defines 'derivative' to mean 'any financial product whose value in whole or in part is determined directly or indirectly by reference to the price of an underlying security but which does not include the possibility of delivery of such underlying securities'[1]. The Panel's note explains that the City Code does not intend to restrict dealings in, or require disclosure of, derivatives which have no connection with an offer or an anticipated offer. The Code will regulate the speed by which the acquisition of shares and rights over shares take place both before and during a takeover transaction when the SARs do not apply[2].

1   *Gore-Browne on Companies*, s 29.10.
2   See s 29.10.

10.20 Rule 4 prohibits any kind of dealings in the securities of a company (including options and derivatives in reference to such securities) by any person, other than the potential offeror, who is privy to confidential, price-sensitive information. Such information must concern an offer or a contemplated offer between the time when there is reason to suppose that an approach to, or an offer for, the company is contemplated and the time of announcement of the approach or the offer or the termination of discussions. It is also prohibited to make any recommendations to any other person as to dealing in the offeree's shares. Similarly, any dealings in the securities of the offeror company are also prohibited except where the securities of such proposed offer are not price sensitive. Although these restrictions generally do not apply to the potential offeror, other restrictions on dealings apply by RIEs and ordinary standards of business practice. Moreover, there may be restrictions that prevent the offeror from dealing before the announcement of an offer if confidential price-sensitive information has been received by the offeree[1].

1   Special disclosure provisions will apply to persons who are part of a consortium making an offer and to other persons acting in concert with the offeror.

10.21 Rule 4 also prohibits any financial adviser or stockbroker (or any person controlling, controlled by or under the same control as any such adviser or stockbroker) to an offeree company from purchasing, for its own account, the shares or derivatives or options of such shares of an offeree company[1]. Moreover, during the offer period, the Code restricts an offeror's ability to sell shares in the target company by prohibiting the ability of the offeror and persons acting in concert with it to sell securities in the offeree company except with prior consent of the Panel. Rule 5 restricts the speed by which voting shares and rights over voting shares may be obtained. This requirement prevents a unilateral offeror from taking its holding of shares and rights to 30% or more of the offeree company until after the first closing date of the offer period. Rule 6 requires that the level of any general offer is no less favourable than the highest price paid by the offeror to acquire any shares in the offeree within a three-month period prior to commencement of the offer period. Moreover, Principle 6 requires all parties to a takeover to take early measures to avoid the creation of a false market in the securities of the offeror or offeree and to use reasonable care to avoid making statements which may mislead shareholders or the market. Other restrictions apply to the substantial acquisition of shares by insiders and those with control[2]. Rule 8 sets out an array of requirements regarding the announcement of dealings during an offer period. The overall objective of public disclosure of dealings is to ensure the maintenance of an orderly, informed and efficient market during the course of a takeover.

1   Although these Rules do not apply, however, to exempt market makers and exempt fund managers, Rule 38.5 requires that such dealings be disclosed to the market and to the Panel on the next business day following the transaction. See *Gore-Browne on Companies*, s 29.22.
2   *Gore-Browne on Companies*, s 29.10.

FSA Rules and the Codes

10.22   The FSA has the parallel responsibility of pursuing its objectives of promoting market confidence and integrity by deterring and detecting market abuse. It does so by interpreting and applying the principles and requirements of the Code of Market Conduct, its Listing Rules, price stabilisation rules and rules regarding Chinese Walls. Moreover, the FSMA 2000, s 120 confers a power on the FSA to include a provision to the effect that behaviour conforming to the City Code does not amount to market abuse, provided approval has been obtained from the Treasury. The FSA has created such safe harbour status for various provisions of the City Code and certain rules of UK recognised investment exchanges (ie SARs). This section will analyse some of the provisions of these codes and rules and how they can create safe harbour status[1].

1   Chapter 9 discussed how these safe harbours provided defences to charges of market abuse and this section will add to the analysis.

The Code of Market Conduct

10.23   The FSMA 2000, s 119 requires the FSA to issue a Code of Market Conduct[1]. The FSMA 2000, s 122 sets out the status of the Code[2], namely that it has evidential weight as to whether market abuse (as defined in the FSMA 2000, s 118) has occurred, except where the Code contains a description of behaviour that does not, in the FSA's opinion, amount to market abuse. The FSA's determinations as to whether certain behaviour amounts to market abuse is legally binding under s 118. The Code was issued by the FSA board on 19 July 2001 and came into effect at N2 (midnight on 30 November 2001). The Code addresses three broad types of market abuse that have been analysed in previous chapters: misuse of information, creating false or misleading impressions and distorting the market. The Code applies to behaviour which occurs in relation to trading on the UK's recognised investment exchanges. Section 118(3) allows the Treasury to prescribe markets and qualifying investments, which it has done by issuing the Prescribed Markets and Qualifying Investments Order 2001. The Code notes that this Order makes certain kinds of investment 'traded on' *prescribed markets qualifying investments*[3]. The Treasury had prescribed all markets established under the rules of a UK recognised investment exchange as markets to which s 118 applies[4].

1 FSMA 2000, Sch 1, para 1(2) sets out the FSA's legislative functions, one of which is to 'issue' a Code of Market Conduct under the FSMA 2000, s 119.
2 The final version of the Code was published in April 2001, but was still subject to some technical changes, which were made and approved when the FSA board 'issued' the final version of the Code on 19 July 2001. This issued version is now available on the FSA website: www.fsa.gov.uk
3 MAR 1.11.2G.
4 As of 1 September 2001, the prescribed UK RIEs are: COREDEAL Ltd, the International Petroleum Exchange of London Ltd, Jiway Ltd, LIFFE Administration and Management, the London Metal Exchange Ltd, London Stock Exchange plc, OM London Exchange Ltd and virt-x Exchange Ltd.

10.24 The Code provides general categories of safe harbours with respect to the offences of misuse of information[1], creating false or misleading impressions[2] and market distortion[3]. For example, the safe harbours that apply to the offence of market manipulation describe behaviour that does not amount to market abuse in that the behaviour does not give rise to false or misleading impressions. One such example of behaviour that will not give rise to false or misleading impressions, provided certain conditions are satisfied[4], would apply to transactions which effect the taking of a position, or the unwinding of a position taken, so as to take legitimate advantage of:

- differences in the income or capital returns generated by investments or commodities (whether such differences solely arise because of the identity of the person entitled to receive such income or capital or otherwise);
- differences in the prices of investments or commodities as traded in different locations; or
- transactions which effect the lending or borrowing of *qualifying investments or commodities* so as to meet an underlying commercial demand for the *investment or commodity*[5].

1 MAR 1.4.20C, 1.4.21C, 1.4.24, 1.4.26C, 1.4.28C and 1.4.31C.
2 MAR 1.5.24C, 1.5.25C, 1.5.27C and 1.5.28C.
3 MAR 1.6.19.
4 These conditions are found in MAR 1.5.8E(1)–(5).
5 MAR 1.5.24C(1)(a)–(c).

10.25 Another safe harbour provides that the reporting or disclosure of transactions will not, of itself, give rise to a misleading or false impression if:

- the report or disclosure was made in accordance with the way specified by any applicable legal or regulatory requirement; and
- the report or disclosure was expressly required or expressly permitted by the rules of a *prescribed market*, the rules of the Takeover Code or SARs or by any other applicable statute or regulation or the rules of any competent statutory, governmental or regulatory authority[1].

As discussed in Chapter 2, an example of disclosure is that required or expressly permitted in Listing Rule 9.10(j) which allows a company to delay certain announcements at its discretion and the Companies Act 1985, s 198 which requires disclosure of certain interests in shares.

1   MAR 1.5.25C(1)–(2).

10.26   Another safe harbour involves organisations that may not be aware of information that is known to certain individuals within the organisation. If an individual within the organisation disseminates information which he would know, or could reasonably be expected to know, is false or misleading if he were aware of information held by other individuals within the organisation, then the organisation will be presumed not to know, or to be reasonably expected to know, that the information was false or misleading if:

- the other information in question is held behind an effective Chinese Wall or is restricted using other similarly effective arrangements; and
- when nothing was known, or ought reasonably to have been known, to the individual who disseminated the information which should have led him to conclude it was false or misleading.

10.27   As discussed above, the FSMA 2000 provides statutory exceptions for two types of behaviour in relation to the market abuse regime: behaviour which is described in the Code as not amounting to market abuse[1] and behaviour which conforms with an FSA rule where that rule includes a provision to the effect that behaviour conforming with that rule does not amount to market abuse[2]. The Code refers to specific instances of both these exceptions as 'safe harbours'. Behaviour will be regarded as conforming to an FSA rule only if it is required or expressly permitted by that rule. To qualify for this safe harbour, there must be a specific rule that either requires or expressly permits a person to engage in the behaviour in question.

1   MAR 1.1.10G.
2   FSMA 2000, s 118(8).

10.28   The FSA Rules which contain a provision to the effect that behaviour conforming with that rule does not amount to market abuse are: the price stabilising rules[1], rules relating to Chinese Walls[2] and those parts of the Listing Rules which relate to the timing, dissemination or availability, content and standard of care applicable to a disclosure, announcement, communication or release of information[3] and Rule 15.1(b) of the Listing Rules (relating to share buy backs). This would cover conduct which complies with the FSA's stabilisation rules and control mechanisms established to comply with the requirements of Chinese Walls. The FSMA 2000, however, does not provide a blanket safe harbour for all FSA rules because most FSA rules address matters wholly unconnected to market abuse, eg capital adequacy or marketing standards for the sale of securities. To establish a blanket safe harbour protection for all FSA rules and regulations could create uncertainty such that, in the absence of the safe harbour, the conduct governed by these rules might otherwise amount to market abuse.

1 MAR 2.1.1R(2).
2 COB 2.4.4R(1)–(4) and see MAR 1.4.21C and 1.5.27C.
3 MAR 1, Annex 1G.

The Listing Rules[1]

10.29 The FSA assumed the responsibility of acting as the UK Listing Authority ('UKLA') in 2000. The FSA also has authority over updating and interpreting the Model Code.

1 See the Listing Rules in *Gore-Browne on Companies*, Appendix A, A.001–A.017.

10.30 A central requirement of the FSA's Listing Rules is that issuers should make information available to the market in a timely and comprehensive manner and that such information which is disclosed should be accurate and not misleading. The Listing Rules also regulate dealings in listed securities by issuers, their directors and their relevant employees. As a result, the Listing Rules and the market abuse regime have a certain degree of overlap as defined under the FSMA 2000 and the Code. The FSA has addressed the issue of how best to reconcile the overlapping features of both regimes and has recognised that both play a vital role in protecting investors and supporting market confidence.

10.31 The FSA has been reviewing its Listing Rules to determine whether they should expressly provide that certain conduct that conforms with the rules does not amount to market abuse. In its capacity as UKLA, the FSA seeks to maintain the regulatory effectiveness of its Listing Rules by ensuring that when the Listing Rules expressly require or expressly permit certain behaviour, a safe harbour will be available to cover that conduct which is undertaken in compliance with the Listing Rule in question.

10.32 The FSA has designated four categories of its Listing Rules which it considers to require either a safe harbour as set out in the Code or explanatory guidance adopted by the FSA pursuant to its power to give guidance in the FSMA 2000, s 157. The overall objective is to ensure that behaviour in conformity with such rules does not amount to market abuse. The four categories of Listing Rules are:

- rules requiring public disclosure of information;
- rules allowing delay in public disclosure of information;
- rules allowing the selective disclosure of relevant information before it becomes generally available; and
- rules that regulate dealings in the listed securities of an issuer.

10.33   Most Listing Rules require issuers to disclose information, either through the Regulatory News Service ('RNS') or in documents released or made available through the UKLA. Listing Rule 9.3A addresses the extent and type of disclosures and requires a company to take reasonable care in ensuring that any statement or forecast or other disclosure is not misleading, false or deceptive and does not contain any material omissions. Moreover, the Code addresses market abuse that may occur because of the dissemination of information through an accepted channel of communication (eg RNS) (MAR 1.5.18–1.5.20).

10.34   The FSA intends to insulate issuers from liability for conduct that arises from disclosures, which are expressly required or expressly permitted by the Listing Rules. Listing Rule 9.1, for example, requires issuers to inform the Company Announcements Office when there are any new major developments in its activities which are not public knowledge. The FSA seeks to ensure, in the absence of a safe harbour, that the issuer has taken all reasonable care to ensure that the announcement is not misleading and thus not in breach of Rule 9.3A and therefore not a breach of the market abuse regime.

10.35   The delay of public disclosure of information is addressed in Listing Rule 9.10(j). It allows issuers to delay announcements of new issues where the securities are subject to an underwriting agreement. This delay enables issuers to sell securities to the secondary market that were not distributed before the announcement of the results of the issue. This delay in announcing the results of the issue creates the risk that there could be a false or misleading impression for the demand of those securities and might therefore result in market abuse.

10.36   Under Listing Rules 9.4 and 9.5, issuers are allowed to disclose information arising from impending developments or matters in the course of negotiation to a number of specified parties, including professional advisers and counterparties to proposed commercial, financial or investment transactions. These exceptions to the general disclosure obligations in Chapter 9 are viewed as necessary because issuers would find it otherwise impossible to conduct their affairs. Thus, the FSA has proposed guidance in the Code that would protect issuers who rely on Rules 9.4 and 9.5 from liability. The FSA has proposed that Listing Rule 9.5 should be amended to require that issuers make a statement to the recipients of information under these provisions to the effect that the disclosures are made in confidence and that they must not deal in the issuer's securities before the relevant information has been made publicly available[1].

1 See CP 76, para 19.

10.37 Under Listing Rule 8.3, listed companies are permitted to disseminate draft listing particulars for the purpose of arranging a placement, a syndication or underwriting or for marketing the approval of an intermediary without obtaining prior FSA approval. In doing so, however, issuers should consider the implications of the 'false and misleading impression' condition contained in the Code when it circulates draft listing particulars. Issuers may also be confronted with the possibility that compliance with Listing Rule 8.3 might result in behaviour that could 'require or encourage' others to deal. This could occur in the following circumstances: an issuer's selective disclosure of information to a select group (as set out in Listing Rule 8.3) could be considered to be 'requiring or encouraging' dealing based on non-public information. The FSA does not seek to extend liability to issuers for such conduct, so long as they have taken the necessary precautions as proposed in the Code:

> 'The FSA will not regard a person as requiring or encouraging others to deal if he circulates draft listing particulars, clearly marked as such, which contain relevant information which is not generally available, solely for the purposes of arranging a placing, a syndication or underwriting or for marketing an intermediary offer'.

This guidance recognises the importance of Listing Rule 8.3 in facilitating dealing in securities that are to be listed by, for example, participation in placement, syndication or underwriting, all of which would occur before publication of listing particulars.

The regulation of dealing in listed securities: the Model Code[1]

10.38 The Listing Rules require that the Model Code apply to the directors and other insiders of listed companies. The Model Code and the Code's provisions both address the misuse of information in the context of preventing the improper use of relevant information, which is not generally available. Consequently, the FSA gives significant consideration to the issue of whether compliance with the Model Code's provisions should be granted safe harbour status under the Code.

1 The Model Code appears as an Appendix to Chapter 16 of the Listing Rules. See *Gore-Browne on Companies*, Appendix B, B.001–B.008.

10.39 The Model Code's para 4 contains the general prohibition on dealing by a director or relevant employee at any time when he is in possession of unpublished price-sensitive information. Regarding the misuse of information, market abuse can only occur when the decision to deal is based on relevant information that is not publicly available. Several provisions of the Model Code, however, permit directors to deal in exceptional or special circumstances at a time when they are in possession of price-sensitive information which is not available to the public[1]. Therefore, these exceptions in the Model Code permit dealing that could amount, in some circumstances, to market abuse.

1 These provisions are found at paras 9, 13, 13A, 14, 16 and 17.

10.40 Furthermore, it should be mentioned that there is some difficulty in allowing a safe harbour to be created for para 9 of the Model Code (allowing a chairman of a listed company to decide when dealing can occur) as this would effectively result in an unlawful delegation of the FSA's powers under the market abuse regime because it would allow a chairman of a listed company to decide whether a director's dealing in certain circumstances should benefit from safe harbour status.

10.41 The FSA has resolved that safe harbour status should not be granted to behaviour in accordance with the Model Code. The FSA provides a flexible interpretation of the Model Code to permit directors to deal in certain circumstances when their decision to deal is based on relevant information that was not publicly available. The absence of a safe harbour means that the Model Code will be in a similar position with respect to the market abuse regime as it has been with the insider dealing regime. A director's compliance obligations with regard to the insider dealing regime and the Model Code will now be the same as that with the market abuse regime.

10.42 Moreover, in determining whether market abuse has occurred, the FSA will take into consideration what efforts have been made to comply with regulatory obligations, ie the Model Code. The FSA has summarised the position for directors and relevant employees under the market abuse regime to be as follows:

- where the director has no relevant information in his possession which is not publicly available, any dealing will not breach the misuse of information element of the market abuse regime, though the Model Code provisions may still prevent a director's dealings;
- where the director does possess relevant information which is not publicly available, he will generally not be permitted to deal under the Model Code and therefore market abuse concerns will be likely not to arise; and
- market abuse may occur where the director possesses relevant information which is not generally available and either he considers that he falls within one of the special or exceptional circumstances provided by the Model Code or his dealing is one of those mentioned in para 20 of the Model Code. This means that the director should be aware that if his dealing is allowed under the Model Code, he must satisfy himself that his behaviour will not amount to market abuse.

10.43 Under the Model Code, in considering whether to give clearance, a chairman need not consider the market abuse regime when neither he nor the director seeking clearance are in possession of relevant information. Moreover, in a close period where the chairman gives clearance under one of the exceptional or special circumstances and neither he nor the director possesses relevant information, no market abuse will arise. A company chairman in possession of relevant information should be aware that if clearance is provided under one of the exceptions in the Model Code, it must satisfy itself that their conduct does not amount to market abuse.

The City Code and the Panel on Takeovers and Mergers

10.44 The FSA has a common interest with the Panel to prevent market abuse in the context of takeovers. The FSA and the Panel have co-operated in their efforts to ensure that the two regimes will interact effectively and efficiently. To accomplish this, the FSA has created safe harbours for those provisions of the City Code that deal with disclosure and publication, the timing of such disclosure, standards for disclosing such information and rules whereby the Panel may authorise the lifting of restrictions on dealing by insiders or others with controlling interests. In applying the market abuse regime, the FSA will have to conclude whether or not alleged manipulative conduct complies with provisions of the City Code that have been given safe harbour status. The FSA and the Panel have adopted operating procedures that allow the FSA to designate certain conduct to be in compliance with the City Code. The FSA will act to enforce such standards when it determines that a provision given safe harbour status has been breached or when conduct occurs during a takeover that suggests market abuse. These safe harbours, however, are not available for the misuse of information element of market abuse as this has been based on the criminal offence of insider dealing and thus has been handled for a number of years by other bodies such as the Department of Trade and Industry and London Stock Exchange.

10.45 Regarding enforcement action, the FSA has adopted, pursuant to the FSMA 2000, s 143, rules endorsing the Takeover Code and SARs . The FSA's endorsement is recognised in the Conduct of Business Rules (COB) X3.1 in which it is stated:

'At the request of the Takeover Panel, the FSA may take enforcement action against a firm which contravenes the Takeover Code or the SARs under Part IV'.

10.46 Under the FSMA 2000, s 157, the FSA has identified four categories of Listing Rules that will qualify for safe harbour status or that require explanatory guidance.

Safe harbours

10.47   The FSA has decided to apply safe harbour status to parts (but not to all) of the City Code, RIE rulebooks and its own Listing Rules, but not to the entire body of these Codes. The rationale for applying safe harbour status is based on the notion that compliance with the City Code and the RIE rules would involve certain acts or omissions that could be interpreted as market abuse under the FSMA 2000. Moreover, the FSA's determination of safe harbour status for portions of the Codes and RIE rules must also take account of the provisions in these regulations that prohibit behaviour which might also amount to market abuse and that this would be relevant to the regular user test as it applies to the person whose behaviour has fallen below the standards that are reasonably expected.

10.48   The FSA's determination of what parts of the Codes and FSA Rules should be subject to safe harbours is based on criteria that can be divided into four categories:

- rules which expressly require or expressly permit behaviour that, in the absence of the safe harbour, could amount to market abuse;
- rules which require that announcements be subject to certain timings and procedures of disseminations that respect certain contents and standards;
- rules which are specifically designed to prohibit behaviour which, if undertaken in breach of the rule, might amount to market abuse; and
- rules which have no connection to the issue of whether or not the behaviour addressed by that rule might amount to market abuse[1].

The FSA has determined that only rules that come within the first two categories should be granted safe harbour status. Safe harbour status for the first category is based on the grounds that it would be wrong to sanction behaviour that arose from regulatory requirements that expressly require or expressly permit certain conduct. To prevent this, the FSA has resolved to create a safe harbour where it is satisfied that the conduct which is required or permitted does not violate the market abuse regime. Similarly, the FSA has adopted safe harbour status for the second category on the grounds that stability of standards and conventions is necessary for effective timing in disclosure, methods of dissemination and the contents of announcements or disclosures and the standard of care to be observed. Safe harbours covering these areas make it difficult for the regulator to argue that a particular announcement or disclosure should have been made at a different time, disclosed in a different manner or disseminated differently[2]. These announcement and disclosure rules are primarily located in the City Code and Listing Rules. Moreover, under these Codes, if the requisite disclosure or announcement standards are not met, it may give rise to a false or misleading statement or contribute to a course of conduct that distorts the market. The FSA relies on these disclosure standards, as set out in the Codes, as necessary for determining what the regular user of that market would expect as to the standards applicable to particular announcements or disclosures. The safe harbour is intended to protect conduct that, with respect to disclosures that meet the standards of the relevant Code, would satisfy the expectations of the regular user.

1   See CP 76, paras 10–11.
2   CP 76, para 13.

10.49   The FSA views the application of safe harbours to these rules as recognition that they are standards that the regular user would expect and, if complied with, would not result in market abuse. Failure to comply with these standards, however, does not necessarily amount to market abuse. This is because there might be other ways or methods by which disclosure could be made which might satisfy the regular user of the market or which could ensure that there was no false or misleading impression or distortion of the market. This would not preclude, however, the particular regulator of the Code from taking action against a breach of that Code.

10.50   The FSA does not apply safe harbour status to the rules in the third category because of two reasons: (a) the significant risk of overlapping responsibilities for interpreting the Codes to determine market abuse and (b) the FSA does not think that complying with the third group of rules is necessarily market abuse. The FSA would also not apply safe harbour status to the rules in the fourth category because the behaviour against which these rules are directed does not amount to market abuse.

10.51   The FSA uses the power to grant safe harbour status to certain provisions of the City Code, the RIEs' rulebooks and to its own Listing Rules as set out above. The two categories of rules it has chosen to apply safe harbour status to are those where there is a real possibility that compliance with the requirement in question could amount to market abuse and to rules where it considers that, without a safe harbour, there could be uncertainty in the market that the standards set by those requirements do not amount to market abuse.

Conclusion

10.52   This chapter surveyed the development of the Model Codes and rules that regulate the disclosure of price-sensitive information and trading on the basis of inside information in the UK's financial markets. Traditionally, these codes and rules were extra-legal in nature and served as a supplement to the criminal law in enforcing standards and principles that restricted insider dealing. However, with the exception of the City Code, the FSMA 2000 has transformed these Model Codes and rules (that were once administered by industry self-regulatory bodies) into a comprehensive civil and criminal legal regime to regulate insider dealing and market abuse in the financial markets. Under the FSMA 2000, the FSA has issued a Code of

Market Conduct that is legally binding and enhances market transparency by describing what is and is not market abuse. Moreover, the FSA has assumed regulatory responsibility for the Listing Rules and the Model Code and has made them binding for all UK listed companies and their directors. Moreover, the FSA now has responsibility for administering and enforcing the price stabilising rules, inter-professional conduct rules and listed company share buy back rules. The Code of Market Conduct and the FSA Rules, combined with the CJA 1993, aim to ensure that directors, certain employees and persons connected with them (within the meaning of the Companies Act 1985, s 346) do not abuse and do not undertake to exploit price-sensitive information they may have, or may be thought to have, especially during periods leading up to an announcement of company results or a takeover. The FSMA 2000 regime represents the consolidation and legalisation of the self-regulatory codes and rules that had once governed the financial markets and further represents a more concerted government role in policing financial markets through a comprehensive set of civil and criminal sanctions to deter market misconduct.

CHAPTER 11

Dealing with investigation and enforcement

Introduction

11.1 In practice, the letter of the law alone is unlikely to influence behaviour or maintain consumer confidence. Consequently, the Financial Services and Markets Act 2000 ('FSMA 2000') underpins the substantive law of market misconduct with a wide range of investigation and enforcement powers.

11.2 Ms Melanie Johnson, the Economic Secretary to the Treasury, said of the powers of investigation:

'we make no apologies for wanting to be sure that investigations can take place as and when the circumstances suggest that they are needed. Nothing is gained by having a regulator that cannot respond quickly. Nothing is gained by encouraging wrongdoers to seek to prevent the launch of inquiries through procedural challenges in the courts'[1].

Extensive powers of investigation are introduced in respect of all types of market misconduct (ie market abuse and the criminal offences of market manipulation and insider dealing). These powers of investigation are reinforced by a number of sanctions.

1   Standing Committee A, 23 November 1999, column 887.

11.3 The FSA also has at its disposal a number of new enforcement powers. The range of sanctions available in combating market abuse is one of the most fundamental innovations of the FSMA 2000. The FSA may impose financial penalties and restitution orders administratively or may exercise its disciplinary powers in respect of authorised persons. Such person may then refer the matter to the newly formed Financial Services and Markets Tribunal ('FSMT'), run under the auspices of the Lord Chancellor's Department. The FSMT is central to preserving the right to a fair trial and correspondingly to the new regime. This may be contrasted with the Financial Services Tribunal, which has had only one referral since 1998[1].

Further, the FSA may apply to the civil courts for injunctions and restitution orders and request the court to impose a financial penalty. Finally, the FSA has received power to prosecute criminal offences of market misconduct. All these enforcement powers will run in tandem with other regulatory provisions such as the City Code.

This chapter first considers investigations before examining the enforcement tools available to the FSA.

1   See the government's consultation paper 'Review of Tribunals'.

Investigations

The appointment of investigators

11.4   The FSA and the Secretary of State both have power to appoint one or more investigators 'if it appears that there are circumstances suggesting' that the criminal offences of market manipulation or insider dealing have been committed or where market abuse may have taken place[1]. The FSA has indicated that it will usually appoint investigators from its own staff as it is permitted to do by the FSMA 2000, s 170(5)[2].

1   FSMA 2000, s 168(2) and (3).
2   ENF 2.11.3.

11.5   Considerable debate surrounded the low threshold for the appointment of an investigator. Members of Standing Committee A argued that this drafting was an attempt by the government to immunise itself from judicial review[1]. The earlier text of the Financial Services and Markets Bill required 'reasonable grounds for suspecting that' certain circumstances existed before the power to appoint an investigator arose. The Economic Secretary said that this was 'an unnecessarily high test for launching an investigation' and justified the recast text on the basis of investigation powers contained in the Financial Services Act 1986, s 177 and the Companies Act 1985, s 432[2].

1   Standing Committee A, 23 November 1999, column 879.
2   Standing Committee A, 23 November 1999, column 886.

11.6   The Secretary of State for Trade and Industry has retained the power to appoint an investigator for a number of reasons. First, such body's expertise in company law investigations, secondly, the potential for a company investigation to move into one concerned with financial services issues and, finally, a fallback in the event of a conflict of interest with the FSA[1].

1   Standing Committee A, 23 November 1999, column 862.

11.7 Amongst the factors that the FSA will take into account when considering whether to conduct formal investigations into market misconduct are the gravity of its concerns, the type of market involved and whether a regulatory authority is in a position to investigate and has adequate powers to conduct such investigation[1]. The FSA has power to prevent a recognised investment exchange ('RIE') or recognised clearing house from commencing an investigation or to limit, terminate or suspend an existing inquiry under the FSMA 2000, s 128.

1   ENF 2.6.2.

Control of the investigation

11.8 The powers to control the investigation are conferred by the FSMA 2000, s 170(7) and (8). They resemble the powers conferred upon the Secretary of State in investigations into potential insider dealing offences by the Financial Services Act 1986, s 177. The investigating authority may direct the scope of the investigation, the period during which the investigation is to be conducted, the conduct of the investigation and the reporting of the investigation. Such directions may in particular confine the investigation to particular matters, extend the investigation to additional matters and require the investigator to discontinue the investigation or only to take specified steps and require the investigator to make an interim report or reports.

Powers of investigators

11.9 The powers of investigators appointed in these circumstances are contained in the FSMA 2000, ss 173 and 175. These powers are extensive and are easily triggered. Where an investigator considers that any person 'is or may be able to give information which is or may be relevant to the investigation' he may require such person to attend before the investigator at a specified time and place and answer questions or otherwise to provide such information as the investigator may require for the purposes of the investigation[1]. In addition, the investigator may require such person to produce at a specified time and place any specified documents or documents of a specified description 'which appear to the investigator to relate to any matter relevant to the investigation'[2]. Finally, the investigator may also require such person to give the investigator all assistance in connection with the investigation 'which he is reasonably able to give'[3].

1   FSMA 2000, s 173(2).
2   FSMA 2000, s 173(3).
3   FSMA 2000, s 173(4).

Interviews

11.10   The powers to compel an interview are considered in the preceding paragraph. The FSA has indicated that it will not always use its statutory powers to require individuals to be interviewed and where appropriate will seek an interview on a voluntary basis[1]. Such statements would not attract the protection from admissibility afforded by the FSMA 2000, s 174(2)[2] (see further below) as the decision of the European Court of Human Rights ('ECHR') in *Staines v United Kingdom*[3] illustrates. The applicant (who was tried in connection with insider dealing) had first given voluntary statements and then attended a formal interview where she gave evidence under oath. The prosecution later made use of the statements that she had given under compulsion. She objected on the basis that her right to a fair trial had been breached. The ECHR distinguished the renowned case of *Saunders v United Kingdom*[4] on the facts in part because the statement in the voluntary interview did not depart from the compulsory. Consultees sought further clarification from the FSA on voluntary interviews following CP 65a. The FSA has now indicated at ENF 2.14.2 that a person attending a voluntary interview has the right to be accompanied by a legal advisor. Further, if the person interviewed is the subject of the investigation, they will be given a copy of the record of the interview according to ENF 2.14.2. However, if the person interviewed is not subject to investigation, an interviewee will be given a record of the interview if the investigator has made one (ENF 2.14.2).

1   ENF 2.14.1.
2   ENF 2.10.5.
3   (16 May 2000, unreported).
4   (1997) 23 EHRR 313.

11.11   Where interviews are conducted under compulsion, the FSA has indicated that it will give an interviewee an appropriate warning. Such person may elect to be accompanied by a legal advisor and will be provided with a record of the interview. Additionally, an explanation of the limited use which can be made of answers in criminal proceedings or where the FSA seeks a penalty for market abuse will be given[1]. Where the FSA is conducting an interview for the purpose of obtaining evidence in criminal proceedings, the FSA is subject to the requirements of the Police and Criminal Evidence Act 1984 and its codes and of the Criminal Procedure and Investigations Act 1996[2].

1   ENF 2.14.3.
2   ENF 2.14.4.

Admissibility of statements

11.12   The general rule is that 'a statement made to an investigator by a person in compliance with an information requirement' is admissible so long as it also complies with any requirements governing the admissibility of evidence in the circumstances in question[1]. This rule is modified in relation to market misconduct with wording resembling that used in the Company Directors Disqualification Act 1986, s 20(2). Where a person is charged with one of the criminal offences of market misconduct or is subject to proceedings under the FSMA 2000, s 123 for market abuse, no evidence relating to a statement made to an investigator in compliance with an 'information requirement' may be adduced and no question relating to it may be asked by or on behalf of the prosecution or (as the case may be) the FSA, unless evidence relating to it is adduced, or a question relating to it is asked, in the proceedings by or on behalf of the interviewee[2].

1   FSMA 2000, s 174(1).
2   FSMA 2000, s 174(2).

11.13   This may be contrasted with the FSA 1986, s 177(6) which specifically provided that statements made to investigators could be used in evidence against such person. This change of approach probably derives from the criticism that without such provision the legislation was contrary to art 6 of the European Convention on Human Rights[1]. However, compelled evidence may still be used to suggest new lines of inquiry, to justify an injunction or an order for restitution or disgorgement or to proceed against a person other than the one who gave evidence[2].

1   See the joint opinion of Lord Lester of Herne Hill QC and Javan Herberg at Annex C of the Joint Committee on Financial Services and Markets First Report.
2   Joint Committee on Financial Services and Markets Second Report, para 20.

Third parties

11.14   The scope of the power of investigation is broadened to third persons, in particular auditors, employees, lawyers and accountants by the FSMA 2000, s 175. An investigator may require such third parties to produce a document if it appears that the document is in their possession. The person to whom the document is produced may take copies or extracts from the document or require the person producing the document or any 'relevant person' to provide an explanation of it. The FSMA 2000, s 175(3) provides that if a person who is required to produce a document fails to do so, the FSA or an investigator may require him to state, to the best of his knowledge and belief, where the document is, no doubt with a view to an application for a search order pursuant to the FSMA 2000, s 176.

Legal advisors

11.15   A lawyer may be required by an investigator to furnish the name and address of his client and to this extent the law goes beyond the Financial Services Act 1986, s 177[1]. However, legal professional privilege is preserved as it was under the FSA 1986, s 177(7). The FSMA 2000, s 413(1) provides that a person may not be required under the FSMA 2000 to produce, disclose or permit the inspection of 'protected items'[2]. 'Protected items' are defined by s 413(3) and include a variety of communications between a professional legal advisor and his client. However, an item may not attract such protection if it is held with the intention of furthering a criminal purpose[3]. It should also be noted that where a person voluntarily discloses documents that benefit from legal professional privilege, such privilege may be waived unless the person making disclosure makes clear that it is waived for limited purposes[4].

1   FSMA 2000, s 175(4).
2   FSMA 2000, s 413(1).
3   FSMA 2000, s 413(4).
4   Standing Committee A, 7 December 1999 and, eg, *Halsbury's Laws of England* (4th edn) vol 3(1), para 526.

Bankers

11.16   The powers of the investigators in respect of bankers are extensive and go beyond the FSA 1986, s 177. Disclosure is not limited to circumstances in which the person owed the obligation of confidence consents. Pursuant to the FSMA 2000, s 175(5), disclosure may also be required where the person to whom the obligation of confidence is owed is the person under investigation or a member of that person's group or the banker himself or a member of that person's group is under investigation. The former appears to render the notion of banker's confidence virtually redundant in this context. However, given that the key evidence of market misconduct may lie in a person's bank account, such step is clearly significant to making powers of investigation effective.

Authorised persons

11.17   The above powers apply irrespective of whether a person is authorised or unauthorised. The FSA has a further range of extensive powers in respect of authorised persons including a general power to appoint an investigator, broad powers to require authorised persons to provide the FSA with information and documents and the power to require a report on any matter about which the FSA has required or could require the provision of information or production of documents under the FSMA 2000, s 165[1].

1   FSMA 2000, ss 165, 166 and 167.

Notification of the investigation

11.18   By contrast with other investigations, there is no statutory obligation to give a person under investigation for market misconduct written notice of such investigation[1]. This may be justified on the basis that many of the enforcement powers such as applications to freeze assets where there is a risk of dissipation of assets would be undermined by early notification of investigation.

1   FSMA 2000, s 170(2) and (3).

11.19   The FSA has, however, indicated that it will notify those under investigation once it proceeds to exercise its statutory powers to require information from them, unless this would prejudice the FSA's ability to conduct the investigation effectively[1]. Respondents at the early stages of consultation generally approved the FSA's suggested approach to notification[2]. Similarly, the FSA will provide an indication of the nature and subject matter of the FSA's investigations to those who are required to provide information to assist with the investigation where, for example, the identity of the perpetrator may not be known[3]. If such informal notification has been given, the FSA would then also need to ensure that it gave notice of a change in the scope of an investigation to a person subject to investigation if he was likely to be significantly prejudiced by not being made aware of it[4]. In response to concerns raised following CP 65, the FSA has given further guidance at ENF 2.12.7 as to the circumstances in which it will notify a person subject to investigation of the termination of the investigation. This provides that the FSA will confirm the discontinuance of the investigation without present intention to take further action where it considers it appropriate to do so having regard to the circumstances of the case.

1   ENF 2.12.6.
2   Response to CP 17, para 96.
3   ENF 2.12.5.
4   FSMA 2000, s 170(9).

11.20   Notwithstanding that notice has not formally been given, a person may know or suspect that an investigation is being or is likely to be conducted by the FSA. If such person falsifies, conceals, destroys or otherwise disposes of a document which he knows or suspects is, or would be, relevant to the investigation or causes or permits the falsification, concealment, destruction or disposal of such a document he is guilty of an offence unless he shows that he had no intention of concealing facts disclosed by the documents from the investigator[1].

1   FSMA 2000, s 177(3).

11.21   In general, the FSA will not state publicly whether or not it is investigating a particular matter unless this will help with investigations or dispel a rumour that an investigator has been appointed[1]. Respondents also generally approved this approach at the early stages of consultation[2].

1   ENF 2.13.1.
2   Response to CP 17, para 98.

Enforcement of investigations

11.22   The FSMA 2000, s 177 creates a number of sanctions that reinforce the powers of the investigators. These are:

- being dealt with by the High Court (or the Court of Session in Scotland) as if in contempt of court, if the court is satisfied that such person failed without reasonable excuse to comply with a requirement imposed upon him by the FSMA 2000, Pt XI;
- the criminal offence relating to falsification, concealment or destruction of documents considered above; and
- criminal offences in respect of the provision or reckless provision of false or misleading information.

11.23   Further, the FSA, the Secretary of State or the investigator may apply to a magistrate for a warrant to search premises and seize documents or information pursuant to the FSMA 2000, s 176. The FSA or Secretary of State must give information to the magistrate on oath in order to satisfy the magistrate that the prescribed conditions for a search and seizure order are satisfied[1]. These conditions are wide ranging and relate not only to information concerning documents that have been withheld, but also, in the case of an authorised person, to documents or information which could be the object of an 'information requirement' in circumstances where such requirement would not be complied with or the documents or information would be removed, tampered with or destroyed[2]. A search warrant is reinforced by a criminal offence attracting a term of imprisonment not exceeding three months or a fine not exceeding level 5 on the standard scale for any person who intentionally obstructs the exercise of any rights conferred by a warrant[3].

1   FSMA 2000, s 176(1).
2   FSMA 2000, s 176(2), (3) and (4).
3   FSMA 2000, s 177(6).

Confidentiality

11.24   Consistent with the need for effective global co-operation in combating market abuse, confidential information may be disclosed through gateways for disclosure intended to assist domestic or overseas regulatory or law enforcement bodies[1]. These gateways are to be prescribed by regulations made by HM Treasury under the FSMA 2000, s 349. To this end, the draft Disclosure of Confidential Information Regulations 2001 have been produced by HM Treasury and are subject to consultation at the time of writing.

1   FSMA 2000, s 349 and the Economic Secretary in Standing Committee A, 7 December 1999.

11.25   However, in general, the FSA must not disclose 'confidential information', which includes information received by the FSA or Secretary of State during an investigation, unless the source of the information and, if different, the person to whom it relates consents[1]. A firm would probably seek such publicity where the fact of an FSA investigation had been made public and had subsequently proved unwarranted[2].

1   FSMA 2000, s 348.
2   ENF 2.13.7.

Interaction with other investigatory authorities

11.26   A set of guidelines on investigation of cases of interest or concern to the FSA and other prosecuting and investigating agencies has been drawn up and lies at ENF 2, Annex 1G.

Sanctions for market abuse – an introduction

11.27   Protections and procedures already exist in the civil and criminal courts. The FSA's administrative powers introduced by the FSMA 2000 are entirely new and require their own set of procedures. This section considers such procedures before examining applications to the court for orders, interaction with regulatory authorities and finally criminal prosecution.

Administrative powers

Procedure

Separation of functions

11.28   One of the major concerns voiced during the passage of the Financial Services and Markets Bill was the need to ensure proper separation between the exercise of the FSA's powers of investigation and enforcement. One member of Standing Committee A expressed the point as follows: 'various legal experts who made submissions on the matter referred frequently to Chinese Walls and I remain unclear as to how thick and sturdy the walls of the FSA's structure will be'[1].

1   Per Mr Tim Loughton, Standing Committee A, 4 November 1999, column 717.

11.29   The FSMA 2000, s 395 obliges the FSA to maintain its own Chinese Wall. Section 395(2) provides that the decision to initiate action against an alleged offender through supervisory notices, warning notices and decision notices must not be taken by a person directly involved in establishing the evidence on which that decision is based. The FSA has created the Regulatory Decisions Committee in order to comply with this obligation. Further, the FSA has now isolated the decision making procedure in a decision making manual.

Regulatory Decisions Committee

11.30   The Regulatory Decisions Committee ('RDC') is a body outside the management structure of the FSA[1]. The chairman of the RDC is the only member who is an employee of the FSA[2]. The RDC is, however, fully accountable to the FSA for the decisions it takes[3].

1   DEC 4.2.3.
2   DEC 4.2.3.
3   ENF 4.2.1.

Warning notice and representations

11.31   Following investigation, if the FSA staff consider that action is appropriate, they will recommend to the relevant decision maker that a warning notice be given[1]. Following such recommendation, the decision maker may decide not to take further action[2]. If the FSA had previously informed the person concerned that it intended to recommend action, it must communicate the decision not to take further action promptly to such person[3]. However, if instead the FSA decides to take action, it is obliged by the FSMA 2000, s 126(1) to give a warning notice to a person against whom it proposes to impose a penalty for market abuse under the FSMA 2000, s 123. Such notice must state the amount of the proposed penalty[4]. Further, a warning notice about a proposal to publish a statement must set out the terms of the proposed statement[5]. A similar procedure applies where the FSA proposes to require a person to pay restitution pursuant to its administrative powers[6].

1   DEC 2.2.1.
2   DEC 2.2.2.
3   DEC 2.2.6.
4   FSMA 2000, s 126(2).
5   FSMA 2000, s 126(3).
6   FSMA 2000, s 385.

11.32   The mandatory contents of the warning notice are set out in the FSMA 2000, s 387. The warning notice must (a) state the action which the FSA proposes to take, (b) be in writing, (c) give reasons for the proposed action, (d) state whether access to certain FSA material applies pursuant to the FSMA 2000, s 394 and (e) if that section applies, describe its effect and state whether any secondary material exists to which the person concerned must be allowed access under it. The warning notice must also specify a reasonable period (which may not be less than 28 days) within which the person to whom it is given may make representations to the FSA, which period the FSA may extend[1]. The FSA has indicated that the period will usually be 28 days from the date the person receives the warning notice, subject to his right to seek an extension of time[2]. A person dissatisfied with the time allowed for representations may request more time from the FSA in writing within 14 days of receiving the warning notice[3]. The FSA considers that this may be particularly appropriate where a person wishes to enter into settlement discussions with FSA staff[4]. However, if a request for an extension of time will be considered by the decision maker, he will notify the recipient of the notice promptly of the outcome of his request[5]. The FSA has also indicated that, where appropriate, it will include a statement that the mediation scheme is available[6]. Notwithstanding the requirements relating to a warning notice, should the FSA issue a decision notice that was preceded by a warning notice, the action to which the decision notice relates need only be under the same part of the FSMA 2000 as the action proposed in the warning notice according to the FSMA 2000, s 388(2).

1   FSMA 2000, s 387(2) and (3).
2   DEC 4.4.3.
3   DEC 4.4.4.
4   DEC 4.4.4.
5   DEC 4.4.5.
6   DEC 2.2.9.

11.33   Following receipt of a warning notice, the person concerned may make representations to the FSA. The decision making manual considers representations at DEC 4.4. Making any representations following the warning notice and ensuring that these are made within the relevant time limits is critical. In particular, the FSMA 2000, s 123(2) provides that the FSA may not impose a penalty on a person if it is satisfied on reasonable grounds following representations by the person concerned in response to a warning notice that the person either believed on reasonable grounds that his behaviour did amount to market abuse (within s 123(1)) or took all reasonable precautions and exercised all due diligence to avoid behaving in a way which fell within s 123(1).

11.34   This is a significant section for a compliance officer to note, as the defence will often rest on the compliance procedures in place within a firm. The following points in the Enforcement Manual are important:

- whether, and if so to what extent, the FSA has issued guidance relating to the behaviour in question and the extent to which the person sought to follow that guidance;
- whether, and if so to what extent, the behaviour complied with the rules of any relevant prescribed market or any other relevant market or other regulatory requirements (including the Takeover Code or the SARs) or any relevant codes of conduct or best practice;
- whether, and if so to what extent, the person has followed established internal consultation and escalation procedures, for example, having previously discussed the behaviour with internal line management and/or internal legal or compliance departments;

- whether, and if so the extent to which, the person has sought the appropriate expert legal or other expert professional advice and followed such advice; and
- whether, and if so to what extent, the person has sought advice from the market authorities of any relevant prescribed market or, where relevant, consulted the Takeover Panel and followed any advice received[1].

1 See ENF 14.5.1.

Access to FSA material

11.35 The FSMA 2000, s 394 confers a right of access to key documentation in the possession of the FSA on a person who has been given a warning or decision notice. In particular, access must be allowed to (a) the material on which the FSA relied in taking the decision that gave rise to the obligation to give such notice and (b) any secondary material that, in the opinion of the FSA, might undermine that decision. The FSA may refuse access to material in circumstances set out in the remainder of s 394, although such refusal must be given by written notice together with reasons. The circumstances in which access may be refused include where material has been obtained under warrant, documents are subject to legal professional privilege and where disclosure would not be in the public interest or would harm the commercial interests of another party.

Settlement and mediation

11.36 The FSA is clearly keen to encourage negotiations, informal settlement and mediation in appropriate cases[1]. Mediation will be available in enforcement cases involving market abuse, subject to exceptions set out in DEC, Appendix 1.4.2.G[2]. The relevant exceptions are where cases involve allegations of a criminal offence or offences, or cases involve allegations of unfitness or impropriety based on judgments about dishonesty or lack of integrity. There has been general support for the FSA's mediation proposals, which will be operated for one year as a pilot scheme[3]. The Securities and Exchange Commission has been criticised for its settlement policies in light of the penal nature of securities statutes[4].

1 DEC, Appendix 1.
2 DEC, Appendix 1.4.1.
3 Policy Statement at 7.21.
4 Anne C Flannery, 'Time for Change: a Re-examination of the Settlement Policies of the Securities and Exchange Commission'.

Decision notice and notice of discontinuance

11.37 After considering the representations made to it following a warning notice, the RDC will state its decision in a decision notice or, where appropriate, a notice of discontinuance. The FSMA 2000, s 388 imposes similar requirements to warning notices in relation to giving decision notices. In the case of a penalty, the amount of such penalty must be stated in the decision notice[1] and similar provisions apply to restitution orders and publishing a statement.

1 FSMA 2000, s 127(2).

11.38 The decision notice is different from the warning notice in that any right to refer the matter to the FSMT and the procedure for making such referral must be indicated at this stage. There is a rather curious provision allowing the FSA to give a further decision notice which relates to different action in respect of the same matter provided a person consents which is expanded upon at DEC 2.3.6 and 2.3.7[1].

1 FSMA 2000, s 388(3)–(6).

11.39 The FSA may not take action specified in a decision notice during the period within which the matter to which the decision notice relates may be referred to the FSMT and if the matter is so referred, until the reference and any appeal against the FSMT's decision have been finally disposed of[1].

1 FSMA 2000, s 133(10).

11.40 The FSA is obliged to give a notice of discontinuance to a person to whom it has given a warning or decision notice if it decides not to take the action proposed in the warning notice or the action to which a decision notice relates[1]. The FSA has also indicated that it will send such notice to a third party served with a warning or decision notice[2].

1 FSMA 2000, s 389.
2 DEC 2.4.10.

Third party rights

11.41 Where a warning notice is in the opinion of the FSA prejudicial to a third party and such party is identified in a warning notice to which the FSMA 2000, s 393 applies, the FSA must give a copy of the notice to a third party[1]. This section does not apply if the FSA has given him a separate warning notice in relation to the same matter or gives him such notice at the same time as it gives the warning notice which identifies him[2]. Such notice must specify a reasonable period (not less than 28 days) within which such third party may make representations to the FSA[3]. However, this right to be informed is qualified. The FSA is not obliged to give a copy to such third party if the FSA considers it impracticable to do so[4]. The FSMA 2000, s 394 relating to access to material, considered above, applies equally to a third party served with a warning notice[5]. The FSMA 2000, s 393 makes similar provision for decision notices.

1 FSMA 2000, s 393(1).
2 FSMA 2000, s 393(2).
3 FSMA 2000, s 393(2).
4 FSMA 2000, s 393(7).
5 FSMA 2000, s 393(12).

Referral to the FSMT

11.42 The government has described the FSMT as 'a single, fully independent tribunal which will safeguard the rights of individuals and firms'[1]. The FSMT has been widely recognised as the notional guarantor of the right to a fair trial[2]. It should be noted that legal assistance may be available in the FSMT in cases of market abuse[3].

1 Miss Melanie Johnson, Standing Committee A, 4 November 1999, column 710.
2 See, eg, the joint opinion of Lord Lester of Herne Hill QC and Javan Herberg at Annex C to the First Report of the Joint Committee on Financial Services and Markets, para 2(d)(i).
3 FSMA 2000, s 134.

11.43 The FSMA 2000, s 127(4) confers a right upon a person to refer the matter to the FSMT if the FSA decides to take action against him by imposing a penalty for, or publishing a statement that a person has engaged in, market abuse. Similarly, where the FSA has imposed a restitution order administratively, a person may refer the matter to the FSMT[1]. Any such reference must be made within 28 days of the date on which the decision notice is given[2]. However, the FSMT may allow a reference to be made after the end of such period[3].

1 FSMA 2000, s 386(5).
2 FSMA 2000, s 133(1).
3 FSMA 2000, s 133(2).

11.44 Some aspects of the FSMT procedure have been set down by the FSMT Sch 13, which in particular limits the circumstances in which the FSMT may award costs. Further rules have been made by the Lord Chancellor's Department pursuant to the FSMA 2000, s 132. These are set out in the Financial Services and Markets Tribunal Rules 2001, SI 2001/2476. One aspect of procedure that has provoked debate is the applicable burden of proof in the FSMT, given the argument that market abuse provisions are criminal in nature[1]. Is it the civil burden of balance of probabilities or a burden of proof nearer the criminal standard of beyond reasonable doubt or should it be a sliding civil scale? It has been suggested that the recent decisions of SRO tribunals have demonstrated an ability on the part of such tribunals to apply a fair sliding civil standard, ie requiring exacting evidence before imposing fines[2].

1 See Chapter 6.
2 Joint opinion of Lord Lester/Javan Herberg at para 58.

Final notice

11.45 If the matter is not referred to the FSMT, the FSA must give final notice to the person concerned pursuant to the FSMA 2000, s 390. Similarly, if the FSMT or a court on an appeal on a point of law (pursuant to the FSMA 2000, s 137) gives the FSA directions to take certain action, the FSA must give the person to whom the decision notice was given a final notice pursuant to s 390(2). Section 390 sets out mandatory requirements that must be included within such notice.

11.46 A penalty becomes a debt at the end of the period given for its payment in the final notice, which must be not less than 14 days beginning with the date the final notice is given[1]. Similar provisions apply to a restitution order, which may be enforceable by the FSA making application for an injunction[2].

1   FSMA 2000, s 390(8).
2   FSMA 2000, s 390(10).

Publication

11.47 The FSA is required to publish such information about the matter to which a final notice relates as it considers appropriate and in such manner as it thinks fit, unless publication would, in the opinion of the FSA, be unfair to the person with respect to whom the action was taken or prejudicial to the interest of consumers[1]. Neither the FSA nor a person to whom a warning notice or decision notice has been given or copied may publish the details concerning it[2]. However, the FSA may publish such information as it thinks appropriate in relation to a matter in which a notice of discontinuance has been served provided that the person concerned consents[3].

1   FSMA 2000, s 391(4), (6) and (7).
2   FSMA 2000, s 391(1).
3   FSMA 2000, s 391(2) and (3).

Penalties and statements

11.48 Chapter 14 of the Enforcement Manual is the current statement of policy that the FSA is obliged to produce by the FSMA 2000, s 124 concerning the imposition of penalties under the FSMA 2000, s 123 and the amount of such penalties.

11.49 The FSA has indicated that it will not institute enforcement action in all cases of market abuse[1]. The factors that the FSA has stated it will take into account are largely intuitive, such as the amount of benefit gained or loss avoided by the transaction, the FSA action taken in previous cases and co-operation with the FSA or other regulatory authority[2]. The FSA will be guided by the statutory objectives underpinning this aspect of regulation, namely the maintenance of market confidence and protecting the interests of consumers[3]. The imposition of a penalty does not make the transaction in question void or unenforceable[4].

1   ENF 14.4.1.
2   ENF 14.4.2.
3   See, eg, ENF 14.1.3, 14.4.2(6) and the FSMA 2000, ss 3–6.
4   FSMA 2000, s 131.

11.50 From the point of view of a compliance officer, it is particularly worth noting the following factors that the FSA will take into account in determining whether to take enforcement action:

- the likelihood that the same type of behaviour (whether on the part of the person concerned or others) will recur if no action is taken;
- any remedial steps that the person concerned has taken to address the behaviour, whether at his own initiative or in meeting the requirement of another regulatory authority, and how promptly that person has taken those steps, such as identifying those who have suffered loss and compensating them and taking disciplinary action against staff;
- whether the person concerned has complied with any requirements or rulings of another regulatory authority such as the Takeover Panel; and
- the previous disciplinary record and general compliance history of the person, including whether the FSA has previously taken any action against the person for market abuse or 'requiring or encouraging' which resulted in adverse findings or issued a private warning to the person and whether the previous conduct of the person in relation to the markets has caused concern to another regulatory authority or been the subject of a warning or other action by a regulatory authority[1].

1   ENF 14.4.2.

11.51 It will be recalled that the FSMA 2000, s 123 limits the circumstances in which the FSA may impose a financial penalty. The factors that determine whether the FSA may impose a financial penalty for market abuse are set out at ENF 14.5.1 and are similar to those considered in the context of s 123 in the passage entitled 'warning notices' above.

Financial penalty or statement of misconduct

11.52 The FSA has power under the FSMA 2000, s 123(3) to publish a statement that a person has engaged in market abuse rather than impose a penalty. The FSA clearly regards the imposition of a penalty as more appropriate for serious cases. The publication of a statement as another sanction affords the FSA the flexibility to adapt to different situations. For instance, where a person has taken steps to ensure that those who have suffered loss due to the behaviour are fully compensated, it may be more appropriate to issue a public statement rather than impose a financial penalty[1].

1   ENF 14.6.2.

Determining the level of financial penalty

11.53 Consistent with the obligation imposed by the FSMA 2000, s 124(2), the FSA's policy in determining the amount of a penalty has regard to (a) whether the behaviour in respect of which the penalty is to be imposed had an adverse effect on the market in question and, if it did, how serious that effect was, (b) the extent to which that behaviour was deliberate or reckless and (c) whether the person on whom the penalty is to be imposed is an individual[1]. The additional factors that the FSA has indicated that it will take into account in determining the level of financial penalty that it may impose are similar to those it takes into account in determining whether or not to take action. For instance, the FSA will consider conduct following the contravention and the previous disciplinary record and general compliance history of the person[2]. The FSA has made clear that while it will seek to adopt a consistent approach, it will not adopt a tariff of penalties for market abuse cases[3].

1 ENF 14.7.3 and 14.7.4.
2 ENF 14.7.4.
3 ENF 14.7.2.

Restitution orders

11.54 The administrative power to seek restitution is considered under the heading 'restitution' below.

Applications to the court

11.55 The warning notice procedure does not apply to applications to court. If the FSA is applying to the court for a restitution order or an injunction, the practice that surrounds similar applications under the CPR, particularly on the question of costs, will prevail. Where there is no particular urgency or secrecy required before an order is obtained, the courts usually expect the parties to have set out their respective cases and sought to reach agreement before issuing proceedings.

Injunctions

11.56 Application may be made by the FSA to the High Court in England (or the Court of Session in Scotland) for a variety of injunctions in cases of market abuse pursuant to the FSMA 2000, s 381. There are three types of order that the court may make pursuant to this section: (a) an order restraining (or in Scotland an interdict prohibiting) the market abuse, (b) an order requiring a person to take such steps as the court may direct to remedy market abuse and (c) an order restraining (or an interdict prohibiting in Scotland) the person concerned from disposing of, or otherwise dealing with, any assets of his which it is satisfied that he is reasonably likely to dispose of or otherwise deal with. These orders could be combined. Those familiar with civil litigation will recognise these orders as types of prohibitory injunction, mandatory injunction and freezing order respectively. An injunction is a powerful sanction, breach of which may result in an application by the FSA for contempt of court. Additionally, the FSA has indicated that it will publish details of successful applications for injunctions, although it will not adopt this course if publication could damage market confidence or impact upon a takeover bid[1].

1   ENF 6.11.1.

Prohibitory injunction

11.57   The FSA must satisfy the court that (a) there is a reasonable likelihood that any person will engage in market abuse or (b) that any person is or has engaged in market abuse and that there is a reasonable likelihood that the market abuse will continue or be repeated in order to obtain a prohibitory injunction[1].

1   FSMA 2000, s 381(1).

11.58   One instance given by the FSA of a likelihood of re-offending is where the Takeover Panel has required a person to cease particular conduct and that person has not done so[1]. Guidance may also be derived from a case such as *SEC v Tome*[2]. Amongst the factors that persuaded the court in granting a permanent injunction in that case were the lack of remorse for intentional trading and the opportunity to repeat such violations in the future by reason of the offender's employment as a registered securities sales representative.

1   ENF 6.6.2.
2   833 F 2d 1086 (2nd Cir, 1987).

Mandatory injunction

11.59   The FSA must satisfy the court that (a) any person is or has engaged in market abuse and (b) there are steps which could be taken for remedying the market abuse (which includes mitigating the effect of market abuse) in order to obtain a mandatory injunction[1]. The FSA's interpretation of this power is broad and includes repatriating funds from an overseas jurisdiction, as well as reinforcing the powers of other regulatory authorities, for instance if a person has failed to take steps identified by such authority[2].

1   FSMA 2000, s 381(2).
2   ENF 6.6.2.

Freezing order

11.60   The court may make a freezing order on the application of the FSA if it is satisfied that any person (a) may be engaged in market abuse or (b) may have been engaged in market abuse[1]. The FSA has also indicated at ENF 6.5.1 that it may ask the court to exercise its inherent jurisdiction to grant a freezing order. This power may be used by the FSA to freeze funds from which restitution may be made.

1   FSMA 2000, s 381(3) and (4).

The FSA's policy as to seeking injunctions

11.61   The FSA has indicated that it will take into account the disciplinary record and general compliance history of the person who is the subject of a possible application for an injunction, including whether the FSA (or any of its predecessor regulators) has taken any previous disciplinary, remedial or protective action against the person or such person has offered undertakings to the FSA in determining whether to seek an injunction[1]. The FSA has also emphasised the regulatory objective of reducing financial crime in relation to the power to seek injunctions[2] and it will be interesting to follow how the FSA uses these powers to that end.

1   ENF 6.6.2.
2   ENF 6.6.2(10).

Restitution orders

11.62   The FSA has power to apply to the High Court (or the Court of Session in Scotland) for a restitution order and also to impose a restitution order administratively in cases of market abuse pursuant to the FSMA 2000, ss 383 and 384. These powers arise where:

- a person has either engaged in market abuse or by taking or refraining from taking any action, required or encouraged another person or persons to engage in behaviour which, if engaged in by the person concerned, would amount to market abuse; and
- profits have accrued to such person as a result or one or more persons have suffered loss or been otherwise adversely affected as a result[1].

1   FSMA 2000, ss 383(1) and 384(2).

11.63   The court may not make a restitution order nor may the FSA impose such order if they are satisfied that:

- the person concerned believed, on reasonable grounds, that he was not engaging in market abuse or requiring or encouraging another to engage in market abuse as set out in the preceding paragraph; or
- he took all reasonable precautions and exercised all due diligence to avoid engaging in market abuse or requiring or encouraging another to engage in market abuse as set out in the preceding paragraph[1].

1   FSMA 2000, ss 383(3) and 384(4).

11.64   The FSA has indicated that it will use its own administrative powers in the majority of cases where it is seeking restitution from firms[1]. However, the FSA has indicated the strategic circumstances in which it may instead apply to the court for a restitution order from a firm, for instance when combining restitution with a freezing order, bringing related court proceedings against an unauthorised person or the FSA suspects that the firm may not comply with an administrative requirement to give restitution[2].

1 ENF 9.7.2.
2 ENF 9.7.3.

11.65 The general factors that the FSA has indicated that it will take into account in considering whether to seek or obtain restitution reflect its concern to advance the statutory objectives combined with its need to prioritise its resources[1]. Consequently, the FSA will consider whether there are identifiable victims of the market abuse, the number of persons who have suffered loss and the extent of those losses, the costs that would be incurred by the FSA in securing redress and whether these costs are justified by the benefit to persons that would result from such action, whether persons who have suffered losses are in a position to bring civil proceedings on their own behalf and whether those who have suffered adverse effects have contributed to their own losses by failing to take reasonable steps to protect their own interests are amongst the factors that the FSA will consider.

1 ENF 9.6.

11.66 The figure of restitution is fixed by having regard to the profits appearing to have accrued, the extent of the loss or other adverse effect and, where a profit has been made and a person has suffered loss, to the profits appearing to the court to have accrued and to the extent of the loss or other adverse effect[1]. The court has powers to require a person concerned to supply it with such accounts or other information as it may require in order to consider these factors and may require any accounts or other information so supplied to be verified in such manner as the court may direct[2]. Similarly, the FSA may exercise its powers to appoint investigators or require a firm to provide a report prepared by a skilled person under the FSMA 2000, ss 166, 167 or 168 in considering the factors affecting the amount of the restitution order.

1 FSMA 2000, ss 383(4) and 384(5).
2 FSMA 2000, s 383(5), (6) and (7).

11.67 Payments made pursuant to a court order are paid in the first instance to the FSA, which must be paid by the FSA to such 'qualifying person' or distributed by the FSA between such 'qualifying persons' as the court may direct[1]. A 'qualifying person' is a person appearing to the court to be someone to whom the profits made by the offender are attributable or who has suffered loss or other adverse effect[2]. The powers of inquiry apply in relation to this exercise[3]. Similarly, when the FSA is exercising its administrative powers to require restitution, it must pass the payment from the offender to 'the appropriate person' (who is defined in the same way as a 'qualifying person'[4].

1   FSMA 2000, s 383(4) and (5).
2   FSMA 2000, s 383(10).
3   FSMA 2000, s 383(6)(c).
4   FSMA 2000, s 384(6).

11.68   Finally, it should be noted that where an application is made by the FSA for a court order, this does not affect the right of any person other than the FSA to bring proceedings in respect of matters to which the section applies[1]. The FSA will generally publish details of successful restitution orders[2].

1   FSMA 2000, s 383(9).
2   ENF 9.10.1.

The FSA's market abuse powers and other regulatory bodies, particularly the Takeover Panel

11.69   The various regulatory Codes are considered in detail in Chapter 10.

The Enforcement Manual suggests that the FSA will be sensitive to the impact of enforcement action for market abuse, particularly in the context of a takeover bid[1]. The FSA has repeatedly emphasised in such passages in the Enforcement Manual that it will work in close co-operation with the Takeover Panel and give due weight to its views. Similarly, the FSA will co-ordinate enforcement action with RIEs who may bring action for breaches of their own rules.

1   See, eg, ENF 6.6, 9.6, 9.10 and 14.9.

11.70   Further, behaviour may breach Principle 5 requiring firms to observe proper standards of market conduct and amount to market abuse. In these circumstances, the FSA has indicated that where the principal mischief arising from the 'behaviour' appears to be market abuse or 'requiring or encouraging', the FSA will take enforcement action under such regime[1].

1   ENF 14.8.

11.71   The importance of global co-operation in combating market abuse has been emphasised in this publication. In the Enforcement Manual, the FSA has indicated that it will work closely with overseas regulatory authorities in seeking to co-ordinate enforcement action[1].

1   ENF 14.11.3.

Prosecution of criminal offences

11.72   The FSA has acquired power under the FSMA 2000, ss 401 and 402 to prosecute both the criminal offence of misleading statements and practices under the FSMA 2000, s 397 and insider dealing under the Criminal Justice Act 1993, Pt V in England, Wales and Northern Ireland. The FSA has agreed guidelines with the other authorities in England, Wales and Northern Ireland who have an interest in prosecuting criminal offences. For instance, in particularly serious cases or those involving complex fraud, the Serious Fraud Office might prosecute.

11.73 The FSA will apply the principles set out in the Code of Crown Prosecutors when considering whether to bring criminal proceedings or to refer the matter to another prosecuting authority[1]. The FSA will consider both whether there is sufficient evidence to provide a realistic prospect of conviction against the defendant on each criminal charge and whether criminal prosecution is in the public interest having regard to the seriousness of the offence and all the circumstances of the case[2]. Instead of instituting proceedings, the FSA may issue a formal caution, in which case it will follow Home Office Circular 18/1994[3].

1 See ENF 15, Annex 1G and 15.5.1.
2 ENF 15.5.2.
3 ENF 15.6.

11.74 The further factors that the FSA has indicated that it will take into account in considering whether to initiate criminal proceedings includes the seriousness of the offence, whether there has been repeat market misconduct and whether dishonesty is involved[1].

1 ENF 15.7.2.

11.75 The FSA's policy is not to impose a sanction for market abuse where a person is being prosecuted for market misconduct or has been finally convicted or acquitted of market misconduct (following the exhaustion of all appeal processes) in a criminal prosecution arising from substantially the same allegations[1]. However, the FSA may take civil or regulatory action such as applying for an injunction or seeking restitution where criminal proceedings have been commenced or will be commenced[2]. In determining whether such proceedings should be taken, the FSA will have regard to whether the taking of regulatory action might unfairly prejudice the prosecution or proposed prosecution of criminal offences, whether the defendants might be unfairly prejudiced in the conduct of their defence and whether it is appropriate to take such action having regard to the scope of the criminal proceedings and the powers available to the criminal courts[3].

1 ENF 15.7.4.
2 ENF 15.7.5.
3 ENF 15.4.4.

11.76 A person convicted of misleading statements and practices or insider dealing is liable on summary conviction to imprisonment for a term not exceeding six months or a fine not exceeding the statutory maximum or both and on indictment to imprisonment for a term not exceeding seven years or a fine or both[1].

1   FSMA 2000, s 397(8) and the Criminal Justice Act 1993, s 61.

CHAPTER 12

Insider dealing: the civil law

A wrong to the market or the company?

12.1   We have identified insider dealing as a wrong that should be discouraged and tended to emphasise the character of the relationship through which the insider acquired the relevant non-public, material information. Although there are examples of conduct resembling insider dealing being condemned much before this on the harm that it did to the market, such conduct was not specifically described as or even really identified with insider dealing. It was considered to be rather more akin to manipulation or fraud. The very name of the concept – insider dealing – imports a relationship of proximity and privilege. Consequently, much of the discussion on insider abuse has fastened on those in a close relationship with or to companies. Therefore, misuse by insiders of privileged information has been regarded by many commentators as involving primarily issues of company law. Indeed, in many countries it is discussed almost as part and parcel of the law relating to directors' duties. Of course, today we recognise that the problem of insider dealing is a much wider one than directors taking advantage of information that comes into their possession whilst sitting on their board. Furthermore, it is recognised that the wrong committed by the insider in misusing unpublished price-sensitive information is not simply a matter of breaching his duties as a director or an officer of a company, but harms the proper operation of the market.

Conflicts of interest

12.2   Directors and, in many countries, officers of corporations are properly regarded as 'stewards' of the corporate enterprise or at least the company. It is a matter for debate in each legal system as to the extent it might also be appropriate to encompass within such a concept others such as controlling or even substantial shareholders, employees and other agents of the enterprise. Suffice to say that most systems of law, given the onerous responsibilities of stewardship, sensibly confine the notion to those who really are in a proper relationship of trust and confidence to the company.

12.3   The notion of stewardship is ancient and has changed little over time. Lord Chancellor Herschell, in the leading English case of *Bray v Ford*[1], emphasised that it is an inflexible rule that the courts will not permit a person in a fiduciary relationship to place himself in a position where his own interests conflict with those he is bound to serve. Nor is he to be permitted to derive an unauthorised benefit – a 'secret profit' – from his position of trust. He must be loyal to his principal. Of course, with all such simple rules, their application in practice is anything but simple. For example, there is still debate as to whether Lord Herschell intended to require those in a fiduciary position to eschew all conflicts of interest and duty no matter how insubstantial or theoretical. Nor is it certain whether the rule that a fiduciary should not benefit – without express authority – from his position is a separate rule or stems from the primary obligation to avoid all conflicts of interest. It is also uncertain as to how far it is appropriate to apply these rules to the situation where a fiduciary is in a conflict of duties to different principals, as opposed to merely his own self-interest. A broad approach could create serious problems for those holding directorships in several companies. Also, there is the real problem of financial intermediaries who engage in activities which might well produce conflicts between their different customers. While Chinese Walls and similar devices may inhibit the flow of actual information from one function within the bank to another, they do not address the essential conflict of duty that the bank has placed itself in.

1   [1896] AC 44.

12.4   While it is certain that those in a position of stewardship or a fiduciary relationship must not subordinate without a clear mandate, the interests of the person for whom they act or serve to their own, it is unclear how conflicting duties might be resolved. For example, would a trustee be under a duty to use inside information that he learnt by virtue of some other relationship for the benefit of the trust? It might be less easy for him to excuse himself when the information in his possession indicates that the trust will suffer a serious loss unless he takes action. Indeed, it has been said that a stockbroker may be under a duty to ensure that privileged information that he possesses does not work to the disadvantage of his client[1]. To what extent it could be argued that a broker may come under a duty to search out such information or act upon information of a positive quality which results in profits rather than the avoidance of an otherwise certain loss is rather more debatable[2]. Suffice to say that the law is sufficiently uncertain in a number of jurisdictions for governments to be actively addressing these issues through legislation.

1   See G Cooper and B Cridlan, *The Law of Procedure of the Stock Exchange* (1971, Butterworths) p 104. But see the comment of Lord Browne-Wilkinson in *Kelly v Cooper* [1993] AC 205, 'stockbrokers … cannot be contractually bound to disclose to their private clients inside information disclosed to the brokers in confidence by a company for which they also act'.
2   See, generally, B Rider, 'The Fiduciary and the Frying Pan' (1978) Conveyancer and Property Lawyer 114 and Law Commission CP 124, 'Fiduciary Duties Regulatory Rules' (1992, HMSO).

12.5 While the trust is a creature of the common law, other systems of law impose obligations on individuals not too dissimilar to those under discussion. For example, in civil law jurisdictions, agents and those operating under mandate might well be held to duties of good faith and care which would give rise to issues not unrelated to those discussed above[1]. It is also the case that even if these matters were of parochial interest to common law systems, in the global financial world of today it would be inappropriate not to have regard to their impact internationally.

1 See C Nakajima, *Conflicts of Interest and Duty* (1999, Kluwer).

12.6 There are few decided cases in which judges have specifically referred to the issue of dishonesty. In most common law jurisdictions, it is generally thought that liability under the fiduciary law is, in large measure, strict. Thus, if a person in a fiduciary position does take an unauthorised benefit from his position, then he should be held accountable whatever his state of mind. While such a draconian approach might be appropriate in the case of trustees in the strict sense of the word, there are many situations involving those in a fiduciary or analogous position where the courts have considered that proof of lack of probity is a material factor[1].

1 See, for example, *Royal Brunei Airlines Sdn Bhd v Philip Tan Kok Ming* [1995] 2 AC 378.

12.7 In the business and financial world, those in a fiduciary position will, it seems, be allowed to enter into situations where there is a possible and even, on occasion, real conflict of duties, provided they act with integrity. On the other hand, where there is a conflict between a duty to another and the self-interest of a fiduciary, the courts will be far more prepared to examine what has in fact taken place. Self-interest has been considered to be almost presumptive of abuse. The greater the degree of self-interest or benefit, the stronger will be the inference of corruption. On the other hand, it must be recognised that even in the case of conflict of duties, an intermediary will often expect to receive a benefit, be it in terms of commission or simply the retention of a business relationship. Consequently, it will rarely be the case that there is absolutely no element of self-interest in the equation.

Secret profits

12.8 Let us turn to a rule that is perhaps even more clear in its articulation than the 'no conflict rule'. Those in a fiduciary relationship must not derive from their position, or rather by virtue of the relationship, a 'secret profit'. In other words, any calculable benefit that comes into their possession that has not been expressly approved or permitted by the principal must be handed over to the principal[1]. This is an important rule of stewardship and is a core principle in any system of good governance. It strikes at the very root of self-dealing. Furthermore, it is one of the few rules that can be applied to directors and certain other corporate fiduciaries who have taken advantage of inside information[2].

1   See *Regal (Hastings) Ltd v Gulliver* [1942] 1 All ER 378 and *Industrial Development Consultants Ltd v Cooley* [1972] 2 All ER 162.
2   See, for example, *Nanus Asia Co Inc v Standard Chartered Bank* [1990] 1 HKLR 396.

12.9   The justification for imposing such strict obligations on those who accept positions of trust is essentially pragmatic. The legal system cannot be expected to detect and monitor every transaction and therefore strict and pragmatic rules are required for the ordering of all dealings between the fiduciary and his principal and with third parties on matters in which the principal has a legitimate interest. The rule therefore requires all remuneration and benefits to be agreed and therefore strikes at self-dealing, abuse of position and the diversion of opportunities that in good conscience should have gone to the principal. The rule against taking unauthorised profits works reasonably well in the context of principal and agent, but when applied to the position of fiduciaries whose relationship is with a company, it gives rise to a number of difficulties. As the company is a separate legal person, this fiduciary obligation is owed directly to the company and to no other person. Consequently, if a director uses information that he obtains as a director to deal in the securities of another company, his liability to account for his profit is to his own company and not to the issuer in whose securities he has traded. When the insider remains involved in the management of the company, there are serious practical and occasionally legal difficulties in bringing him to account. It is his company that has the right to sue for breach of the duty of good faith that he owes to it. In practice, this will mean that the action is to be commenced by his colleagues on the board or in senior management. The possibilities for minority shareholders to intervene and bring an action on behalf of their company are severely limited.

12.10   The law relating to the circumstances in which minority shareholders may prosecute an action on behalf of their company in the face of opposition from the management and majority shareholders is not particularly clear. A strict application of the so-called 'rule in *Foss v Harbottle*'[1] would render it almost impossible for such a derivative action to succeed in regard to what might be termed a 'simple' case of insider dealing.

1   (1843) 2 Hare 461.

Loss to the insider's company

12.11   While the cases indicate that liability to account for a 'secret profit' arises notwithstanding there is no qualifiable loss to the principal[1], the possible 'injustice' of such a strict rule has been questioned[2]. While it is necessary to sanction breaches of good faith and the company to whom the insider owes his fiduciary duty not to make secret profits is better placed than most to enforce this obligation, it is often difficult to identify any specific loss. Even in those jurisdictions in which issuers are allowed to trade in their own securities in certain circumstances, it is hard to show that an insider's misuse of inside information has occasioned quantifiable loss to the company. The company may contend that its confidence in the fair dealing of its agent has been undermined. It might also be argued that if it becomes known that a particular company's directors engage in insider dealing, the reputation of the company for integrity will diminish. It will be seen as an 'insider's company'. This may have implications for its business, financial and employment relations. While there is little, if any, empirical evidence to support this, anecdotal evidence abounds. On the other hand, in many developing markets, even quite significant enterprises are manifestly insiders' companies. It is often said that it is the very fact that their promoters remain in control which indicates to the market that the company is a good investment opportunity. Whether it is thought to be a good or bad thing for promoters to remain in control of their companies, it is hardly appropriate that this be determined by laws designed to inhibit insider dealing. It might be said that companies that allow their insiders to speculate on the basis of their inside information are permitting their management to, at best, waste time or, at worst, subordinate management to the ends of short-term market speculation. There is also a real danger that management will manipulate or at least influence the timing of corporate disclosures to facilitate their own trading. It is perhaps more sensible simply to recognise that corporate issuers do have a proper and real interest in the market for their shares and consequently allegations of abuse in this market are of concern to them. Where dealing takes place in shares other than those issued by the insider's corporation, it may be more convincing to argue that the insider is competing with his own company in the relevant market. However, in most cases, the impact that insider dealing is likely to have in such circumstances, even accounting for the use of derivatives trading, is hardly likely to result in calculable loss.

1   In *United Pan-Europe Communications NV v Deutsche Bank AG* [2000] 2 BCLC 461, the Court of Appeal emphasised '... it is not in doubt that the object of the equitable remedies of an account on the imposition of a constructive trust is to ensure that the defaulting fiduciary does not retain the profit; it is not to compensate the beneficiary for any loss' per Morritt LJ. See also *New Zealand Netherlands Society Oranje v Kuys* [1973] 2 All ER 1222.
2   See, for example, G Jones, 'Unjust Enrichment and the Fiduciary's Duty of Loyalty' (1968) 84 LQR 472.

12.12   While it is probable that an insider who is in a fiduciary position makes a profit through using inside information may be accountable to his principal, it is not clear whether a fiduciary could be required to account to his principal for 'negative profits', ie that is where he uses his priviledged position to avoid a loss that he would otherwise have sustained. For example, could a director be held to account for 'profit' that he makes through avoiding a loss by selling out his shareholding on the basis of unpublished, price-sensitive information that he has obtained by virtue of his fiduciary position? Although there is no English authority directly on the point and the courts have been reluctant to allow what are essentially compensatory claims for breach of a fiduciary duty, it is obviously desirable that someone who abuses his position by avoiding a more or less certain loss should be held accountable to the same extent as one who has benefited by making a profit. The Court of Appeal, with which the House of Lords agreed, in *A-G v Blake*[1], while hesitating to award damages for a breach of what might in other circumstances have been regarded as a fiduciary relationship, held that, in exceptional circumstances, the court has power to award a 'restitutionary' measure of damages for breach of contract even if, according to ordinary principles, there would be no basis for a claim to compensation. Of course, where there is a viable claim based upon something other than the fiduciary taking advantage of his privileged position to avoid a loss, such as in *Coleman v Myers*[2], since the fusion of the administration of law and equity, damages may be awarded for breach of a fiduciary obligation, at least where there is a parallel claim for negligence.

1   [1998] 1 All ER 833; affd [2000] 4 All ER 385.
2   [1977] 2 NZLR 225.

A narrow obligation

12.13   When we contemplate the duty that a corporate fiduciary owes to his company not to take advantage of his position or, for that matter, information that comes to him by virtue of his privileged position, we must recognise the narrowness of the relationship within which this duty operates. Directors and other corporate fiduciaries owe their duties to the company and, as the company has a separate legal personality, only to that entity. They do not, as fiduciaries, owe duties to other, albeit related, enterprises, shareholders, creditors, employees or anyone else. Of course, if they step into another legal relationship, they might well find themselves owing duties directly to such persons as well as to their company. For example, as we shall see, there have been cases[1] where a director has stepped into a special relationship with one or more of the shareholders and by virtue of this has been held liable for taking advantage of privileged information in his dealings with them. Such cases, outside the United States, are, however, exceptional. It is important to remember that, while as a matter of good governance, directors are required to have regard to the interests of different constituencies, as a matter of law, their duties are owed to and are enforceable by their company. Thus, while members of the board both collectively and individually must act in what they consider to be the best interests of the company and in doing this they should consider the interests of all those 'represented' in the enterprise, their duties of stewardship are owed to the company.

1   See, for example, *Allen v Hyatt* (1914) 30 TLR 444; *Briess v Woolley* [1954] AC 333 and, in particular, *Gadsden v Bennetto* (1913) 9 DLR 719 (Man).

12.14   Consequently, the shareholders, individually or collectively as the providers of capital, have no right to sue on a claim based on an infraction of a duty owed to the company. The company's property is not theirs and it has been decided that even conduct on the part of directors which damages the share price does not give individual shareholders or the even the general body of shareholders the standing to sue[1]. The claim is that of the company's for the misconduct in question. To allow the issuer to sue and also give shareholders a right of action to recover for the diminution in the value of their investment might result in them recovering twice over for essentially the same wrong, as although a share does not represent a divisible part of the corporate assets, its value is tied, or at least should be, to the aggregated value of the enterprise, including all those assets belonging to the company. While there are examples in a number of countries where shareholders have successfully pursued directors and other corporate insiders for essentially insider dealing, their suit has been firmly based on breach of a relationship other than to the company. In all cases, liability has been based on the breach of a special relationship that has come into existence because of the special facts of the case. In other words, the insiders have come into another and external relationship with the shareholders which has given the shareholders a legitimate expectation of fair dealing.

1   *Prudential Assurance Co v Newman Industries Ltd (No 2)* [1982] Ch 204.

12.15   There are other reasons why individual shareholders have not been permitted to pursue insiders with whom they happen to deal on the market. Although an insider taking advantage of unpublished, price-sensitive information in circumstances where the other party did not have or could not have had access to it may be characterised as 'unfair', the courts have, in most jurisdictions, appeared reluctant to recognise a cause of action. Their caution is based on a concern not to disrupt the proper operation of bargaining in the markets. While equality of access to information may be desirable, it is rarely, if ever, attainable. The law has long recognised that disparities or imbalances in information, let alone the ability to interpret or apply the information, cannot justify intervention in a bargain that has been completed without fraud[1].

1   *Bell v Lever Bros* [1932] AC 161.

12.16   The mere failure to reveal information, even when it is appreciated that the other party does not have that information or could not obtain it with the exercise of reasonable diligence, does not give rise, in the ordinary course of events, to a duty to disclose or refrain from dealing. It matters not how significant or material that information might be to the decision of the other to deal and upon what terms. The notion of *caveat emptor* reflects more than a *laissez faire* approach to the market. It is based on a host of considerations that have developed over time and which lie at the very heart of how we do business. The law does, of course, make exceptions. Perhaps, apart from statutory intervention, the most significant is where there exists a pre-existing relationship between the parties in which there is an expectation on the part of at least one of the parties of fair dealing.

213

12.17 Where a fiduciary relationship can be found, it is probable that the obligation of fair dealing will import a duty of full disclosure and probably also a duty of care. Where such a relationship exists between an insider and the person with whom he is dealing, it is likely that the law will provide a remedy. However, the fiduciary obligation must generally arise from a pre-existing fiduciary relationship as it is far less clear that such obligations can arise, other than in the most exceptional circumstances, by virtue of the transaction in question. While it is probable that directors, the classic insider, may be in a contractual relationship with shareholders of their company, this is not a fiduciary relationship so as to give rise to the fiduciary obligation of fair dealing. It follows that a director who deals with someone who becomes a shareholder by virtue of that very transaction is in no pre-existing relationship whether contractual or otherwise. The traditional attitude of English law, and for that matter all common law jurisdictions, is that a director owes his fiduciary duties to his company which is a separate legal person. He does not owe duties directly, or for that matter even indirectly, to the shareholders who also have no legal interest in the company's property. The rule established by Swinfen-Eady J in *Percival v Wright*[1] that directors do not owe duties as directors to members of their company either individually or collectively has been criticised, particularly in the context of insider dealing, but it remains a cornerstone of company law.

1   [1902] 2 Ch 421 and see also Lord Lowry in *Kuwait Asia Bank v National Mutual Life Nominees Ltd* [1990] BCLC 868 at 888. But see also *Re Chex Nico (Restaurants) Ltd* [1992] BCLC 192 and *Peskin v Anderson* [2000] 2 BCLC 1.

12.18 On the other hand, whilst the courts are not generally receptive to arguments that they should discover new fiduciary relationships, they are prepared to reconsider the factual circumstances in which duties can arise and in particular take account of changes in social and perhaps moral views. Thus, the High Court of New South Wales in *Glandon Pty Ltd v Strata Consolidated Pty Ltd*[1] expressed the view that as attitudes to insider dealing had changed since 1902, a court faced with the issue today might not be as unwilling as Swinfen-Eady J was to discover a fiduciary obligation. In practice, what the New South Wales court was alluding to was a long-established approach, namely the recognition that in special and exceptional circumstances the facts of a particular case might well persuade the court that an unusual fiduciary relationship arises on the particular facts of the case. Although there are a number of examples of the courts being prepared to find that, for example, directors have stepped outside their normal corporate relationship into a special relationship with their shareholders, or for that matter third parties, perhaps the most dramatic illustration is *Coleman v Myers*. Although, at first instance, Mahon J was prepared to hold that *Percival v Wright* was simply *per incuriam* and should not be followed in New Zealand, the Court of Appeal, while taking the view that Swinfen-Eady J had been correct on the facts before him, held there were circumstances which could, and did in the present case, justify the court in finding that a relationship of fair dealing, involving both a duty of good faith disclosure and also one of care, arose as a legitimate expectation on the particular facts. In this case, the closely held nature of the company, the exceptional materiality of the information in question, the dishonesty of the insiders and the fact that the relevant shareholders had, over a long period, come to rely upon their probity, all served to justify the implication of a fiduciary obligation of fair dealing.

1   (1993) 11 ACSR 543.

12.19   The approach of the New Zealand Court of Appeal was in line with earlier English decisions[1] and has been followed by the Court of Appeal of New South Wales in *Brunninghausen v Glavanics*[2]. The circumstances in which an English court would be prepared to find a specific duty of disclosure to an existing shareholder, let alone a person buying into the issue for the first time, are not entirely clear. It is probable that the insider would have to be in possession of highly relevant and material information which the other party could not have obtained even with the exercise of diligence. Furthermore, the situation must, it would seem, be such as to raise on the part of the person dealing with the insider a reasonable expectation of fair dealing[3]. The comment of Newberger J in *Peskin v Anderson*[4] seeking to summarise the English law after *Brunninghausen* may well go too far[5]. The learned judge observed:

'I am satisfied, both as a matter of principle and in light of the state of the authorities [including *Brunninghausen*], that *Percival v Wright* is good law in the sense that a director of a company has no general fiduciary duty to shareholders. However, I am also satisfied that, in appropriate and specific circumstances, a director can be under a fiduciary duty to a shareholder ... So far as the authorities to which I have referred on this issue are concerned, the decisions ... in which a duty was held to arise were cases where a director with special knowledge was buying the shares ... for his own benefit from shareholders, where the director had special knowledge which he had obtained in his capacity as a director of the company, and which he did not impart to the shareholders, and where the special knowledge meant that he knew that he was paying a low price'.

1   See, for example, *Royal Brunei Airlines Sdn Bhd v Philip Tan Kok Ming* [1995] 2 AC 378.
2   (1999) 32 ACSR 294.
3   See *Platt v Platt* [1999] 2 BCLC 745, but note the reservations of the Court of Appeal [2001] 1 BCLC 698.
4   [2000] 2 BCLC 1 at 14.
5   See *Platt v Platt* [2001] 1 BCLC 698.

12.20   For a special relationship to develop giving rise to an obligation of fair dealing, it is most likely that the parties will be engaged in direct and personal negotiations. Even in those states in the United States that have developed the so-called 'special facts' doctrine[1], remedies, are in practical terms, confined to non-market transactions. It is also likely that in most cases the company will be closely held. Indeed, there are cases where the company resembles a partnership in which the courts have been prepared to view the relationship between shareholders and directors as analogous to that of partners[2] bound by obligations of mutual good faith.

1   See *Strong v Repide* 213 US 419 (1909).
2   For example, *Ebrahimi v Westbourne Galleries* [1973] AC 360.

12.21   It is not, however, just shareholders who might feel that they should be able to bring insiders to account either for their breach of 'duty' to the enterprise or as counterparties to an objectionable transaction. Those who invest in corporate bonds, who are not shareholders in the sense of being members of the company, may consider that they have been disadvantaged by an insider utilising privileged information in a trade with them on the market. Trading in bonds and other financial paper may be just as attractive to an insider than more conventional dealing in corporate shares and options. In most jurisdictions, the duties, if any, that the board, let alone individual directors of a company, may owe to creditors is even more underdeveloped than in regard to the position of directors to shareholders. There is little chance of an insider who trades in debt securities, on the basis of privileged information, being liable to any counterparty unless exceptional circumstances give rise to a special relationship along the lines we have discussed.

Benefiting another – a breach of duty?

12.22   We must also remember in our present discussion that the remedies available for a breach of the fiduciary's duty of loyalty are rather limited. Where the fiduciary allows another to benefit in place of himself, the law has been less robust. What if a director passes on to another the relevant inside information in the expectation that the other person will use it for dealing? The person who uses the inside information, in many legal systems, will not be liable to the insider's company as he is not in a fiduciary relationship. The position of the insider who passes on the relevant information is also problematical[1]. As the profit is not his, can it be said that he has taken advantage of his position? Of course, if the person to whom he has given the information and who has profited through its use can be regarded as his agent or alter ego, the position may be different. However, the courts have been reluctant to attribute the profit made by, for example, a wife[2] or a company associated with the insider to the director. Provided the profit is that of a separate person who is not acting on behalf of the director, then it seems that the fiduciary law is powerless. In no small measure, this may well be due to the difficulty that the law has in finding a suitable remedy. There is no profit in the hands of the fiduciary that the company can call to account.

1   Note the position of the chairman in *Regal (Hastings) Ltd v Gulliver* [1942] 1 All ER 378.
2   See *Daniels v Daniels* [1978] Ch 406.

12.23 Judges have understandably been reluctant to stand by and see insiders facilitate the looting of their companies by others with whom there is often a fair suspicion that they are in cahoots. A series of recent decisions have underlined the significance of the constructive trust as a means of reaching out and imposing an essentially restitutory liability on those who receive the benefits of a breach of trust or who knowingly facilitate the breach. Whilst the principles are by no means new, the way in which the judges have applied them has been dynamic, while in the House of Lord's decision in *Westdeutsche Landesbank Girozentrale v London Borough of Islington*[1], Lord Goff stated, 'it is not the function of your Lordships' house to write the agenda for the law of restitution, not even to identify the role of equitable proprietary claims in the part of the "law" has there been a burst of judicial activity in the area of intermeddlar liability'. In recent cases, the courts have fashioned a relatively effectively device to impose restitutory liability on those who, knowing the facts that amount to a breach of trust, knowingly participate in it or facilitate the laundering of the proceeds in circumstances where an ordinary person would consider what they have done, or perhaps not done or asked, is dishonest. The liability in such cases is not that of a constructive trustee in the conventional sense of the word; their liability is as an accomplice and the monetary liability that they are exposed to is to make restoration as if they were a constructive trustee. It is interesting that Lord Browne-Wilkinson in the *Westdeutsche* case observed that the distinction between the concept of remedial constructive trusts, as developed in US law and the traditional approach of the English law, remains, despite judicial ingenuity and the desire of judges, to make the 'crooks' pay. He pointed out that the essentially institutional constructive trust under English law arises by operation of law and that it is for the court merely to recognise and give effect to it and it is not open to the judge simply to impose such a device to afford a remedy which would not otherwise exist.

1   [1996] AC 669.

12.24 The view has been taken that this area of the law is of little practical significance in the area of insider dealing as, before a trust can be found, it is necessary to identify property which can in the contemplation of the law be considered viable as trust property. In *Lister v Stubbs*[1], the Court of Appeal established the rule that a bribe, in so far as such involved only a personal obligation to account, could not be the basis of a tracing claim and was not susceptible to being regarded as trust property. Of course, there has always been a substantial grey area in company law in regard to what the textbooks refer to as the 'corporate opportunity' cases. In one or two Commonwealth cases, the courts have seemingly regarded the benefit of a contract which in fairness should have gone to a company[2], but which has been wrongfully. diverted to another person, as a form of corporate property. In many of these cases, however, the issue is made more complex by the so-called 'rule in *Foss v Harbottle*'[3]. Simply stated, this rule provides that where a wrong has been done to the company, then it is the company which is the proper plaintiff in any suit for redress. In determining whether suit will be brought and upon what terms, the view of the directors and, in default, the shareholders in general meeting, will be respected unless a minority shareholder can bring himself within certain defined exceptions. Perhaps the two most significant in the present context are the so-called 'fraud on the minority' exception and that relating to misappropriation of corporate property. Where the wrongdoers could exercise control over the company and its organs in a manner effectively to prevent the company seeking redress, then the courts would allow and, indeed, facilitate a minority shareholder proceeding, in effect on the corporate cause of action. The same is true in regard to conduct which amounts to the majority giving away or appropriating the company's property in an unlawful manner. Thus, as Professor Sealy observed in the first edition of his casebook on company law[4] published in 1971, in practice, the arguments put before the courts in these cases in all probability had rather more to do with engineering a way round the rule in *Foss v Harbottle* and escaping the implications of shareholder ratification than any fundamental issue of substantive law.

1   (1890) 45 Ch D 1.
2   *Cook v Deeks* [1916] 1 AC 554; *Canadian Aero Service Ltd v O'Malley* (1974) 40 DLR (3d) 371.
3   (1843) 2 Hare 461.
4   L S Sealy, *Cases and Materials in Company Law* (1971, Cambridge University Press) p 391.

12.25   In *A-G for Hong Kong v Reid*[1], the Privy Council, on an appeal from New Zealand, following the approach of the Court of Appeal of Singapore in *Sumitomo Bank Ltd v Kartika Ratna Thahir*[2], opined that the rule in *Lister v Stubbs* was inappropriate today. The Privy Council considered that on the basis that equity looks as done that which should be done, there was a sufficient basis in law for tracing into the proceeds of a bribe. Furthermore, their Lordships' comments and particularly those of Lord Templeman were wide enough to include the proceeds of a 'secret profit'. If the proceeds of, for example, insider trading could be traced and be the basis of a constructive trust, the law in this area would be radically changed. For example, it would mean, as was in effect held by the High Court of Hong Kong in *Nanus Asia Inc v Standard Chartered Bank*[3], that the proceeds of insider dealing could be traced into the hands of a recipient who took otherwise than as a bona fide purchaser without notice. It would also follow that accomplice liability could be imposed on those who facilitated the insider dealing provided they had the requisite degree of knowledge and were objectively speaking dishonest. It would also be arguable that in so far as the proceeds were the 'property' of the company, the exception to the rule in *Foss v Harbottle*, placing beyond the reach of the majority of shareholders to ratify or excuse cases where there had been a misappropriation, would be available. While it has been assumed that the observations of, in particular, Lord Templeman in all probability were unintended to be applied broadly to all breaches of fiduciary duty resulting in unjust enrichment, recent cases have shown that some judges are willing to throw the net very widely. In *United Pan Europe Communications NV v Deutsche Bank AG*[4], the Court of

Appeal had no difficulty in applying such reasoning to the misuse of confidential information obtained within a duty of loyalty and imposing a constructive trust on shares bought by the bank. With respect, however, in *Reid*, their Lordships clearly did not have these wider issues in mind when they showed so much determination in ensuring the unsavoury Warwick Reid should not be allowed to whisk his ill gotten gains, as Lord Templeman said, 'to some Shangri-La which hides bribes and other corrupt moneys in numbered bank accounts'. Indeed, this is one of the real problems in this area of the law. The judges, once they sniff fraud, are prepared to go some way in ensuring that the crook's ill gotten gains are taken away from him. They are not always too concerned with traditional compensatory, let alone restitutory, jurisprudence. In looking at some of the decisions, particularly those relating to directors' duties, it is important to remember that to a very real degree the end has justified the means and a search for all prevailing and entirely rational principles of restitution may well be a search in vain.

1   [1994] 1 All ER 1.
2   [1993] 1 SLR 735.
3   [1990] HKLR 396.
4   [2000] 2 BCLC 461.

12.26   It is still probably the law that not all breaches of fiduciary duty are capable of giving rise to a constructive trust relationship. In *Nelson v Rye*[1], Laddie J followed Sir Peter Millett's view expressed extra-judicially in 'Bribes and Secret Commissions' published in the Restitution Law Review[2]. Sir Peter took the view that a constructive trust is appropriate when an agent receives property himself in circumstances where it should have gone to his principal. This is a principle which has long been recognised in the company law cases. The Australian High Court in *Warman International Ltd v Dwyer*[3] also threw some light on this issue by distinguishing situations where a fiduciary benefits by use of his principal's property or an opportunity coming to him by virtue of acting for his principal where a constructive trust might be appropriate and other cases where he is merely guilty of a breach of his duty of loyalty. In the latter case, while there may well be an obligation to account for all or part of the 'secret profit', the more exacting relationship of a trustee may well be inappropriate. However, the Court of Appeal in *United Pan Europe NV* took the view that a constructive trust might be an appropriate remedy to deprive a fiduciary of his ill gotten gains when 'the conduct complained of falls within the scope of the fiduciary duty' to exhibit loyalty and it need not be shown that the profit resulted 'by virtue of his position'. Furthermore, the Court of Appeal did not accept that a constructive trust 'will only be granted where the applicant can trace into the property over which it is sought'. The remedy would depend upon the circumstances. Furthermore, in this context, it must also be remembered that the Privy Council has also shown a greater degree of flexibility in dealing with that old inflexible rule that a fiduciary should not place himself in a position where his interest and duties conflict[4]. Disclosure with assent and contractual delimitation of the scope of duties and expectations[5] may well render what would otherwise be a conflict of interest nothing objectionable to the law.

1 [1996] 2 All ER 186.
2 (1993) RLR 7.
3 (1995) 128 ALR 201.
4 See para **[12.3]**.
5 *New Zealand Netherlands Society Oranje v Kuys* [1973] 2 All ER 1222; *Kelly v Cooper* [1993] AC 205 and *Clarke Boyce v Movat* [1994] 1 AC 428.

12.27 A further problem which has manifested itself in the law relating to insider dealing is whether inside information can be considered to be a form of property, thereby bringing in the law relating to constructive trust and all this might entail. The law is unclear as to in which circumstances the courts will protect information of a confidential nature in a manner which is analogous to property. The Divisional Court has decided that confidential information is not property for the purposes of the law of theft in England[1]. Whether such a view adequately takes account of the civil law and can in any case stand after the view expressed by the Privy Council in *Reid*[2] remains seriously open to doubt. In *Reid*, Lord Templeman certainly regarded the majority of their Lordships in *Boardman v Phipps*[3] as imposing a constructive trust on the defendants on the basis that they had misused confidential information. In *United Pan Europe NV*[4], the Court of Appeal had no difficulty in considering a proprietary remedy, namely a constructive trust, might well be an appropriate remedy to improve on shares purchased by a fiduciary who had used confidential information. Indeed, as we have seen, Morritt LJ did not think it an issue whether the applicant could trace into the relevant property; what was at stake was depriving a fiduciary who had stepped into a conflict of interest of its 'secret profit'.

1 *Oxford v Moss* (1978) 68 Cr App R 183.
2 [1994] 1 All ER 1.
3 [1967] 2 AC 46.
4 [2000] 2 BCLC 461.

12.28 Whilst it might well be appropriate to protect confidential information as if it were a form of property in certain circumstances[1], it would be pushing the boat out far too far to contend that most inside information is properly regarded as property for the law of trusts. In many instances, inside information may not have the qualities often associated with confidential information. On the other hand, as the Court of Appeal in *United Pan Europe NV* appears to have accepted, it would be somewhat illogical if the courts allowed one to trace the proceeds of a 'secret profit' obtained in breach of the general obligation of loyalty and yet did not allow such protection for the misuse of the actual information which gave rise to the profit in the first place. Perhaps the answer is to separate the issues of tracing into the proceeds of a profit made in breach of a fiduciary duty and the imposition of a constructive trust as an appropriate remedy to deprive a fiduciary of his illicit profit. Notwithstanding the uncertainty whether the principles relevant to the law relating to constructive trusts and the tracing remedy can be applied to all 'secret profits' and the misuse of information, it is useful to refer to a series of relatively new cases which imbue liability on those who receive the benefits or assist in the laundering of the proceeds of a breach of fiduciary duty.

1   See *Dunford and Elliot Ltd v Johnson and Firth Brown Ltd* [1977] 1 Lloyds Rep 505; *Indata Equipment Supplies Ltd v ACL Ltd* [1998] 1 BCLC 412 and *A-G v Blake* [1997] Ch 84.

12.29   The 'flood' of cases seeking to impose civil liability on those which might broadly be described as 'fiduciary facilitators' are based on a principle of law most clearly set out by Ungoed-Thomas J in *Selangor United Rubber Estates v Craddock*[1]. In this case, the learned judge referred to an established principle of equity that where a person knowingly participates in another's breach of trust he will be regarded as standing in the same place as the trustee. While there has been much discussion in the books and cases as to the exact nature of this liability and whether it is properly considered a constructive trust relationship in all cases, suffice it to say in this context there would appear to be only two problems in fashioning this rule to become a most effective weapon against insider abuse.

1   [1968] 1 WLR 1555.

12.30   The first is simply what sort of misconduct on the part of a fiduciary will be sufficient to bring the principle into play. Most of the cases have involved either a conventional trust relationship or at least something so close as to make little practical difference. It would seem, however, that the property divided or misappropriated by the trustee must be capable of sustaining a proprietary or tracing claim. This point arose in *Nanus Asia Co Inc v Standard Chartered Bank*[1]. In this case, the Hong Kong court was required to determine whether Standard Chartered was in a position analogous to that of a constructive trustee with regard to profits from insider dealing in the United States made by a Taiwanese who, with an employee of Morgan Stanley, had misappropriated price-sensitive information from Morgan Stanley and then traded on it on the New York Stock Exchange. There was no problem with regard to the bank's state of knowledge as it had already been joined in civil enforcement proceedings in New York.

1   [1990] HKLR 396.

12.31   The Hong Kong court held that proceeds of the abuse of inside information were 'held' by Standard Chartered on trust for the US authorities and various other claimants in the United States. At the time, some thought this decision, although welcome, went somewhat further than the English law as it was not thought that the misuse of confidential information, let alone mere inside information, was capable of sustaining a trust relationship thought to be a prerequisite for a viable tracing claim in equity.

12.32   In view of our discussion above, it now appears that while not all breaches of a fiduciary duty will support a claim for tracing, there will be situations involving the sort of abuses we are discussing that will.

12.33   There has been also considerable discussion as to the requisite state of knowledge for liability. The cases have indicated two basic standards, one requiring subjective knowledge and the other a rather more objective or constructive standard. It was thought that the distinction could be justified in terms of whether the third party who facilitates the breach of trust comes into possession of the relevant property or simply facilitates its control or attention by another. In the first case, a more objective standard was considered appropriate and knowledge of facts which would put a reasonable man on notice that something dishonest was afoot would be sufficient to justify liability akin to that of a trustee. On the other hand, where the participation of the third party does not extend to possession of the property, it was thought that the requisite degree of *scienter* should be actual knowledge. In the view of recent cases, it would seem that the question of knowledge is rather more bound up with the nature of liability that is being imposed. Where the third party does not come into possession of the trust property or its proceeds, then it is difficult to conceive of him as a constructive trustee or, for that matter, as having any status which would involve a proprietary nexus. The liability of such a person for participating in the breach of trust will be personal. In *Agip (Africa) Ltd v Jackson*[1], the Court of Appeal found no difficulty in regarding a chartered accountant who had facilitated laundering the proceeds of a fraud by incorporating companies and opening bank accounts in the names of these companies liable as if he were a constructive trustee and thereby holding him personally liable to restore the funds in question. Of course, in such cases, the liability is personal to the defendant and does not involve a propriety liability. In this case, the court found that the person concerned had acted dishonestly. He knew of facts which in the circumstances made him suspicious, but he then deliberately refrained from making the enquiries which an honest man would have made and which would easily have uncovered the fraud. Although the cases do indicate varying qualities of knowledge, it would seem the better view today is that before a third party can be held liable as a facilitator, the court will have to be shown that he knew the facts or deliberately turned a blind eye and then acted with a lack of probity. In *Royal Brunei Airlines Sdn Bhd v Philip Tan Kok Ming*[2], the Privy Council handed down an opinion which does bring some clarity to this area of the law. The Privy Council emphasised that the liability of a person who assists or procures a breach of trust, but does not himself actually receive the property in question, is based on his dishonesty. The Privy Council considered it matters not whether the trustee has himself been dishonest. Furthermore, the probity of the facilitator is to be judged, in the opinion of the Privy Council, on an objective basis. The test was whether he had acted in a way otherwise than an honest man would have in the circumstances. This would invariably involve conscious impropriety on the part of the facilitator, rather than mere negligence, let alone simple inadvertence. However, a person might well be considered to be acting dishonestly for the purpose of imposing liability where he recklessly disregarded the rights of others. The Privy Council underlined that in determining whether a facilitator had acted dishonestly, his actual knowledge at the relevant time had to be considered by the court and this was a subjective issue. What might have been known by a reasonable man in the position of the facilitator might be probative, but was not conclusive. Furthermore, the personal and professional attributes of the facilitator must also be considered in determining what he did and for what reason.

1   [1991] Ch 547.
2   [1995] 2 AC 378.

12.34 The issue was most recently discussed in *Heinl v Jyske Bank (Gibraltar) Ltd*[1]. In this case, the judges used, as the basis of their reasoning, the judgment of Lord Nicholls in *Brunei* and concluded that it was not enough that on the whole of the information available to him he ought, as a reasonable man, to have inferred that there was a substantial probability that the funds originated from the bank in question, but that the inference had, indeed, been drawn. This clearly supports the idea that a high level of suspicion will be needed to incur liability in these cases. Another recent case bearing on the issue of liability in these circumstances is *A Bank v A Ltd (Serious Fraud Office Interested Party)*[2]. This again saw the probability of liability of those who negligently participate in money laundering reduced as the court held that banks did not become constructive trustees merely because they entertained suspicions as to the provenance of money deposited with them. The level of dishonesty needed for dishonest assistance was not satisfied by a general suspicion; there needed to be substantial suspicion pertaining to the specific transaction with which they were involved for liability to be incurred.

1   [1999] 34 LS Gaz R 33.
2   (2000) Times, 18 July.

12.35 There are situations where, to establish the requisite state of mind for liability under the civil and criminal law, it will be necessary to attribute knowledge from one person to another. Where companies are involved, as has already been pointed out, this involves a number of issues. A similar problem arises in fixing a company with a particular state of mind or knowledge. In *R v Rozeik*[1], the Court of Appeal, referring to the earlier case of *El Ajou v Dollar Land Holdings plc*[2], accepted that whether a company is fixed with the knowledge acquired by an employee or officer will depend on the circumstances and it is necessary to identify whether the individual in question has the requisite status and authority in relation to the particular act or omission. Therefore, it does not follow that information in the possession of even a relatively senior official will be attributed to the company if that employee is not empowered to act in relation to the transaction in question. On the other hand, as was dramatically illustrated in the House of Lord's decision in *Re Supply of Ready Mixed Concrete (No 2)*[3], an employee who acts for the company within the scope of his employment, even if against the express instructions of his employer, may well bind the company as he is the company for the purpose of the transaction in question. A similar view was expressed by the Privy Council in *Meridian Global Funds Management Asia Ltd v Securities Commission*[4].

1 [1996] 1 BCLC 380.
2 [1994] 2 All ER 685.
3 [1995] 1 AC 456.
4 [1995] 2 AC 500.

12.36 As the decision of their Lordships in *Ready Mixed Concrete* clearly shows, a company may be liable to third parties or be guilty of the commission of an offence even though the relevant employee was acting dishonestly and/or in breach of his contract of service or even against the interests of the company. In that case, the House of Lords accepted that the management had gone to considerable lengths to ensure compliance with their instructions, but once a transaction had been entered into by an employee who had the power to deliver on behalf of the company, such considerations went merely to the issue of mitigation.

12.37 Whilst the Privy Council recognised in *Meridian Global Funds Management* that it is a matter of interpretation as to whether a particular statute seeks to 'fashion a special rule of attribution for the particular substantive rule', both the Privy Council and the House of Lords were quite prepared to adopt this notion of 'merger' of minds in the case of restrictive trade practices law and securities regulation, given the discerned public policy in avoiding a result which might defeat the purpose of the legislature.

12.38 Where the employee in question is perpetrating a fraud against his employer, then it is obviously inappropriate to take his knowledge of the fraud as being that of the victim company. This much is clear from *Re A-G's Reference (No 2 of 1982)*[1]. In such situations, the employee cannot be both a party to the deception and represent the company for the purpose of it being deceived.

1 [1984] 2 All ER 216. See also generally Cheong-Ann Png, *Corporate Liability* (2001, Kluwer).

12.39 When the company is the victim, the person or persons who may be taken to represent its state of mind may well differ from those whose state of mind will be attributed to the company in cases where it is the company that is charged with an offence. In *Rozeik*, the Court of Appeal thought that in this latter situation such persons are more likely to represent what Viscount Haldane called 'the directing mind and will of the corporation'[1].

1 *Lennard's Carrying Co Ltd v Asiatic Petroleum Co Ltd* [1915] AC 705.

The position of investors

12.40 Investors who subscribe directly or indirectly through an issuing house to a new issue of securities may suffer a loss if the securities in question are sold at a price in excess of their 'real' worth. While this is not really insider dealing in the conventional sense, the issuer and its agents are in a privileged position in that they are aware that the securities are worth less than the market thinks. In many jurisdictions, the law has long recognised that such conduct is highly damaging to the market. Indeed, a special commission appointed by the House of Commons in 1697[1] described such practices, when compounded by insiders dumping their shares on the market, as undermining the 'trade and wealth' of the country. Consequently, in cases of the new issue of securities, most legal systems, as we have seen, impose strict disclosure obligations on those involved in promoting the issue. Consequently, a failure to disclose material information would be unlawful and result in civil and possibly criminal liability. Of course, if those privy to the relevant information seek to use it in their own dealings, then this would be insider dealing. The justification for imposing onerous disclosure obligations on a company at the time it issues securities to the public is that all the facts pertaining to the nature and extent of the investment risk are exclusively in the possession of the issuer and its insiders. It has also been argued in South Africa[2] that the sale of over-priced securities in such circumstances is akin in legal terms to selling chattels that have latent defects.

1   Commission Appointed to Inquire into the Trade of England, House of Commons Journals, 20 November 1697.
2   *Pretorius v Natal South Sea Investment Trust Ltd* 1965 (3) SA 410 (W).

12.41   On the other hand, the courts have been concerned to limit the scope and thus the extent of the issuer's liability. Consequently, in most jurisdictions, there is a reluctance to afford market purchasers and sellers actionable claims against those whose action might influence the price of securities already in the market. Thus, it will often only be those who have transacted directly with the relevant issuer that will be able to sue. Those who deal in the market with other parties will have no right to complain. By the same token, it has been held that auditors only owe their duty of care to the company for which they are appointed to act. They do not owe a duty in the ordinary course of events to those investors in the market who may well be influenced in their investment decisions by what the auditors say in their reports[1]. Although often expressed in terms of principle, the court's decision in such cases is clearly based on policy considerations. The need to consider the proportionality as to the possible extent of liability, when compared with the wrong in question, is recognised in other areas of the law. For example, in the United States, Congress enacted legislation limiting the exposure that insiders dealing on the market might have to contemporaneous market traders.

1   See, for example, *Caparo Industries plc v Dickman* [1990] 2 AC 605.

12.42   In the case of investors who are already in the market, the question as to whether they suffer loss or not from insider abuse is more problematic. They are not, as in the case of those who subscribe for securities in a new issue, left with over-priced securities that the market has had no opportunity to evaluate. In most organised markets, the matching of parties is essentially random and in the case of an active and relatively deep market there will be willing sellers or purchasers at whatever the market price happens to be. In the majority of situations, this price will be wholly uninfluenced by the insider's conduct. Consequently, the mere failure of an insider to 'share' his information with whoever happens to end up as his counterparty, cannot really be said to have misled that person into dealing at that price or with the insider on the terms he has. Therefore, the insider's failure to disclose has not in any real way caused that particular individual to deal on the terms he has. Thus, in market transactions, the elements that are usually required for a viable civil action are either absent or can only be found as fictions.

12.43   On most markets, the securities that are traded represent capital that was contributed to the relevant company in the past. Therefore, it is not unlikely that modern investors operating on the market will be primarily concerned with current valuations and returns rather than the longer term fortunes of the enterprise. Consequently, a relatively high proportion of trading on the markets will be dictated by the current price. With the advent of computer assisted trading programs and the development of related and derivative markets, trading will be far more responsive to price fluctuations. Therefore, it is argued that the only 'real' price is that currently on offer and thus there is no way in which an investor can logically complain that he has been harmed by the existence of information outside the market.

12.44   It has also been said that it is only those investors who trade in the time lapse between the insider's transaction and the disclosure of the relevant information who have any real complaint. Longer term investors who remain in the security in question will reap the rewards or suffer the consequences of the information when it does come to the market, regardless of the insider's conduct. While derivatives may have the effect of gearing gains or losses, essentially the same considerations apply. If we cannot attribute price movements to the action of the insider, then it is difficult to claim that, whatever way the price moves, it is caused by, or is the fault of, insider dealing.

12.45   While the above discussion has centred on dealings in equity securities or rights derived from or related to equity securities, we need to consider whether loss arises when insider dealing occurs in dealings in debt securities. Those holding debt securities may be regarded as standing in the position of creditors to the relevant issuer. Of course, in most cases, this will be a somewhat indirect relationship. The attitude of holders of debt securities to the activities of management will be influenced by the extent to which the relevant borrowings are secured. A significant difference between an equity and a debt security is that the latter is likely to have a relatively determined life expectancy. Of course, given the complexity of structuring corporate finance today, this may be a distinction without a difference.

However, in the case of securities with fixed maturity or, for that matter, any pre-determined right or obligation, their very sensitivity to time renders them a more attractive instrument for certain forms of insider manipulation.

12.46 The attitude of those who provide capital to a company to the conduct of management will be influenced by many other factors. The emphasis that has been placed around the world on the benefits of good governance and ethical management has no doubt had some effect on the way in which management operates and their conduct is assessed. Small investors may well be annoyed that those in positions of trust have abused inside information, but in most legal systems there is little they can do about it. In the vast majority of jurisdictions, even if they were contemporaneous traders, the chances of their being able to frame and pursue any claim for compensation or rescission are remote. Larger institutional investors may be in a rather different position. An institutional investor may not have the same degree of flexibility that a smaller private investor has. For example, an institutional investor with a significant holding in a particular company may find that it is almost 'locked in'. This may result not only from the size of its holding, but also from the knowledge that it acquires by virtue of its position. Although most systems of regulation tend to focus attention on protecting the weak rather than assisting the strong to ensure better treatment for all, institutional investors have been encouraged to take more interest in the proper management of the issuers in which they invest. Some, in furtherance of their own policies of good governance and ethical investment, have been prepared to stand up to those suspected of committing abuses. Of course, it must always be remembered that institutional investors are not spending their own money in pursuing those that they suspect of bad management practices and abuse. Therefore, it is necessary for institutional investors to consider the balance carefully between the costs and benefits of such a course of action.

12.47 While it is difficult to demonstrate the sort of loss resulting from insider dealing that legal systems would normally be willing to compensate, where the insider does more than trade on the basis of the information or encourages another to do so, the position may be very difficult. If the insider engages in acts of fraud or manipulation, then his actions may well result in quantifiable losses for which most systems of law would provide remedies. As has been pointed out, there must be some justification for allowing the investor to transfer the loss that has resulted in the movement of the market price on to the insider. In virtually every legal system, this can only be done if it can be established that the investor's loss was in some way caused by the insider's actions or default.

12.48 Much of what has been said with regard to the position of those who happen to be matched as the counterparty to an insider transaction is on the basis that the dealing takes place on a market. In the case of most developed markets, the dealing will be indirect, impersonal and anonymous.

Consequently, as we have noted, the matching of counterparties will be essentially random. Where, however, the transactions take place in circumstances where the parties are known to each other and there is therefore an opportunity for negotiation, it is possible that the legal position may be somewhat different. For example, in direct and personal transactions, it is rather more likely that a court might be persuaded that the conduct of the insider amounts to a misrepresentation. Of course, in such cases, it is still necessary to impose on the insider an obligation to disclose so as to convert his failure to speak into a misrepresentation. Nonetheless, where the parties are contracting with each other directly, it is easier for a court to find an implied undertaking of fair disclosure than in the context of market transactions. Having said this, however, except in rather special circumstances, there is little, if any, jurisprudence or authority directly on the point[1]. On the other hand, it is no doubt true that a judge may well be rather more sympathetic to a plaintiff who has been disadvantaged in dealings with an insider who has acted in a manner that most people would have no difficulty in regarding as dishonest[2].

1   See para **[12.13]** et seq.
2   See, for example, Lord Lane CJ in *Re A-G's Reference (No 1 of 1988)* [1989] BCLC 193.

12.49   It is hard to find in the law or, for that matter, the institutional structures of modern enterprise, a concern for inhibiting insider abuse, other than on the basis that it undermines the time honoured notion of stewardship. While it is true that investors and other 'stakeholders' may deplore and feel personally aggrieved by the abuse of inside information, in the vast majority of jurisdictions, the law has not recognised this by imposing any duty on insiders that could be enforced, otherwise than through the company. However, as we have seen, even this cause of action is based not so much on logic, but the notion that those who are placed in positions of trust should not be allowed to abuse them.

CHAPTER 13

The impact of other laws: domestic and overseas

Introduction

13.1   The globalisation of financial markets has resulted in increased interaction among securities firms and investors in different jurisdictions. The securities and derivatives markets underpin economic growth and development and the overall strength of market economies by, for example, supporting corporate initiatives, providing finance for new ideas and facilitating the management of financial risk. Sound and effective regulation can, in turn, enhance market confidence and the integrity and development of securities markets. Increasingly, globalised and integrated securities markets pose significant challenges for regulators. Share transactions are taking on an increasingly international character. In a global and integrated securities market, national regulators must be able to assess the nature of cross-border conduct if they are to ensure the existence of fair, efficient and transparent markets.

13.2   The increasingly global market also brings with it the increasing interdependence of national regulators. Accordingly, there must be strong co-operation and co-ordination between regulators and capability to give effect to those links. Cross-border trading in securities has caused a great deal of overlap in the regulatory responsibilities of national regulators and, in some instances, where economically powerful countries (eg the United States) impose their regulations extra-territorially, it can result in a diminution in sovereignty of affected nation states. Indeed, the world's largest and most liquid securities market is the United States and many non-US companies are subject to extra-territorial jurisdiction under US securities and banking laws because of their contacts with US commerce and financial markets. This chapter will discuss the interaction of European Union securities regulation with UK financial regulation in the area of market abuse and insider dealing. The chapter then examines US securities regulation and its extra-territorial impact on foreign persons and markets. Finally, the chapter analyses emerging international standards and principles that seek to control insider dealing and market abuse in an international context. These international standards, principles and rules that relate to market abuse and insider dealing have been promulgated by the world's leading international body of securities regulators, the International Organisation of Securities Commissioners ('IOSCO'). IOSCO has adopted international standards and principles to protect investors against market abuse and has set out standards for national regulators to use while investigating and prosecuting those who attempt to use unlawful means to manipulate securities markets.

13.3   The barriers to a global securities market are diminishing: financial information is becoming available and inexpensive to obtain and it has become easier to effect share transactions abroad[1]. Ultimately, the forces of liberalisation and technology will link most financial markets with the result that regulators should develop improved regulatory links to improve the effectiveness and efficiency of their financial markets. National regulatory authorities should enter agreements that allocate jurisdictional authority amongst regulators so that they have the authority to impose extra-territorial jurisdiction on those who seek to manipulate markets from other countries. This chapter discusses the extra-territorial application of US securities laws with respect to its anti-fraud provisions and disclosure requirements. The close links between US and UK securities markets necessitate some discussion of how US securities laws can expose UK persons and other non-US persons to civil and criminal liability for insider dealing and market manipulation. The chapter then discusses recent efforts by IOSCO to develop international standards in the areas of market abuse and insider dealing. The IOSCO standards are important for understanding how the FSA will interpret the market abuse regime and how the UK courts will apply these principles in legal proceedings.

1   See Merritt B Fox, 'Securities Disclosure in a Globalising Market: Who Should Regulate Whom' (1997) 95 Mich L Rev 2498.

Impact of EU law on insider dealing and co-operation in investigations and enforcement

13.4   As discussed in Chapter 3, the Criminal Justice Act 1993, Pt V implemented the requirement set out in Council Directive 89/552[1] that all member states of the EU adopt laws outlawing insider dealing. Although the implementation process of EU directives often results in national legislation that is interpreted differently relative to other member jurisdictions, the Insider Dealing Directive's requirement that member states make it an offence to commit insider trading has been uniformly adopted by all 15 EU member states[2]. Equally important, the Investment Services Directive 1993 ('ISD') imposes obligations on member states to co-ordinate investigations and enforcement of certain breaches of financial regulations. Articles 18–21 require host states to assume supervisory and regulatory responsibility for all firms operating within host state territory. Article 19(1) and (2) provides that the 'competent regulatory authority' may periodically require all investment firms with branches or agency offices to report on their activities and to provide all information necessary for monitoring their compliance with the prudential conduct of business standards as set out under EU and national law[3].

1   89/552/EEC (13 November 1989).
2   See the discussion in Chapter 3.
3   For example, section C of the Annex to the ISD requires all home state authorities to keep records of all transactions, ie the number of instruments bought and sold and the dates, times and transaction prices. The home state is obliged to exchange this information upon request with host state regulators during investigations of financial service firms based in other EU states who are operating in the jurisdiction.

13.5   EU host member states are required to facilitate transnational investigations and enforcement of financial regulation in the following way. If a financial firm with a passport from another EU state is suspected or found to have violated national or EU financial laws, the host state regulator must take the following steps in order to address the breach: (a) approach the firm's home state regulator to seek assistance in conducting an investigation and then (b) to co-operate with the home state regulator regarding any enforcement action[1]. Generally, the host state must take 'all appropriate measures at its disposal to end the violation' and to adopt measured procedures in seeking co-operation and information before undertaking direct enforcement. Article 25 addresses issues of confidentiality which provides that officials of the competent authority are bound by professional secrecy in relation to the information they receive in the course of their duties[2]. These restrictions on disclosure contain exceptions, however, to allow assistance and information to be given to other authorities of member states which might have regulatory oversight over particular transactions and parties.

1   Article 20 (encouraging co-operation in enforcement matters by allowing national regulators to obtain necessary information).
2   This is similar to the confidentiality provisions of the Financial Services Act 1986, Pt III.

13.6   Article 25 also permits member states to enter into mutual assistance agreements with third countries (eg countries outside the EU) so long as the information exchanged is covered by guarantees of secrecy equivalent to those provided in art 25. The UK has entered into many mutual assistance agreements and memoranda of understanding ('MOU') with countries outside the EU that provide for the exchange of information and evidence to support investigations and enforcement actions by national authorities. For instance, the UK–US 1986 MOU[1] is a non-binding statement of principles and procedures for making requests for information in regard to investigations and enforcement actions in regard to alleged breaches of securities laws. Each national authority retains discretion whether to co-operate in the disclosure of requested information[2]. The UK–US MOU covers insider dealing, misrepresentations in the course of dealing and market manipulation and it applies to securities or futures traded within the territorial jurisdiction of each regulatory authority[3]. The impact of EU law and mutual assistance agreements has been substantial in requiring UK authorities to take account of international developments in financial regulation and to adopt practices that are similar to those taken by other regulatory authorities. Conflicts occur, however, when the laws of some jurisdictions are imposed unilaterally and in an extra-territorial manner without the consent of UK authorities. This has become a major issue in regard to the extra-territorial application of US securities laws as discussed below.

1   The relevant agencies today would be the US Securities and Exchange Commission and the Commodities and Futures Trading Commission and the UK Department of Trade and Industry and the Financial Services Authority.
2   For example, the UK Secretary of State may deny requests for co-operation on the grounds of public interest.
3   Paragraph 11 of the MOU provides for spontaneous provision of information by one agency to another.

Recent efforts to reform European securities regulation

13.7   The increasing integration of the EU's internal market has necessitated consideration of whether there should be Europe-wide rules and regulations governing capital markets. In particular, some securities regulators believe that there should be a reconfiguration of national regulatory schemes that support a Europe-wide securities regulator with authority to promote the objectives of market integrity and investor protection. These objectives include proposals to adopt clear EU standards to regulate market abuse. In May 1999, the European Commission submitted the Financial Services Action Plan ('FSAP') for comment. The FSAP sets out an agenda to achieve a common European market in financial services. One of its many proposals is to '[s]et common disciplines for trading floors to enhance investor confidence in an embryonic single securities market' through the adoption of a directive on market manipulation[1].

1   See European Commission, 'Financial Services: Implementing the Framework for Financial Markets: Action Plan' (1999) COM 232 (11 May 1999) p 23.

13.8   The Forum of European Securities Commissions ('FESCO') responded to the Commission's FSAP by issuing a paper that presents its views on how market abuse should be regulated at both European and national level. The FESCO paper stated that 'to establish an effective regime against market abuse' the directive should go beyond enhancing 'co-operation between supervisors [and] to establish a more common approach to detection and investigation ... as well as enforcement'[1]. This statement clarifies the prevailing objective to establish a common standard across the EU to regulate market abuse and insider dealing. Although many EU national regulators agree that there should be some standard for regulating market abuse, difficulties arise regarding the implementation and enforcement of an EU-wide scheme. The 'Committee of Wise Men' (also known as the Lamfalussy Committee) on the regulation of the European securities markets[2] has addressed these issues in a report that calls for the establishment of an EU securities regulatory framework. The 'Committee of Wise Men' proposes to create a European securities regulatory committee to set EU standards for the regulation of EU securities markets. A European securities regulatory committee would co-ordinate enforcement of such standards with EU national authorities. The Commission has delegated to the 'Committee of Wise Men' the task of devising a process to ensure the adoption and implementation among the EU states of a similar regulatory treatment for market abuse. This would avoid the adverse effects of relying on dissimilar national approaches.

In May 2001, the Commission of the European Communities released a proposed European Communities Directive on Insider Dealing and Market Manipulation (Market Abuse) which, if implemented, will replace the current Insider Trading Directive 1989. The proposed Directive contains many of the features of the Insider Trading Directive, including the rationale that those persons who trade on the basis of insider information have an unjustified economic advantage over other market participants and that insider trading laws are necessary to enhance investor confidence. The proposed Directive also covers the main principles of the 1989 Directive by distinguishing between primary and secondary insiders and applying the insider trading laws to financial instruments that are traded or capable of being traded on a regulated market.

The proposed Directive, however, contains important differences from the 1989 Directive. For example, it would apply not only to securities, but also to all financial instruments, including derivatives over commodities[3]. The commentary to the proposed Directive provides that 'the scope of financial instruments significantly affected by privileged information is not limited to those of the issuer, but enlarged to related derivative financial instruments (eg options on equity, futures and options on index)'. The proposed Directive would also require all member states to impose criminal sanctions for insider dealing on 'any natural or legal person'[4]. This would make all corporations, partnerships and other business entities criminally liable for insider dealing.

Draft art 2 of the proposed Directive expands the scope of personal liability for primary insiders by excluding any requirement that they have 'full knowledge of the facts' in order for criminal or civil liability to be imposed. The repeal of this requirement recognises the market reality that primary insiders may have access to insider information on a daily basis and are aware of the confidential nature of the information they receive. In addition, the proposed Directive adopts an 'information connection' requirement to the definition of secondary insider. According to this definition, a secondary insider would be any person, other than a primary insider, 'who with full

233

knowledge of the facts possesses inside information'[5]. They would be subject to the same prohibitions on trading, disclosing and procuring as primary insiders[6].

Moreover, draft art 6 requires that issuers of financial instruments inform the public as soon as possible of inside information, subject to various confidentiality and other exemptions[7]. Draft art 6 also requires that any 'natural person, or entity, professionally arranging transactions in financial instruments shall refrain from entering into transactions, and reject orders on behalf of its clients, if it reasonably suspects that a transaction would be based on inside information'[8]. Draft art 8 exempts from the insider trading prohibitions buy backs and market stabilisations during an initial or secondary public offer, except where the insiders have complied with such provisions as prescribed by the Commission. The proposed Directive states in its commentary that '[t]rading in own shares and stabilisation however must be carried out transparently in order to avoid insider dealing or giving misleading signals to the markets. Trading in own shares could be used to strengthen the equity capital of issuers and so would be in investors' interests'[9]. The proposed Directive has other draft articles setting out standards for mutual assistance and co-ordination in detecting, investigating and prosecuting insider trading and other market abuse in EU member states.

1   See FESCO, 'Market Abuse: FESCO's Response to the Call for Views from the Securities Regulators Under the EU's Action Plan for Financial Services' (1999) COM 232 (29 June 2000).
2   The Lamfalussy Committee was created by the EU Council of Economic and Finance Ministers to propose a plan to implement the Financial Services Action Plan. See the initial report of the 'Committee of Wise Men' on the regulation of the European securities markets (9 November 2000) pp 26, 35 and Annex 1.
3   Draft arts 2, 3 and section A of the Annex.
4   Draft art 2.
5   Draft art 4.
6   Draft art 4.
7   Article 6 contains related restrictions on selective disclosure: paras 1–4.
8   Draft art 6, para 5.
9   Commentary to the proposed Directive.

13.9   In assessing the impact of EU regulation of insider dealing and market abuse on UK financial regulation, it should be noted that the well-developed regulatory framework of UK financial services legislation under the Financial Services and Markets Act 2000 ('FSMA 2000') and the comprehensive regulations promulgated by the FSA are likely to serve as a model for the Commission in considering possible regulatory frameworks to police market abuse and manipulation. Moreover, it may be said that the FSMA 2000 market abuse regulations and statutory framework appear to adopt a regulatory approach that is very similar in its degree of focus and coverage as that of another major national securities market regulator, the US Securities and Exchange Commission. Indeed, the FSMA 2000 could promote a kind of convergence among regulatory systems that facilitates co-ordination of enforcement and reduces instances of unilateral acts by securities regulators. Until such convergence takes place, UK financial operators will have to be aware of the onerous requirements of US extra-territorial securities regulation.

Extra-territorial application of US securities laws, foreign issuers and anti-fraud provisions

13.10   This section addresses the extra-territoriality of US securities laws in the context of how the anti-fraud provisions apply to foreign issuers and to transactions involving activities that take place, in part, in non-US territories. The section then discusses what reporting requirements apply to foreign issuers. Most US case law addressing the extra-territorial application of US securities laws focuses on the anti-fraud provisions of the Securities and Exchange Act 1934[1]. The courts have developed two tests for determining subject matter jurisdiction in securities fraud cases. One test relies on the 'effects test' that assesses the effects in the United States of conduct that occurs in foreign countries, while the other focuses on the conduct of foreign persons within the United States.

1   15 USCA, s 78 et seq.

Anti-fraud provisions of the Securities and Exchange Act 1934, s 10b

13.11   Section 10b of the Securities and Exchange Act 1934 makes it unlawful, inter alia, to use or employ any manipulative or deceptive device or contrivance 'in connection with the purchase or sale of any security'. Moreover, s 27 of the Act vests the district courts with jurisdiction of all actions 'to enforce any liability or duty created by this title or the rules and regulations thereunder'. The federal courts, therefore, have jurisdiction to enforce the provisions of s 10b and Rule 10b-5. The federal circuit courts have interpreted the anti-fraud provisions to have extra-territorial effect in a number of circumstances. Generally, the courts apply alternative tests: the 'conduct' test or the 'effects' test[1]. Under the conduct test, the court has subject matter jurisdiction 'where conduct material to the completion of the fraud occurred in the United States'[2]. Mere preparatory activities and conduct far removed from the conduct of the fraud will not suffice[3]; rather, '[o]nly where conduct "within the United States directly caused" the loss will a district court has jurisdiction ... ' Under the 'effects' test, the court has jurisdiction 'whenever a predominantly foreign transaction has substantial effects within the United States'[4]. Thus, remote or indirect effects in the United States do not confer subject matter jurisdiction.

The Second Circuit Court of Appeals held in *Schoenbaum v Firstbrook*[5] that extra-territorial jurisdiction could be imposed on a transaction involving securities issued by a foreign corporation that were listed on a US stock exchange and held by US citizens on the grounds that such a transaction affected US securities markets. The court found that extra-territorial subject matter jurisdiction was justified under the federal securities laws on the basis that the challenged foreign transaction had an 'effect' on domestic US securities markets. Similarly, the Ninth Circuit also found extra-territorial jurisdiction based on the 'effects' test[6] in a case involving a takeover of a Canadian corporation by a US corporation that involved the improper use of the US corporation's securities, which were registered and listed on a US national exchange and had adversely affected both the foreign plaintiffs and the US securities markets. Further, extra-territorial jurisdiction can be imposed on foreign actors who make misrepresentations to US investors in the sale of foreign securities that were only traded in foreign markets[7]. In this case, the Second Circuit premised jurisdiction upon domestic conduct and the direct effect on US investors. However, extra-territorial jurisdiction will not be conferred on a transaction or occurrence if its only connection to US territory are activities in the United States that are 'merely preparatory' to the actual fraud[8].

1 *Butte Mining plc v Smith* 76 F 3d 287 (9th Cir, 1996).
2 *Psimenos v E F Hutton & Co* 722 F 2d 1041, 1046 (2nd Cir, 1983).
3 *Psimenos v Hutton.*
4 *Consolidated Gold Fields plc v Minorco SA* 871 F 2d 252, 261–262 (2nd Cir, 1989).
5 405 F 2d 200 (2nd Cir, 1968); cert denied 395 US 906 (1969).
6 *Des Brisay v Goldfield Corpn* 549 F 2d 133 (9th Cir, 1977).
7 *Leasco Data Processing Equipment v Maxwell* 468 F 2d 1326 (2nd Cir, 1972).
8 *Zoelsch v Arthur Andersen & Co* 824 F 2d 27 (DC Cir, 1987); *Bersch v Drexel Firestone Inc* 519 F 2d 974 (2nd Cir, 1975).

13.12 The extra-territorial scope of the anti-fraud provisions also extends to the acts of a defendant based in the United States who perpetrates fraud upon non-US persons in a foreign country. The Second Circuit observed that the jurisdictional basis was sufficient in this case because Congress could not have intended 'to allow the United States to be used as a base for manufacturing fraudulent security devices for export, even when … peddled only to foreigners'[1]. Moreover, foreign nationals who are resident in the United States are protected to the same extent as US nationals so long as their claims arise at the time they are resident in the United States. This rule applies even though the fraudulent scheme is devised and set into motion abroad[2], but a foreign corporation whose sole shareholder and chief executive officer was a foreigner residing in the United States was required to prove that losses incurred on account of the fraudulent scheme were directly caused by acts within the United States[3]. However, deception of a foreigner who is a sole shareholder within the United States, while necessary to demonstrate a fraudulent scheme, has thus been held insufficient proof of direct causation of loss[4].

1 *Consolidated Gold Fields plc v Minorco SA* 871 F 2d 252 (2nd Cir, 1989); see also *IIT v Vencap Ltd* 519 F 2d 1001, 1017 (2nd Cir, 1975); on remand 411 F Supp 1094 (SDNY, 1975).
2 *O' Driscoll v Merrill Lynch, Pierce, Fenner & Smith Inc* Fed Sec L Rep 99, 486 (SDNY, 1983).

3   *O' Driscoll v Merrill Lynch, Pierce, Fenner & Smith Inc* WL 1360, 1361 (1983).
4   *O' Driscoll v Merrill Lynch, Pierce, Fenner & Smith Inc.*

13.13   The Eighth Circuit imposed extra-territorial subject matter jurisdiction on foreign conduct that involved the use of the US telephone system and US mail to further a fraudulent scheme, even though the only victim of the fraud was a foreign corporation purchasing stock in another foreign company[1]. In this case, the foreign defendant sellers relied, in part, on the US telephone system and US mail fraudulently to induce foreign investors to purchase securities of a foreign company not listed on a US exchange. The court imposed extra-territorial jurisdiction, despite the fact that no transaction occurred in the United States nor involved US securities, by finding that the defendants' conduct (use of the US telephone and mail system) was significant – not 'merely preparatory' – and constituted a fraud devised and completed in the United States[2].

1   *Continental Grain (Australia) Pty Ltd v Pacific Oilseeds Inc* 592 F 2d 409 (8th Cir, 1979).
2   *Continental Grain (Australia) Pty Ltd v Pacific Oilseeds Inc* at 420.

13.14   The Second and Third Circuits have also upheld extra-territorial subject matter jurisdiction based on conduct in the United States that directly caused a foreign plaintiff's losses, even though the fraud had no direct effect on US securities markets or upon investors in the United States[1]. Therefore, foreigners purchasing securities in the United States are protected by US federal securities laws[2]. Jurisdiction, however, will not extend to conduct that is, at most, 'ancillary' or peripheral and therefore not the direct cause of the plaintiff's losses. The Second Circuit took this position in *Fidenas AG v Compagnie Internationale Pour L' informatique CII Honeywell Bull SA*[3], when it denied extra-territorial jurisdiction to the claims of foreign investors against a foreign subsidiary that was wholly-owned by a US parent on the grounds that knowledge by the US parent of fraudulent conduct committed by its foreign subsidiary was insufficient US conduct. In a subsequent suit filed against the US parent for the same fraud, the court denied jurisdiction on the basis that mere knowledge of the fraud was insufficient to confer extra-territorial subject matter jurisdiction upon US courts. The court then relied on the Second Circuit's view that the transactions were 'predominantly foreign' and thereby dismissed the suit for failing to satisfy either the 'conduct' or 'effects' test for subject matter jurisdiction.

1   *SEC v Kasser* 548 F 2d 109 (3rd Cir, 1977); cert denied 431 US 938 (1977).
2   *IIT v Cornfeld* 619 F 2d 909, 918 (2nd Cir, 1980). See also *Arthur Lipper Corpn v SEC*
    547 F 2d 171 (2nd Cir, 1976); cert denied 434 US 1009 (1978).
3   606 F 2d 5 (2nd Cir, 1979).

13.15   Similarly, the US District Court for the Southern District of New York has applied the transaction test to deny extra-territorial subject matter jurisdiction in a case where the primary fraud and every fact essential to the plaintiff's claim of fraudulent misconduct was committed or occurred in Costa Rica[1]. The transaction was considered not to have had significant enough effects on US securities markets and the fraudulent conduct in question was ancillary to the US and was 'predominantly foreign'[2]. In addition, extra-territorial subject matter jurisdiction will not be conferred where US investors used circuitous means (by setting up an overseas shell corporation) in order to conceal their US nationality so that they could participate in a foreign public offering in which they purchased the non-US securities of a foreign corporation. The court held that the plaintiffs were estopped from bringing a claim under the US securities laws because they had gone to great efforts to avoid and evade the Act's requirements[3].

1   *Mormels v Girofinance SA* 544 F Supp 815 (SDNY, 1982).
2   *Mormels v Girofinance SA.*
3   *MCG Inc v Great Western SA* 544 F Supp 815 (SDNY, 1982).

13.16   Based on the above cases, the following propositions can be made about the extra-territorial application of the anti-fraud provisions of the US securities laws:

- that jurisdiction will be conferred on acts of material importance that occur in a foreign country if such acts cause losses in the sale of securities to US resident investors in the United States;
- that jurisdiction will be conferred on acts of material importance that occur in the United States if they cause losses in the sale of securities to US residents abroad; and
- that jurisdiction will *not* be conferred on transactions that result in losses in the sale of securities to foreigners outside US territory *unless* acts within the United States directly caused such losses[1].

1   See *Bersch v Drexel Firestone Inc* 519 F 2d 974 at 993 (2nd Cir, 1975); cert denied 423 US 1018 (1975).

Reporting and disclosure requirements

13.17   The extra-territorial scope of reporting and disclosure requirements are more narrowly defined. A foreign issuer's filing of misleading reports to the SEC will not of itself provide a sufficient jurisdictional basis to support a private right of action by foreign investors. This means that there will be no US jurisdiction over claims by foreign investors residing abroad against a foreign corporation for filing misleading reports with the SEC, even though the misrepresentations were contained in documents filed with the SEC and also were circulated in the US press[1]. In contrast, there will be US jurisdiction where a non-US national residing abroad brings an action against a foreign corporation for fraud in connection with the sale of US securities since some of the acts that were apart of the fraud occurred in the United States[2]. Jurisdiction will also extend to misrepresentations in a prospectus delivered outside US territory by a foreign corporation to foreign investors residing abroad if negotiations relating to the prospectus took place in US territory[3]. Generally, however, the extra-territorial application of US securities law's reporting and disclosure requirements will not extend to the claims of a foreign corporation arising out of misrepresentations in a prospectus or other similar documents if the plaintiff cannot provide adequate proof of causation from acts that took place in the United States.

1   *Kaufman v Campeau Corpn* 744 F Supp 808 (SD Ohio, 1990).
2   *Kaufman v Campeau Corpn.*
3   *Alfadda v Fenn* 935 F 2d 475 (2nd Cir, 1991).

Foreign manipulation of US markets

13.18   The term 'manipulation' in the context of financial markets has pervaded markets from the Dutch tulip bulb mania in the early seventeenth century to the recent collapse of Internet technology stock prices in 2000. The Securities and Exchange Act 1934 does not define 'manipulative' or 'manipulation'. The Securities and Exchange Commission has adopted rules that describe 'manipulation' by relating it to specific acts or activities that are then proscribed as 'manipulation' or 'manipulative'. The term 'manipulate' or 'manipulative' is often described as involving 'motive' or 'intent' to punish a result that is socially undesirable. A strict interpretation of the term would lead one to deduce that many types of acts could be characterised as manipulation, including activities regularly engaged in by securities professionals and others, but not necessarily in contexts predetermined to be undesirable. A less than rigid standard may be used to define 'manipulation' as it could cover many activities in the marketplace that are not viewed as harmful or socially undesirable. Indeed, the concept of manipulation is a constantly evolving one that takes on a less than objective standard that is similar to the 'he knows it when he sees it' definition used by US Supreme Court Judge Potter Stewart. The Seventh Circuit Court of Appeals adopted a definition of 'manipulation' as 'the creation of an artificial price by planned action'[1]. The Eighth Circuit utilises a definition that describes manipulation to occur when a price does not 'reflect basic forces of supply and demand'[2], yet no agreement exists regarding the types of behaviour that would qualify as market manipulation. Some agreement has coalesced around certain conduct that can be termed as artificial factors that result in manipulation in financial markets, such as 'corner', 'squeeze', 'domination and control', 'rumour manipulation', 'investor interest' manipulation and even 'price effect' manipulation, but these criteria appear to be hard to define in practice as the US courts have been contradictory in the application of these terms to conduct that is allegedly manipulative[3].

1   *General Foods Corpn v Brannon* 170 F 2d 220, 234 (7th Cir, 1998).
2   *Cargill Inc v Hardin* 452 F 2d 1154 at 1163 (8th Cir, 1971).
3   M G and J R Pickholz, 'Manipulation', a paper presented at the 18th Symposium on Economic Crime, Jesus College, Cambridge (September 2000).

13.19   The US government imposes criminal liability on non-US persons or business entities that are engaged in off-shore manipulations affecting US markets or US issuers. The basis for such jurisdiction is the Securities and Exchange Act 1934, s 9(a) that prohibits 'any person' from using 'any means or instrumentality of interstate commerce' (including e-mails, faxes and telephones) or of the mail, 'or of any facility of a national securities exchange [for a] manipulative or deceptive device or contrivance' in contravention of the SEC rules.

13.20   US courts have generally held that, given the principal purpose of US securities laws to protect US investors exposed to fraudulent or manipulative activities that implicate the jurisdictional means of interstate commerce, foreign activities by foreign nationals producing such a result in the United States or affecting US investors will be subject to US jurisdiction, which will displace the foreign law and will, as a matter of conflict laws, allow US courts to apply US laws to foreign nationals.

Extra-territorial jurisdiction over commodities trading and civil RICO

13.21   Where a cause of action arose from trading on US commodities exchanges, US courts will uphold extra-territorial subject matter jurisdiction, even though the parties to the suit were non-resident US aliens and the fraudulent transactions and conduct occurred in a foreign country[1]. In *Tamari*, the court relied on the 'effects' test to find that 'where the ... transactions involve trading on domestic exchanges, harm can be presumed, because the fraud ... implicates the integrity of the American market'[2]. The court also noted that extra-territorial jurisdiction could attach to a foreign defendant's transmission of orders on behalf of the foreign plaintiffs when such transmissions went from Lebanon to the commodities exchange in Chicago. That such transmissions constituted 'conduct within the United States that was of substantial importance to the success of the fraudulent scheme'[3].

The Racketeer Influenced Corrupt Organisations Act ('RICO') contains no express provision regarding its extra-territorial application[4]. RICO applies to civil actions and provides an express private right of action for those who were defrauded by individuals who used their controlling influence over a business enterprise to commit a fraud. To determine extra-territorial jurisdiction, the courts seek guidance from precedents 'concerning subject matter jurisdiction for international securities transactions and anti-trust matters'[5]. Therefore, the courts will look to the cases discussed above to determine issues of extra-territoriality under RICO.

1   *Tamari v Bache & Co (Lebanon) SAL* 547 F Supp 309 (ND Ill, 1982); order affd 730 F 2d 1103 (7th Cir, 1984); cert denied 469 US 871 (1984).
2   *Tamari v Bache & Co (Lebanon) SAL* at 313.
3   *Tamari v Bache & Co (Lebanon) SAL* at 315.
4   See *John Doe v UNOCAL Corpn* 110 F Supp 2d 1294, 1310 (CD Cal, 2000).
5   *North South Finance Corpn v Al-Turki* 100 F 3d 1046, 1051 (2nd Cir, 1996).

13.22   In addition, jurisdiction may be imposed on the activities of non-US persons residing abroad when their activities affect the US marketplace. The Ninth Circuit in *Bourassa v Desrochers*[1] held that the jurisdictional link was satisfied by a Canadian broker's telephone call from Canada to an investor in the United States. Jurisdiction was not satisfied, however, in a case where defrauded US investors brought an action for aiding and abetting liability against a foreign auditor for producing a report that was used by a foreign company without the consent of the auditor[2]. A US court also dismissed a claim based on lack of jurisdiction when it involved US investors who owned American Depository Receipts ('ADRs') and had received a press release announcing a UK company's tender offer for shares in a UK target company whose securities were trading in the United States through the use of ADRs[3]. The determination of whether to impose extra-territorial subject matter jurisdiction will be a highly factual inquiry which must be made on case-by-case basis[4].

1   938 F 2d 1056 (9th Cir, 1991).
2   *Reingold v Deloitte Haskins & Sells* 599 F Supp 1241 (SDNY, 1984).
3   *Plessey Co v General Electric Co* 628 F Supp 477 (D Del, 1986).
4   *Dept of Economic Development v Arthur Andersen & Co* 683 F Supp 1463 (SDNY, 1988).

13.23   Manipulation and other types of securities fraud will continue to affect financial markets, as it has since the time that the Rothschild's banking house used carrier pigeons to obtain information of Napoleon's defeat before the information became generally available to the investing public. Today, market manipulation occurs across national borders through use of the Internet to manipulate stock prices through, for example, disseminating information that is false and negative about an issuer in an effort to drive down the price of its securities. Prosecuting securities manipulation requires a global approach involving co-operation and co-ordination, transparency of markets and uniform rules for such activities as margin borrowing and short sells.

IOSCO and UK efforts at international co-operation

13.24   IOSCO is the leading international body concerned with the regulation of securities markets[1]. Its membership comprises regulatory bodies from 91 countries who have responsibility for day-to-day oversight and administration of securities laws. The preamble of IOSCO's byelaws states:

'Securities authorities resolve to co-operate together to ensure a better regulation of the markets, on the domestic as well as on the international level, in order to maintain just, efficient and sound markets'.

To accomplish this, IOSCO encourages its member regulatory bodies to co-ordinate the establishment of standards and mutual assistance with other regulators as follows: (a) to exchange information on their respective experiences in order to promote the development of domestic securities markets, (b) to unite national efforts to establish standards and an effective surveillance of international securities transactions and (c) to provide mutual assistance to ensure the integrity of the markets by a vigorous application of the standards and be effective enforcement against offences.

1 See IOSCO's website: www.iosco.org

13.25 IOSCO seeks to develop international standards to provide advice for national regulators which serves as a yardstick against which national regulatory efforts can be measured. IOSCO also recognises that providing minimum international standards and effective international co-operation in establishing, maintaining and investigating standards will not only result in investor protection, but also reduce systemic risk. IOSCO recognises that the increasing integration and liberalisation of global financial markets poses significant challenges for the regulation of securities markets. Moreover, markets, especially emerging markets, have experienced remarkable growth in recent years, but have also been exposed to the volatility of short-term capital flows which have resulted in some countries experiencing financial instability and the increased risk of contagion. This has been exacerbated by the lack of transparency and disclosure of material information for investors to assess risks in emerging markets. National regulators must now take account of transactions and activities that occur in other countries and IOSCO seeks to establish standards to assess the nature of cross-border conduct with a view to ensuring the fair, efficient and transparent operation of securities markets.

IOSCO and market abuse

13.26 IOSCO recognises that investors should be protected from misleading, manipulative or fraudulent practices. IOSCO adopts a broad definition of 'manipulative or fraudulent' conduct to include insider trading, front running or trading ahead of customers and the misuse of client assets. IOSCO has designated the principle of full disclosure of material information to be the primary principle for ensuring investor protection. Full disclosure reduces information asymmetries in the marketplace and thereby improves the investor's position to assess the potential risks and rewards of their investments.

13.27 IOSCO asserts that a key component of full disclosure requirements are adequate accounting and auditing standards, which should be of a high and sufficiently robust standard to inspire international confidence. Moreover, only duly licensed or authorised persons should be allowed to hold themselves out to the public as providing investment services. This should also apply in the case of market intermediaries and the operators of exchanges. IOSCO also encourages national authorities to require initial and ongoing capital requirements for those licence holders and authorised persons. These standards should be designed to achieve an environment in which a securities firm can meet the current demands of its counterparties and, if necessary, wind down its business without losses to its customers.

13.28   IOSCO also encourages national authorities to adopt strict standards of supervision for market intermediaries for the purpose of achieving investor protection by setting minimum standards for market participants. Investors should be treated in a just and equitable manner by market intermediaries based on standards that should be established in rules of business conduct. An effective system of surveillance is needed which would entail inspection, oversight and internal compliance programmes for investment firms and intermediaries.

13.29   Investors are particularly vulnerable in securities markets to misconduct by intermediaries and others, but the capacity of individual investors to take action may be limited. Further, the complex character of securities transactions and of fraudulent schemes require strong enforcement of securities laws. In the event a violation occurs, investors should be protected through effective enforcement of the law.

13.30   IOSCO also sets out the principle that investors should have access to neutral fora, such as courts or administrative tribunals, to seek redress for damages and other injuries arising from market abuse and other misconduct. Remedies should include adequate compensation and/or restitution. The network of mutual assistance agreements that IOSCO has encouraged national regulators to adopt should lead to more effective enforcement. Effective cross-border supervision and enforcement will depend on close co-operation and co-ordination by national regulators. The FSMA 2000 contains provisions that implement many of these principles and standards adopted by IOSCO.

13.31   The FSMA 2000 authorises the FSA to co-ordinate their investigations and to subpoena documents and witnesses from foreign jurisdictions and to prosecute parties allegedly committing acts in foreign jurisdictions that breach the market abuse provisions of the FSMA 2000. Part I of the consultation document issued with the Financial Services and Markets Bill emphasised the need for 'extensive co-operation with regulatory bodies in other countries'. Part X provides for more effective information gathering to be collected as part of investigations in foreign jurisdictions and thereby provides mechanisms for co-operation with foreign authorities. It improves upon the Financial Services Act 1986 and its disjointed approach to obtaining information from abroad and co-ordinating investigations with foreign authorities.

13.32   More specifically, the FSMA 2000, s 139 refers to 'assistance to overseas regulators' and is similar in content to the Companies Act 1989, s 82 amendments where it lists a number of matters that the FSA must take into account before deciding whether to exercise its investigative powers or not. The FSMA 2000, ss 140 and 141 authorise broad powers for the FSA to gather information and documents from an authorised firm, its employees and even a member firm within the authorised firm's corporate or entity group. These powers build on existing powers contained in the Companies Act 1989, s 83 amendments.

13.33 The FSMA 2000 makes two important changes with respect to international co-operation and enforcement from previous legislation under the Companies Act 1985 and the Financial Services Act 1986. The FSMA 2000, s 139(6) makes provision for the requirements contained in the Investment Services Directive making it mandatory for the FSA to respond to requests for co-operation and information from other EU member state authorities. Further, the FSMA 2000 develops safeguards to provisions authorising disclosure to foreign regulators by more narrowly defining and reducing the categories that can be relied on by UK authorities to reject requests for information and to co-ordinate investigations and enforcement actions. For example, the FSMA 2000, s 305(1) tightly restricts the disclosure of all confidential information that arises from fiduciary and privileged relationships. Such information can only be provided with the consent of the person from whom it was sought. The FSMA 2000, s 306(1) provides exceptions to this restriction on disclosure that will be more specifically defined by regulations that are to be adopted by the Treasury. This list of prescribed recipients will be entitled to take, obtain and utilise information that would otherwise be non-disclosable.

13.34 CP 17 discusses the FSA powers to intervene on behalf of foreign authorities. The principle of reciprocity will determine the willingness of the FSA to intervene on behalf of foreign authorities in investigations and enforcement actions. The FSA will act if there is a corresponding legal obligation in the requesting jurisdiction that would allow them to provide comparable assistance to the FSA, if asked. The principle of reciprocity is a key component of the UK MOU and mutual legal assistance treaties that authorise UK authorities to co-ordinate information collection, investigations and enforcement with foreign jurisdictions if those jurisdictions allow UK authorities to have reciprocal rights in UK investigations and enforcement actions. The FSMA 2000, Pts IV and XII both provide detailed procedures that authorise the FSA, acting on a request from an EU member state or other jurisdiction with which it has an agreement guaranteeing reciprocal rights, to support an enforcement action of a foreign regulator by allowing the FSA to vary, cancel and intervene in a regulated firm's ability to conduct permitted financial services activities whilst operating in the UK. Part IV addresses disclosure of information from foreign firms which seek to carry on regulated financial activities in the UK. Part XII authorises the FSA to intervene in order to protect the integrity and good governance of UK financial markets by imposing jurisdiction extra-territorially on persons or transactions outside the UK that may affect UK markets.

13.35   The FSMA 2000, ss 42 and 164 are similar to the Companies Act 1989, s 82(4) in allowing the FSA ultimately to exercise discretion as to whether it should exercise its broad powers. It should be noted that such discretion may appear to be an obstacle to enhanced transnational co-operation, yet this discretion is expressly denied if the foreign authority requesting assistance is an EU member state based on the Investment Services Directive, as implemented by the FSMA 2000, s 139. Outside the EU, this discretion can only be restrained by bilateral or multilateral agreement.

Conclusion

13.36   The barriers to a global securities market are diminishing; financial information is becoming available and inexpensive to obtain and it has been become easier to effect share transactions abroad[1]. Ultimately, the forces of liberalisation and technology will link most financial markets with the result that regulators should develop improved regulatory links to improve the effectiveness and efficiency of their financial markets. National regulatory authorities should enter agreements that allocate jurisdictional authority amongst regulators so that they have the authority to impose extra-territorial jurisdiction on those who seek to manipulate markets from other countries. EU securities regulation has evolved to where it has become a significant factor in setting standards and binding requirements for the UK's financial markets. The Lamfalussy Committee's proposal for an EU securities regulator will have institutional implications for the governance of EU securities markets. Moreover, the proposed Directive on Insider Dealing and Market Manipulation will promote further convergence of standards and rules amongst EU member states.

This chapter also discussed the extra-territorial application of US securities laws with respect to its anti-fraud provisions and disclosure requirements. US courts apply alternative tests: the 'conduct' test or the 'effects' test. Under the 'conduct' test, the court has subject matter jurisdiction where conduct material to the completion of the fraud occurred in the United States. Under the 'effects' test, the court has jurisdiction whenever a predominantly foreign transaction has substantial effects within the United States. The close links between US and UK securities markets require an analysis of how US securities laws can expose UK persons and other non-US persons to civil and criminal liability for insider dealing and market manipulation. Finally, the efforts of IOSCO have been instrumental in developing international standards in the areas of market abuse and insider dealing. The IOSCO standards are important for understanding how the FSA will interpret the market abuse regime and for how the UK courts will apply these principles in legal proceedings.

Overall, the adoption of the FSMA 2000, and in particular its market abuse regime, represents an important step in the development of effective remedies to combat market misconduct in the financial markets. The FSMA 2000 adopts a more expansive notion of extra-territorial jurisdiction that seeks to police acts or omissions that take place in foreign jurisdictions, but have a significant effect or connection with the UK's financial markets. Moreover, the FSMA 2000 adopts enhanced provisions on mutual assistance and co-operation so that the UK authorities may more effectively exchange information with foreign authorities in investigations and enforcement actions.

1   See Merritt B Fox, 'Securities Disclosure in a Globalising Market: Who Should Regulate Whom' (1997) 95 Mich L Rev 2498.

Index

All references in this index are to paragraph numbers